Practicing Law in Frontier California

LAW IN THE AMERICAN WEST

series editor
John R. Wunder,
University of Nebraska–Lincoln

series advisory editors
Lawrence M. Friedman,
Stanford University
Kermit L. Hall,
University of Florida
Harry N. Scheiber,
University of California,
Berkeley

Volume 2

GORDON MORRIS
BAKKEN

Practicing Law in Frontier California

University of Nebraska Press   Lincoln and London

The paper in this book meets the minimum
requirements of
American National Standard for
Information Sciences—
Permanence of Paper for Printed Library
Materials,
ANSI Z39.48–1984.

Library of Congress Cataloging in
Publication Data
Bakken, Gordon Morris.
Practicing law in frontier California /
Gordon Morris Bakken.
p.   cm. – (Law in the American West ; v. 2)
Includes bibliographical references and index.
ISBN 0-8032-1219-4 (Cloth : alk. paper)
1. Practice of law – California – History.
2. Lawyers – California – History.
I. Title. II. Series.
KF301.5.C3B35   1991   349.73'09794–dc20
[347.3009794]   90-40646   CIP

To the memory of my pioneer forebears of the Koshkonong Prairie:
Halvor Jacobson (1829–98) and Johanne Berg (1836–1928)
Jacob Martinius Jacobson (1858–1928) and Anne Lande (1860–1955)
Mildred Jacobson (1886–1984) and Nordahl Anderson (1885–1971)
my parents Evelyn Anderson and Elwood Severt Bakken (1915–1969)
and to my brother Richard Elwood Bakken

CONTENTS

ILLUSTRATIONS

ACKNOWLEDGMENTS

In researching this book, it has been my privilege to do most of the work at the Huntington Library in San Marino, California. Ray Billington and Martin Ridge were constant sources of encouragement and insight. Mary Wright and Fred Perez tirelessly provided me with collection after collection, even under the extreme conditions of library construction. Most nourishing for any researcher at the Huntington are the exchanges of ideas at morning coffees, lunch, or the long walks through the garden or canyon which bring critical perspective to the task. John Phillip Reid has been most important over the years in giving critical, analytic insight about law during these walks. When Paul Zall guided us to quail, hawks, or great horned owls, we gained a greater appreciation of the environment that the pioneer attorneys of this study knew. Only at the Huntington could such marvels of nature enrich the life of the mind with such splendor.

This researcher also is indebted to many supporters. The American Bar Association generously supported my research travel. Dean Don Schweitzer at California State University, Fullerton, made money available for a computer consultant. President Jewell Plummer Cobb manifested her personal commitment to research scholarship with grant money for my travel to the Bancroft Library and the California State Library in Sacramento. My wife, Erika, dedicated many hours to computer manipulation of text and showed extreme self-control when more than three archive boxes of notes were scattered about my study at one time. My children, Angela and Jeffrey, were continuously patient with their father's obsession and late-night print runs.

I also owe a debt to numerous others for inspiration. They include Jeffrey Eugene Kelly, Michael Donovan, John O'Neel, Clinton Scrivner, Mark Straziuso, Billy Thomas III, Devon Alexander, Jenny Buck, Shelly Piper, Marty Cruz, Stephen Ho, Thomas House, Bryan MacGillvray, Brian Salisbury, Bruce Torkelson, John Traylor, Charles Mauzy, Jeffrey Anderson, James Galland, Craig O'Neill, Travis Dowdell, David Candow, James Thorp, Justin Branstad, Kenneth May, Lance Phillips, Eron R. A. Campuzano, Lynne Kelly, Julie Miller, Steven E. Meck, David Medina, Jason Nicoletti, Colin Price, Robert A. Schemel, Ellen Bowman, Kathi Geriak,

Michelle Hales, Jill Hassel, Alison Holman, Shannon Montoya, Tracy Nielson, Lisa Schweitzer, Chris Van Dieren, Julie Vendes, Julianne Vesper, Alicia Moon, Kendra Porter, Meredith Cline, Julie Casdorph, Lonny Snyder, Nate Rogers, Jeffrey Simeon, Brian Wolf, Julie Miltenberger, Cindy Schoner, George Charlesworth, Charles Conaway, James Harman, Jamie Majchrzak, Gerald Nakamura, Cale Pewthers, Todd Reese, Scott Reindl, Tim Sessom, Mark Van Dieren, Mike Watkins, Michael Woore, Matthew Gandin, Aaron Hamilton, Ritchie Ireland, Tommy Rowan, Joe Veltri, Jr., Heather Wood, Ivan Lopez, David C. Greer, Brent A. Stanford, Clint A. Owen, Eric Ambrosius, Robert Bowen, Steve Bryant, Patrick Chavez, Chris Chruma, Mac Cooper, John Daugherty, Jerome Facione, Keef Leasure, Joe Lechner, Rajai Qusar, Lance Kissinger, and Tempe Graves.

This book's errors and omissions are my responsibility.

The social history of the nineteenth-century California bar is primarily made up of the behavior of the men and a few women of a developing profession in a new state. The wave after wave of humanity that inundated Northern California in the first years of the gold rush included members of the early bar. Others followed. By the end of the century, a new breed of college-educated, California-born attorney entered practice, while at the same time the nature of practice also dramatically changed. The questions we ask of these pioneer lawyers are conservative from a methodological perspective. We want to know something of demography and biography. Bar admissions and contemporary biographical data provide the most useful information. More importantly, we must know what they did. How were they educated? How did they "find" law in the fabric of common law? What kind of law did they practice? How did they organize themselves to practice law and to achieve professional identity?

These questions are asked in the tradition of John Phillip Reid, not in the emerging emphasis of critical legal studies. Reid's *Law for the Elephant: Property and Social Behavior on the Overland Trail* is the most important book on law and culture in the American West because it focuses upon the law-mindedness of ordinary people. These people, Reid demonstrates, exhibited habits, actions, and values formed by a behaviorism based on law.[1] Professor Reid found that "law was the taught, learned, accepted customs of a people" and "the expression of an agrestic, community centered world we have lost, a custom bottomed on the sovereign's law, learned by living in a coercive state, and instilled into the marrow of social behavior."[2] On the other hand, David M. Trubek and John Esser have written that critical legal studies scholarship starts "from the premise that legal theory is an ideological product, part of a process through which unequal and unjust relationships are produced and reproduced in society."[3] This Neo-Marxist tendency to focus on ideology as a central concept and to explain ideologies in terms of the capitalist class's manipulation of economic and political institutions is clearly contrary to Reid's findings, which are based upon manuscript sources.

Even more certainly, critical legal studies scholars have yet to demonstrate that their theories have grounding in historical fact. Hendrik Hartog's "The End(s) of Critical Empiricism" essay probably said it best.

> There is indeed something rather odd about a sequence of writings that begins with the various pieces of the Amherst Seminar and ends with this comment. First the Amherstians (notably [Austin] Sarat and [Susan] Silby) write repeated methodological essays about the failure of sociolegal research to produce substantive scholarship that challenges dominant perspectives. Then Trubek and Esser write of the Amherstians' failure to produce "a scholarly article that explicitly champions a specific marginalized group." Now I write about the failure of Trubek and Esser to produce a substantive paradigm. How long can this go on?[4]

We should instead be basing our research and writing on historical data.

In commenting on critical empiricism, William C. Whitford suggested one kind of research design that addressed how people learn law and acquire values. Professor Whitford observed that "learning . . . is the experience of believing that one has acquired an enhanced ability to describe the causal relationship between different events." This process implies "an ability to predict the future with greater accuracy."[5] Whitford's research design suggested that inquiry at "particular locales at particular times" and more in-depth analysis of information not necessarily susceptible to computer manipulation could be fruitful.[6] This book's methods fall somewhere between the computer-manipulated data and the evidences of the learning process, behavior in an environment, and law-in-action.

My methodological approach in answering these questions is eclectic. In this functional analysis of lawyers, I have relied on manuscript sources. Although I am fond of quantification and computer analysis, as the footnotes should reveal, I am committed to analyzing behavior at the operational level of law. Lawyers functioning as attorneys for real clients with real problems provide the best evidence of behavior and the historical realities for the participants. This approach has required the tedious reading of millions of documents since 1970. The well-known fact to historians—that the seat of the pants must meet the seat of the chair—may be the reason for the paucity of historical scholarship based on critical legal studies. Perhaps not.

My presentation of history also is eclectic. My review of the secondary literature and the manuscripts has convinced me that in the affairs of lawyers, the participants often spoke better than their historians. In the alternative, my heavy reliance on writings of another century gives the reader a sense of the times as well as a sense of the people. Further, descriptions tell much of the environment. Whether in a courthouse or a mining camp, the people we see in frozen frame were our forebears in our legal world.

This history of California's early lawyers is, then, an analysis of individual attorneys operating in their times. Their words convey values that might seem wrong-headed to some in our "modern" times. Lenders expected to be paid back. Contracts were to be performed. Land titles were to be quieted. Criminals were personally responsible for their acts and punishment was to be swift and sure. These, with other fundamental faiths, were the values of the day for lawyers and most of their clients.

But these were not the only values. There were countervailing tendencies; creditors and their lawyers perceived that hoards of transient insolvent debtors were escaping bad judgment or hard times. Were the creditors victims of law? Or were the debtors victims of a capitalistic plot? As Patricia Nelson Limerick has observed about the West, it was often difficult to distinguish between victim and victor.[7] Squatters and claim jumpers appropriated real property despite the claims of others. Had they lost respect for private property? Would they be victims or victors? When property claimants consulted counsel, they searched for order and lawyers pursued their claims under law. Other individuals threatened to destabilize the community with personal violence and other criminal behavior. These were turbulent times when law seemed to be a hollow promise of relief from those who would disrupt the social order. These were times when law needed to be certain, sure, and useful.

California also experienced the industrial revolution in this half century. The coming of the railroad and factories forced lawyers to work with clients in a rapidly changing legal environment. The velocity of change in tort law during this time exceeded that in other fields.

The problem of understanding the interrelationship of law and values during this time period is a difficult one. I can only hope that this effort will at least map out some answers and illuminate the law as well as the lawyers of California during this half century.

The purpose of the historical map is multifaceted. Generally, history helps us to find patterns and repetitions. Often those patterns reveal cultural values, some of which are suggested above. History also can display patterns of beliefs, ideals, loyalties, and aspirations capable of transforming a random aggregation of people into a coherent society. California's gold rush and the creation of instant cities challenged the assumptions about patterns, but law was the glue that held institutions and the society together much as it had on the overland trail. Lawyers also were central in holding the society together and in mapping out the trail it would follow into the twentieth century.

The work of James A. Henretta and Theodore S. Hamerow have influenced how I have drawn this historical map. Their work on the nature of history and how it can be written has encouraged me to explore various methods in describing the social and institutional history of the legal profession in California.[8]

In 1979 James Henretta proposed an "action model" for the writing of social history.[9] Henretta found in the methods of the Annales school, the Marxist perspective, and the American reaction to them, a way of overcoming the limitations of the quantitative, conceptual, and narrative approaches to historical writing. The Annales school stressed the prime structural features of social, technological, and cultural life within a relatively small geographic environment. These historians used quantification to reduce the area of incomprehension with statistical analysis, attempting to grasp the totality of a society, and acknowledged a certain social determinism, or a belief that history was at least partially determined by external forces. Marxists wrote with the belief that the productive system was of crucial importance in the life of the society, that the relationship between standing and social production was manifest in class divisions, that change and contradiction were fundamental features of social reality, and that the relationship between social standing and production in a capitalistic society alienated men and women from both their labor and their inherent selves. American historians reacted to the primacy of sense perception of the Annales school and the ideology of the Marxists. They attempted to establish the facts in a spirit of neutral, passive detachment, acknowledging that human reason had limited power to understand the world, that models can comprehend only the immediate data to which they apply, and that there were no fundamental laws that comprehend the totality of human experience. The alternative Americanist position was to focus on the inherent value of the lives of the people, not the structures of power, and to depict the traditions, experiences, and struggles of the people to identify their conception of the world.

Henretta also offered, and I agree, that the work of Clifford Geertz is instructive, particularly the "thick description" to deal with the problem of specialized institutions that reach beyond the experiences of most individuals in a society. The research strategy suggested using "different informants or documentary sources to construct a comprehensive picture of the social world."[10] Law in a society often transcends an event, although a "thick description" of the event may be useful.

Henretta concludes that to overcome the limitations of these quantitative, conceptual, and narrative approaches we need to adopt a composite rhetorical mode of presentation. Historians should focus attention on the importance of human agency even as it depicts the limiting forms, structures, and geographies of the historical context. His conclusion about historical writing is optimistic, in that a presentation can produce history by adopting the proper mode.

Theodore S. Hamerow is less optimistic, but still helpful to this historian.[11] We write and read history, he offered, because the process is essential for the sense of identity of our civilized community. Some historians hope that in some obscure way they provide a glimpse of the future or give us a collective sense of direction or purpose. Others write and study history because it is a vital part of the cultural heritage of mankind, teaching wisdom and fostering virtue and making us into better human beings. These historians take seriously the words of John Stuart Mill that the object of universities "is not to make skillful lawyers . . . but capable and cultivated human beings." Rather, if we "make them capable and sensible men, they will make themselves capable and sensible lawyers." People may become competent lawyers without studying history, but only knowing history can make them thinking lawyers. Finally, Hamerow observed, "By providing a coherent intelligible account of the past, it satisfies a profound human yearning for knowledge about our roots."[12]

I have drawn from many methodological sources in writing this book. From the Annales school, I have attempted to comprehend the totality of law in society, but have looked at a geographical area far too large for the approach. I will argue that the rule of law and the elements of an autonomous legal system were the external forces that determined much of law's social history. From the Wisconsin school of legal history, I will introduce quantitative data and make empiricism central in analysis. In dealing with the problem of law transcending events, I have used a narrative that focuses on the attorney-client conversations of John D. Bicknell, a Los Angeles attorney.

On the level of theory and historiography, I conclude that the new Marxists have failed to grasp the genius and centrality of the rule of law in America. I base this conclusion on the ideas presented below as well as the conceptual approach to life of the participants in their legal history. The new Marxists, commonly called critical legal studies, particularly in our law schools, operate loosely around five concepts: (1) Legal doctrines are often aimed at legitimizing structures of power and distributions of wealth that are unjust and illegitimate; (2) legal literature is full of contradictions and deep-level incoherencies; (3) legal arguments are generally indeterminate; (4) explanations of legal rules and practices, especially those that purport to use general scientific methods and theories, such as economics, are often mere attempts to create an illusion of necessity, in order to lull people into accepting the status quo and adopting a defeatist attitude toward the possibility of radical change; and (5) critical legal studies methodology can set us free to choose new and better assumptions and thought patterns.[13] As is shown in the conclusion of this study, the words and actions of the historical figures of the study do not support these assumptions.

On the broader issues of the rule of law the words of Edward P. Thompson, rather than the critiques of Trubek, Esser, and Hartog are particularly apt:

> I am insisting only upon the obvious point, which some modern Marxists have overlooked, that there is a difference between arbitrary power and the rule of law. We ought to expose the shams and inequities which may be concealed beneath this law. But the rule of law itself, the imposing of effective inhibitions on power and the defense of the citizen from power's all-intrusive claims, seems to be an unqualified human good. To deny or belittle this good is, in this dangerous century when the resources and pretensions of power continue to enlarge, a desperate error of intellectual abstraction.[14]

We will find that the California bar and its clients had a profound respect for the rule of law. We will see that respect in their words and in their actions.

In the history of the American West, the history of the bar and of law is in its infancy. Western historians have found in the frontier and the West themes touching upon the role of law in America's westering process. Democracy in the form of participation, suffrage changes, and access to institutional power gained ground as Americans moved west. In the West legal change was evident in the abrogation of the English common law, in the creation of new institutions for the irrigation and mining frontiers, and in the velocity of change. There was a judicial recognition of Western uniqueness cited as a reason for legal change. Popular justice and frontier law enforcement coexisted in many communities. Despite the growing attention to the legal history of the American West, the role of the bar has drawn little print.[15] This book attempts to demonstrate the vitality of such inquiry. Specifically, it supports the observation of Andrew R. L. Cayton that a frontier people "needed . . . to be disciplined." A properly developed sense of the law as well as common sense would force a man "to connect his own good with that of society, and to enjoy his own rights in a manner that [would] not injure his neighbors."[16] To demonstrate this point, I will focus upon the work of William Higby to bring the rule of law in the abstract into the lives of the participants in the frontier community-building process. Law was the institutional glue that held communities together and enabled the building process to continue.

Finally, this book gives factual grounding for Patricia Nelson Limerick's observation that the lawsuit was very much a part of Western history.[17] Lawsuits were for courts and lawyers, but historians too often forget that lawsuits involved people caught up in controversy and dispute. In one sense, I have attempted to do what Limerick suggested was necessary, to look at Western history "as if one were a lawyer at a trial designed on the principle of the Mad Hatter's tea party—as soon as one begins to understand and empathize with the plaintiff's case, it is time to move over and empathize with the defendant."[18] Historians have too often understood California's history from the perspective of the vigilante rather than in the eyes of a lawyer like William Higby. We seldom have acknowledged the role of lawyers in civilizing the West. While we acknowledge that "the West was not where we escaped each other, but where we met,"[19] we have not yet recognized that one of the burdens of Western history is the state of its legal history.

1

The Lawyers

I . . . am doing what I can to keep "Peace on earth,
Good will among men" by the practice of law in a small way.
John Dustin Bicknell, August 7, 1889

The history of the private bar of California in the nineteenth century involves a rush for gold, the creation of instant cities, the growth of agribusiness, industrialization, urbanization, and the role of lawyers in the socioeconomic process. More specifically, it is a history of frontier turmoil, fluid standards of practice, growing demand for specialization, increased professional education, and an emerging professional identity in a maturing state. This study covers the period 1850–1900 and identifies the "frontier bar" as attorneys entering practice in the first three decades of that period.

The professionalization of the bar has recently attracted scholarly attention.[1] Gerard W. Gawalt's work on the Massachusetts bar has been particularly important because of his exhaustive research and careful use of collective biography.[2] This study of California's bar combines collective biography with an analysis of the role and function of the bar in a rapidly changing socioeconomic setting.

Who constituted the California bar at a particular time and place is not subject to as precise an answer as a social scientist would desire. The federal census of 1900 recorded 4,278 individuals holding themselves out as attorneys, up from the 1,115 lawyers of 1870.[3] The *Roll of Attorneys* in the Cali-

fornia State Archives in Sacramento has inscribed the names of 6,329
people admitted to practice for the period 1850 through 1900. Six hundred
nineteen won admission in the 1850s, 2,412 in the 1890s, and 223 in 1900.
Charles W. Palm reported in his *Lawyers' Directory of California* that 2,206
attorneys were available to provide professional services in 1889.[4] Palm's
directory was an early form of advertisement for attorneys who could afford
inclusion, but it failed to include all persons in practice at the time. *"Pile";
or, A Glance of the Monied Men of San Francisco and Sacramento County. Also
an Accurate List of Lawyers*, published in 1851, listed 153 persons practicing
law in the two California instant cities.[5] The *Roll of Attorneys* provided 164
names of admittees for 1850 and 1851. In the 1850s it was not unusual for
men to practice law in local justice courts without being admitted to the bar.[6]
Bar admission required attainment of twenty-one years of age, "good moral
character," and "the necessary qualifications of learning and ability."[7] The
justices of the peace these attorneys practiced before were not required to
be lawyers and, in the early days of the frontier, were schooled only in experience and the American cultural tradition. Given the slippery early definitions of the bar, it is not easy to provide any precise numbers, but the
extant figures do provide an adequate foundation for analysis.

One group of attorneys published their biographies in bar, county, and
city histories. These 1,168 attorneys, which will be referred to hereafter as
the elite group, provide the collective biographical data for this study.[8] California's elite frontier bar was a small percentage of the total number of lawyers admitted in California in the nineteenth century. One hundred twelve
of the attorneys in this study gained admission to practice in the 1850s and
1860s. One hundred sixty joined the bar in the decade of the 1870s, 340 in
the 1880s, and 529 in the last decade of the century. Of the lawyers that
practiced in the nineteenth century, 402 were members of other state bars
before joining the California bar. In the 1870s and 1880s the percentage
of lawyers with prior bar admission was substantially higher than the percentage in the pre-1870 period (8 percent in the 1850s, 19 percent in the
1860s, 27 percent in the 1870s, 28 percent in the 1880s, and 18 percent in
the 1890s).

The origins of the elite California bar in the nineteenth century shifted
dramatically from East coast and southern states in the frontier period to
California and the Midwest by the 1890s. The tide of migration of the 1850s
contained lawyers as well as miners, merchants, and entrepreneurs. Of the

attorneys admitted to the bar in the 1850s, 46 percent were born in the East, 28 percent in the old South, 11 percent in the Midwest, 11 percent in foreign countries, and 4 percent in the new Southwest. In the 1860s, lawyers from the East Coast and the Midwest accounted for 31 percent each of the total admitted in the decade. The South contributed 19 percent of the bar in the 1860s, the new Southwest 8 percent, foreign countries 8 percent, and California 3 percent. In the last three decades of the nineteenth century, California's contribution to the bar increased steadily. In the 1870s, 14 percent of the admittees were born in California, in the 1880s, 30 percent, and in the 1890s, 35 percent. The Midwest's contribution remained strong throughout the later period. In the 1870s, 23 percent of the admittees were Midwesterners, in the 1880s, 30 percent, and in the 1890s, 27 percent. For the last half of the century, California origins accounted for 27 percent of the bar, and Midwest origins, 27 percent. In each of these last three decades, the percentages for lawyers of East Coast and southern origins declined. Only the numbers of the foreign born remained fairly steady for all five decades, but they never contributed more than 11 percent in any decade.

In Los Angeles County, the frontier phase of the bar ended abruptly in the 1870s. Up to 1870, only a handful of lawyers practiced in the sleepy little town. They concentrated on the stuff of trade: debt collection and land-title litigation. But in 1878, Judge Ignacio Sepulveda reported: "Litigation is abundant here. There are about 50 lawyers in town, and my Court is open all the time. Law is becoming valuable and land titles are fought every day. I have a very busy time, but so far, everything has gone smoothly, the relations between the bench and the bar are unexpectedly pleasant."[9] The table below demonstrates the bar's growth in the 1870s.

THE LOS ANGELES COUNTY BAR

Year	Total No. Att'ys	Mean Age	Pop. per Att'y
1850	7	36.0	504.3
1860	24	37.8	472.2
1870	27	37.2	567.0
1880	85	42.3	398.6

These Los Angeles County attorneys left mid-Atlantic and New England states to establish law practices in the land of promise. The greatest economic promise in law was the uncertainty of land titles. Jonathan R. Scott and J. Lancaster Brent dominated the early title litigation practice. For them, the promise was fulfilled. Scott reported ownership of one thousand dollars in real estate in the 1850 census and Brent none. A decade later Scott possessed twentyfold in real estate plus ten thousand dollars in personalty, and Brent reported fifteen thousand dollars in real property and five thousand dollars in personalty.

The antebellum bar soon gave way to a cast of younger players. John D. Bicknell was a seasoned counselor entering the bar at thirty-four. Others of the new generation entered practice in their twenties: Stephen M. White (twenty-one), Erskine M. Ross (twenty-four), Jackson A. Graves (twenty-three), Will D. Gould (twenty-seven), Henry W. O'Melveny (twenty-two) and Bradner W. Lee (twenty-nine). These men entered practice early in life and they were survivors. Graves practiced for nearly thirty years, and Gould and O'Melveny persevered for over a half century. The new breed also had timing on its side. They entered practice in the 1870s when times were hard and legal business scarce. They established themselves in this competitive market and reaped the harvest of the boom of the 1880s. The work of Graves, O'Melveny, and Bicknell in the 1870s allowed their firms to capture the largest share of the county's legal business and persist for over a century.[10]

Elsewhere, lawyers who arrived in the later 1860s or early 1870s often dominated the practice of their county or city. A. S. Ensworth, a pioneer San Diego attorney, commanded the field in the 1850s and made 55 percent of the appearances in the county's trial courts in 1860. But his dominance dwindled due to the onslaught of the new legal legions of the late 1860s. Levi Chase, William T. McNeally, and William J. Gatewood all arrived at the end of the decade. In 1870 the firms of Chase and Leach, and Gatewood and McNeally made 55 percent of the appearances in the county trial courts. In Santa Barbara, Charles Huse and Charles Fernald had the upper hand in the 1850s and 1860s. Huse made 56 percent of the appearances in the 1862–63 term and 27 percent in the 1870–71 term of the district court. Huse and Fernald controlled 42 percent of the cases by 1871. By the 1890s county practice fell into the hands of men who arrived in the 1870s and associated themselves with Fernald or opened individual offices. Jarrett T. Richards arrived in 1868 and by the 1870–71 term made 15 percent of the appearances. Richards formed a partnership with John J. Boyce, who arrived in 1876, and with Fernald, Richards, Boyce, and several other arrivees of the 1870s came to dominate appearances by the 1890–91 term of the superior court.

During the first two decades of this study, the East Coast lawyers made up a large portion of the elite group of the bar. Sixty-two percent of the lawyers admitted to the California bar in the 1850s with a prior bar admission came from the East Coast. Midwestern lawyers accounted for 22 percent and their southern counterparts for only 9 percent. For the last half of the century the midwestern lawyers accounted for 37 percent and the East Coast lawyers for 29 percent of the total admittees with prior bar admissions. The South contributed fifty-seven barristers, totaling 14 percent.

Data from the *Roll of Attorneys* show that the origins of the previously admitted bar are somewhat different.[11] In 1879, the year when the largest number of lawyers were admitted before 1895, 97 of 298 admittees had prior bar admissions. Twenty were from New York, twelve from Illinois, six from Ohio, three from Michigan, one from Wisconsin, one from Minnesota, one from Indiana, and two from Iowa. The New York attorneys and their midwestern counterparts accounted for 47 percent of the experienced bar. For the period 1891–1900, 724 of the 2,420 admittees, or 29 percent, had prior admissions. Sixty-one hailed from New York, sixty-six from Illinois, twenty-eight from Indiana, twenty-seven from Iowa, ninety-five from Michigan, seventeen from Minnesota, eleven from Wisconsin, and twenty-nine from Ohio. Midwesterners accounted for 12 percent more of the prior admittees in the last decade of the century than in 1879. The number of prior bar admittees from the South in the last decade was dramatically smaller than among the early elite bar. Only one lawyer migrated from Alabama, two from Florida, two from Georgia, one from Mississippi, seven from North Carolina, one from South Carolina, thirteen from Virginia, two from West Virginia, and zero from Louisiana. The figures must be qualified, particularly for Michigan, because, as we will see, Michigan Law School graduates were in the habit of gaining admission in Michigan upon graduation and getting on the next train to California. Further, Californians sent their sons to eastern law schools until Hastings College of Law opened its doors in

1878. Some were admitted to the bar of the state of study before returning home. Although prior bar admission may not indicate actual practice experience, it clearly denotes educational attainment, by the 1890s, often law school. The fact that so many lawyers came to California with prior bar admission also suggests that the state remained a magnet of opportunity in the minds of many lawyers throughout the end of the century.

California's bar was large, and the bulk of those attorneys arrived in the last decade of the century. If we use comparative census data for Massachusetts, as Gerard Gawalt has so ably done, we see that Massachusetts had a bar of 3,412 in 1900, up from 1,270 in 1870. The California bar received 2,420 admittees in the last decade alone. The gold-rush bar came with the national stampede west, but the bar of the last quarter-century came for a variety of reasons—mostly economic—as outlined below.

The men of the frontier bar came to the state for a great variety of reasons, not solely to practice law. Henry Eno wrote from Iowa in 1848 that he was going to leave Iowa because "lawyers swarm like the Locusts of Egypt— there is over 40 in this County and not one who makes a living by his profession." Eno departed for California in 1849 to seek his fortune with the Argonauts without clear direction of vocation: "I may be the Lawyer. I may be an office holder or I may be the merchant and if worse comes to worse, I may be obliged to work for a living."[12] Eno went to the mines, but turned to the practice of law and then officeholding. He was elected as Calaveras County judge and later as Alpine County judge. Public office was economic security in a mining county that provided lawyers with haphazard means of making a living at the bar. Eno's experience was not isolated for members of the frontier bar. Five hundred forty-one of the lawyers in this study held office. During the period of 1849–1900, half of those who held office did so before 1889, and the other half held office after 1889, which indicates that officeholding decreased as the century progressed. The mean age of officeholders was thirty-three. California lawyers in rural counties were more frequently officeholders than their urban counterparts. This California experience was similar to that of Dodge City, Kansas, attorneys. C. Robert Haywood has observed that "the usual channel of advancement for a lawyer unsuccessful in practice was to run for political office."[13] The same applied to the Henry Enos of the Golden State bar.

Ambrose Eastman needed focus in his professional life and looked to California when he wrote to Charles Fernald seeking advice:

I have met a serious reverse in an enterprise which I entered upon a year or two ago outside of my profession. It settles definitely and finally that my true course is to adhere strictly hereafter to my profession, and lean solely upon that. My mistakes in life are due altogether to departures from that course, in the hope of speedier returns from other sources. I have a moderate and growing practice here, but the disappointments I have met make me look for "fresh fields and pastures new," where with hope and energy I can catch up the fight and win a place in my profession which shall be recognized and valuable. I know that I can grow into a good lawyer. I write to ask frankly if its worth while for me to come to Santa Barbara.[14]

This quest for greener pastures was very much a part of the 1870s, leading some lawyers to practice in a new place or to move from private practice into public life.

One of the lawyers who left Greenfield, Missouri in 1872 was John Dustin Bicknell. He dissolved his law partnership, conveyed partnership lands to his partner, paid up his indebtedness, split the assets, and started for Los Angeles.[15] Although he left the Missouri bar behind, his colleagues did not forget his mailing address. George D. Orner, a Joplin attorney, wrote to him on August 14, 1875: "What are the chances on the coast for one of 'my ability' with a capital of just justification to get there. I have been constantly in the practice since 1867—one year I was in politics—and you know from practice and experience that there is no money in the practice at this point or in this section."[16] C. W. Threasher of Neosho made a similar inquiry in 1874, complaining: "law business here has fallen off more than one-half since you left and there is little in the country except what comes from lead and zinc."[17] J. M. Richardson's February 1875 letter echoes Threasher's observation, "Could a lawyer make a living there? Our country has improved little since you left."[18] P. H. Ward did not have the advantage of long experience in Missouri, but wanted out.

I am contemplating settling in California to practice my profession—law. My attention has been called to Los Angeles as a town offering as good inducements to Attorneys as any place of its size in the state. Any information about your city or other places in your state that is a good place for lawyers, will be thankfully received.

I have been here but a few months, having recently come from the

University of Virginia; and I am not satisfied with the prosperity of the Country; or the amount of business done here.[19]

The theme of the 1870s was desperation born of an oversupply of lawyers or a lack of work. Many perceived California as a land of opportunity.[20]

California too had its problems with the ratio of lawyers to law business. J. M. Kennedy of San Francisco wrote to Bicknell to inquire about prospects in Los Angeles.

I have been unable to get into any Law Office, although I have been introduced to many of the best firms here. The trouble is that I being a stranger and not acquainted with the general vocation of the practice in a large city, would not be of sufficient assistance to justify them in paying me enough to live upon. They can get plenty of office boys living with their parents for $10 per month and here again there are hundreds of young fellows just standing in the profession and living at home who are glad to accept positions in Law Offices for the purpose of studying, so that I have concluded to give up the practice of law and try something else.[21]

Kennedy's experience was an exception because unemployment among lawyers was low, although many turned to other pursuits.[22] Whether Henry Eno in a rural county or J. M. Kennedy in the mecca of Golden State law, pursuing another trade was always a possibility.

Others came to California for more personal reasons. Lawyers were among the health seekers that came to California throughout the period.[23] John Downey Works was one lawyer who came to San Diego in search of better health. He established a thriving private practice and served on the California Supreme Court.[24] Milton Smith, writing to John D. Bicknell from Ithaca, New York, in 1888, opined: "I like a milder climate than we have here and expect to locate to Los Angeles after November."[25] But there was more to California than just good weather. John D. Bryan of Las Cruces, New Mexico, thought of moving to Los Angeles to "have the benefit of good schools and churches." Bryan had two boys to educate and was a Catholic. He understood that Los Angeles had "good schools and that the Catholics [were] well represented."[26] Bicknell wrote to Bryan six weeks later: "I think it [Los Angeles] is a good place to practice law yet a great many come here and make failures. In short everything depends upon yourself."[27] The surviving documents tell of lawyers seeking money, better climate, and educational opportunity. Bicknell thought that success depended upon personal effort, but the experiences of J. M. Kennedy and Henry Eno indicated that other factors played a part. Similarly, Henry Eno's turning to public office was mirrored by other lawyers turning to concurrent occupations to support their law practices.

California's nineteenth-century lawyers did not confine their vocational energy solely to law practice, particularly in the third quarter of the century. Many also held public office, a tendency that was more evident in rural than in urban areas. Attorneys also engaged in a wide range of other concurrent occupations. Ranching, banking, and journalism attracted some. Others gravitated to mercantile pursuits or the world of corporate management. Time and place had a great deal to do with the necessity of seeking a living outside the courtroom.

Of the elite bar members who held public office, 14 percent served in the legislature; 21 percent were on the bench; and 15 percent held administrative jobs in government. The frontier bar was substantially different from those that would follow. In the decade of the 1850s only 5 percent of the total took office. The Civil War decade accounted for 5 percent of the fifty-year total; the 1870s, 13 percent; the 1880s, 24 percent; and the 1890s, 53 percent. The changing mix over time reflected the increased competition for clients and the increased size of government. The growth of the "great" law firms in the 1870s and 1880s constricted the business available for the sole practitioner and the smaller new firms. As Jackson A. Graves correctly observed about the 1870s: "I, and the firms I was subsequently associated with, controlled all the legal commercial business of Los Angeles." In the area of real estate, the firm of Graves and O'Melveny "examined more abstracts of title than all the [other] lawyers of Los Angeles put together" in the period 1885–90.[28] For the lawyers operating outside of the great firms and their referrals, public office represented security as well as opportunity in an increasingly competitive profession.

This "great firm" domination was not a California phenomenon. Gerard Gawalt observed that in late-nineteenth-century Massachusetts a few lawyers in each county dominated court practice. Robert Haywood saw the same pattern in Dodge City, Kansas, with "the established attorneys" handling "most cases."[29] Public officeholding and concurrent employment often were alternatives of necessity.

If a lawyer chose public office, he did so early in life. In the elite group, 62 percent of the officeholders held their first office prior to the age of thirty-five. Lawyers admitted to another state bar were the youngest, with 87 percent entering public life prior to age thirty. Even with experience and another bar admission in hand, young lawyers often needed the income and publicity that public office could bring. General practitioners dominated the officeholders, occupying more than 80 percent of all offices for the last half of the century. Generalists more frequently than specialists held subsequent offices. Specialists obtained needed publicity in a few offices and harvested the produce of short terms of public service.

The origins of lawyers holding public office changed dramatically in the last half of the century. In the 1850s, East Coast and southern members of the bar dominated the public officeholding statistics. East Coast lawyers accounted for 52 percent of the officers and southern lawyers for 33 percent. In the decade of the 1860s, the shift in first offices held was extreme, with southerners accounting for only 12 percent, while East Coast lawyers held 40 percent, and midwesterners 28 percent. The Civil War and southern origins became negative associations for California voters, although the substantial staying power of first-time southern officeholders was evidenced by their frequently holding second offices. By the 1890s the shift was nearly complete. Victor Montgomery of Santa Ana observed in a letter to George Smith Patton that southerners would no longer be successful in politics because "the State is becoming yankeeized."[30] In the 1860s the dropout rate for southern officeholders was nil, as it was in the 1870s. The reason for the change was the influx of attorneys from other regions; they increased the competition at the polls for the limited number of public offices. Another, more significant change was the growing number of native sons entering the bar. In the 1890s California-born attorneys held 37 percent of the offices and the southerners a mere 9 percent.

Geography and officeholding for these young men had a very close relationship. If a lawyer chose a rural or mining county to hang out a shingle, he was more likely to hold public office than his urban counterpart. All of the lawyers in the elite bar from Calaveras, Contra Costa, Marin, Modoc, San Benito, Shasta, Sierra, Siskiyou, Tuolumne, Ventura, and Yuba counties held at least one public office during their careers. In Los Angeles County, only 53 of 257 lawyers in this study held public office. In San Francisco, only 50 of 147 attorneys held office. In developing counties like Alameda, the ratio was much closer: 15 never held public office and 13 did. Similarly, in San Diego, 28 never served in public office and 16 did. Sacramento County was little different, with 19 not serving and 13 serving in at least one office. The urban lawyer had more opportunity, albeit limited by the large firms in the latter part of the century, to seek and find income in private practice.

Two attorneys exemplify the public service and private enterprise routes to success. Oliver S. Witherby was born in Cincinnati in 1815 and was a graduate of Miami University. He was admitted to the Ohio bar in 1840 and came to San Diego in 1849 with the U.S. Boundary Commission as quartermaster. He won election to the California assembly and a subsequent appointment as district judge. In 1853 he was appointed collector of customs for the port of San Diego. During his career he made a fortune in real estate.[31] Leland G. Stanford assessed his career as follows: "For the better part of two decades Witherby specialized in holding remunerative public positions that were undemanding of his time and permitted him to pursue professional and business opportunities as he chose."[32] Moses L. Wicks of Los Angeles "gave up law for real estate and in the 1880s was an active subdivider."[33] By the turn of the century, Wicks held himself out as dealing in "law, oil and mining."[34] Law facilitated public service as well as private entrepreneurial activity.

Time and place also was a factor in the profitability of the law business. San Francisco went through boom and bust cycles in the 1850s that had an impact on law business. William Higby wrote to his father in 1851 describing San Francisco: "Our city is busy and bustling and like a sprightly, healthy, fat infant, with a kind and capable mother to nourish it, is growing lusty and increasing in size rapidly. Why not, with the whole world to feed it."[35] With prosperity, all benefited; but San Francisco would suffer because of the chaos of growth.[36] Meanwhile, David Smith Terry was trying to make a living in Stockton. He wrote to his wife, Cornelia, in 1852, "For some time past I have been almost constantly engaged [in practicing law, and] besides this I have been engaged in farming and various other businesses."[37] In 1870 Terry, like so many other California lawyers, was involved in mining litigation in Nevada. From Hamilton, Nevada, Terry thought Stockton looked good.

I do not think this country is at all likely to prove a good place for making rapid fortunes at the law. There is too great a dread of the expense of litigation and very few people have the means if they had the will to carry on mining suits which are greatly more expensive than any other class of cases. Compromise and consolidation are the usual course in all disputes about mines and the litigation outside of mining cases will always be better in Stockton than here.[38]

To Terry litigation was still the ingredient that produced income.

To a young practitioner trying to break into litigation, particularly in a rural county, concurrent employment was a necessity. J.P.C. Morgan opened his practice in Placer County out of his hotel room in the Borland Hotel, offering his legal talents as well as "lessons in bookkeeping, penmanship and German."[39] This trend was even more evident in counties where litigation dried up with the economy. Mining counties like Mariposa showed a sharp decline in lawyers exclusively practicing law, as litigation declined to almost nil in the last decade of the century.

Some members of the California bar became part of the state's newspaper industry, more frequently in rural areas, to provide a source of income. In urban areas, the editor-attorney was a professional journalist. William Thomas Baggett, for example, came to California in 1877 after four years of practice in Tennessee. Settling in San Francisco, he published the *Pacific Coast Law Journal* in 1878, the *San Francisco Law Journal* in 1879, the *Pacific Coast Law Journal* in 1880–81 with William H. Davis also editing the *Daily Examiner*, in 1880–81. In 1882–83, he shared ownership of the *San Francisco Daily Law Journal* with Davis and James H. Stockwell.[40] Cornelius Cole was a forty-niner, an organizer of the California Republican party, and editor of the *Sacramento Daily Times* prior to his election to the U.S. Congress in 1863 and Senate in 1866.[41] Colonel Jeff Gatewood was an experienced publisher from the period of the Mexican War and established the *San Diego Union* upon his arrival there in 1868. He later sold a one-half interest to Charles Taggart, which enabled him to build up his practice in Old Town. In 1872 he founded the *Daily World*. B. Conklin and Jacob M. Julian purchased the *World* in 1875. Both were experienced publishers from Missouri. Two years later Conklin was elected district attorney and to a superior court judgeship in 1900.[42] These professional men worked at both the newspaper business and the practice of law at various times in their careers, but journalism was their main focus.

In the less populated legal centers of California, lawyers mixed journalism, public service, private practice, and other pursuits to make a living. Walter Van Dyke was an Ohio attorney who came to Los Angeles in 1850, won election as district attorney in 1851, and to the state assembly in 1852. For the next few years he was in Fort Humbolt organizing the city, working for election as district attorney, and editing the *Humbolt Times*. With the election of 1861 he went to the state senate for two sessions and then on to private practice in San Francisco and Los Angeles.[43] Theodore Eldon Jones also came to California in 1850 and went straight to the Placerville diggings. In 1853 he turned his attentions to mining in Trinity County. In 1861 he established the *Trinity Gazette* and a decade later edited the *Shasta Courier*. Prior to his election as county judge in 1875, he edited the *Trinity Journal*. In 1879 he won election to the superior court bench, and the people retained him in three subsequent elections.[44] Elijah Carson Hart was a reporter for the *Marysville Daily Appeal*, the editor of the *Oroville Mercury* and the *Journal* in Willows. While in Willows, he studied law and won admission to the bar in 1885. Leaving the countryside and journalism the next year, Hart served in a series of public offices in Sacramento.[45] John C. Gray was a Maine attorney and also an editor of the *Oroville Mercury*. Prior to opening his law office in Oroville in 1872, he taught school for seven years. Gray served in several elected positions before achieving the superior court bench in 1890.[46] J. A. Adair was a Bear Valley teacher before his admission to the bar. After a two-year term as district attorney, he edited the *Mariposa Gazette* in 1895 and became its owner in 1897. Mariposa County litigation evaporated in the 1890s with the decline of the mining industry and most members of the bar remaining in the county were forced into other vocations.[47]

Other attorney-editors moved like the wind. Thomas Fitch was the editor of the *Milwaukee* (Wis.) *Free Democrat* in 1859, the next year a law student in San Francisco, an editor again in 1861 in San Francisco, the next year in Placerville as editor of the *Republican*, in 1863–64 the editor of the *Virginia City* (Nev.) *Union*, an 1864 member of the Nevada Constitutional Convention, and finally a practicing attorney. Fitch put out his shingle in Belmont, Nevada, in 1869, in Salt Lake City, in 1871, in San Francisco, in 1875, in Prescott, Arizona, in 1877, in Minneapolis, Minnesota, in 1880, and in

Tucson, in 1881. Fitch, like 5 percent of California's elite bar, practiced in three or more locations in a career. California's bar was clearly more geographically mobile than the Massachusetts bar of 1870–90. Gerald Gawalt has observed that "geographic mobility was apparently low before 1840, and for lawyers admitted between 1870 and 1890 geographical immobility became nearly universal."[48] California attracted men who chased mining strikes as well as litigation. Another factor faced by the rural bar was the lack of transportation providing spacial mobility for practice; whereas, as Gawalt notes, Massachusetts transportation networks afforded the requisite mobility, enabling a centralized practice.

Other members of the bar dabbled in newsprint, but concentrated more on law practice and public service. Robert Ferral was one such attorney. Arriving in California in 1852 with years of experience in the newspaper business, he became a member of the Aurora bar. In 1869–70 he was elected successively clerk of the California assembly, secretary of the senate, and clerk of the assembly. Ferral also served as district attorney, judge of the city criminal court, and superior court judge. In 1872–73 he was an editorial writer with Henry George for the *San Francisco Evening Post*.[49] Clarence Greathouse was an editorial writer for the *Examiner* in 1885–86, after fifteen years of private practice in San Francisco. Greathouse left journalism and law in 1886 when President Cleveland appointed him U.S. consul-general to Japan.[50] James W. Coffroth was a Pennsylvania-born journalist and editor of the *Spirit of the Times*. He arrived in California in 1851 and settled in Tuolumne County. In that year he was the county delegate to the state Democratic convention and the people sent him to the state senate for the 1853, 1854, 1856, and 1857 sessions. C. Robert Haywood's study of Dodge City, Kansas, lawyers established a similar pattern of concurrent employment in journalism and officeholding in the face of increased competition for law business.[51]

Three important demographic trends emerge from the data. In politics, rural lawyers more frequently held political office than their urban counterparts. Second, rural lawyers more frequently turned to journalism as a concurrent occupation and played a larger role in state journalism as a result. As will be developed subsequently, these two activities played an important role in the development of the social, political, and economic fabric of the state. A third trend is that small town practitioners needed concurrent employment to sustain themselves economically. Advertisements such as this

in general, just as Lelia Robinson Sawtelle in Massachusetts sued for admission to the bar and worked for legislation.[57] Foltz continued to make contributions to California's legal tapestry. She was one of the creators of the California parole system in 1893 and the author of the Foltz Defender Bill, which created the state system of public defenders for the criminally accused.[58] Clara Foltz, indeed, pioneered for all Californians in opening opportunity in the profession to all.

These were the people of the bar doing a miriad of things among which was the private practice of law. In the following chapter I will describe and analyze what they did. As Patricia Nelson Limerick has so ably put it "one skill essential to the writing of Western American history is a capacity to deal with multiple points of view. It is as if one were a lawyer at a trial designed on the principle of the Mad Hatter's tea party."[59] Writing Western legal history is a similar task, particularly in choosing the representative narratives that illuminate the issues. Because I am dealing with the supposedly orderly topic of law, the task should be easier, at least as easy as it was to practice law in nineteenth-century California.

2

Legal Education and Literature

*If you have determined to adopt the law as your
profession, I suggest as the most direct and certain means of qualifying
yourself for the work that you enter some law school.*
—Jackson A. Graves to Mortimer C. Patterson, May 4, 1896

The education of America's lawyers in the nineteenth century was achieved through the apprenticeship system, reading law outside of a law office, in college classrooms, and in law school lecture halls.[1] On the frontier, lawyers gained knowledge traveling with other lawyers and judges from court to court on circuit. Daniel Calhoun's description of the Tennessee bar in the early 1900s was very much like the gold-rush bar of California a half century later. The frontier lawyer in Tennessee rode circuit in close proximity with other lawyers, the judge, and the attorney general. Life on circuit was both professional and social in this circle of practitioners. Standard equipment was a good horse, Blackstone's *Commentaries*, the Tennessee statutes, and a branding iron to brand the livestock received as fees. There was an emotional intensity to life in the frontier bar, which quickly gave way to a more stable, specialized bar with major practitioners garnering most of the cases.[2] This frontier bar was educated in the courtroom, in the local inn, and by Blackstone. There also was an elite group schooled in the classics, Blackstone, and rhetoric. Robert A. Ferguson's *Law and Letters in American Culture* describes an elite bar of classically trained men who saw law as culture and part of a political religion. These generalists used oratory and general historical and philosophical principles to persuade audiences, whether political or legal. This classical tradition gave way in the 1850s to specialists, scholars who saw no need to see the larger framework, but served industrial clients ably. Only on the frontier did the classical tradition survive into the later nineteenth century.[3] Charles E. DeLong's experience as a member of the gold-rush bar best exemplifies the frontier tradition of law learned on the circuit and rhetoric used as a tool of legal persuasion.

Charles E. DeLong came to California lured by gold as a teenager. He later turned to nonmining pursuits, and finally to the law. After the fever of forty-nine abated, he started to collect foreign-miner license taxes from the Chinese. In 1855 he reported that his nocturnal hunt for Chinese miners netted him "about 80 licenses."[4] The next year DeLong turned to the practice of law in the justice courts of the mother lode without the benefit of study or a license. In February 1856, he confided in his diary that the "suit came off. Had a great time, got beat like thunder, right against the law and evidence."[5] By May he was "taxing [his] wits in order to find a loop hole of escape."[6] In September he had moved on to criminal defense work. On September 8 and 9, 1856, he defended Michael Purcell on an assault and battery charge. The trial went well, but the "jury retired and balloted 11 for acquittal and one for guilty." The jury "returned without a verdict" and "were sent back and finally came in with a verdict of guilty. A proof of what one obstinate man can do."[7] DeLong's diary was filled with civil and criminal trial experiences for most of 1856. Amid a heavy litigation and debt collection practice, DeLong decided to study for the bar. Study and practice went hand in hand. In March 1857 he litigated and applied himself to his studies.[8] In April, DeLong "studied Chitty on Contracts" or "stayed home all day studying some but loafing more; drew up two complaints against Samuel Briggs at request of A. E. Cowsby (a negro) one for petit larceny and one for damages on nonfulfilling a contract."[9] In May he was still studying and practicing, but now "reading Blackstone" and "Kent, until ten, commenc[ing] a new rule of life, secular and rational with an eye to the future."[10] Late in May, DeLong was studying "Blackstone pretty steady, through the day, [but] it was most intolerable."[11] In June, Kent was the regular fare, and on June 16 DeLong "called on Judge May [and] criticized him some on law. [It was the] intention of both of [them] to go to Marysville in August to be admitted." Neither the lawyer nor the judge he appeared before had the benefit of admission to the bar. However, both DeLong and May had access to law books and were in the process of becoming members of the bar. May, like the justices of the peace described by John R. Wunder, had access to legal literature and demonstrated legal competency.[12] The frontier bar of the 1850s received its education in law from books and in action in the justice courts of the mother lode.

DeLong continued his studies until he took his bar examination in September. He "studied like a Turk," particularly Blackstone.[13] In July, DeLong wrote that he was "bent over [his] studies closely." He "viewed the distant future with a determination to succeed."[14] "[I] went down to May's and he catechized me in Blackstone and I did him. I got through quite well."[15] In September he returned to Judge May's and "had a set-to of examination out of Blackstone under the old tree, prepatory to application for admittance."[16] All this work paid off, because on September 30 DeLong passed, "received congratulations from [his] friends and put up [his] shingle as an Attorney at Law over [his] door after dark." Although DeLong prepared for the bar by the traditional path of reading law, he did not do it in a lawyer's office. Rather, his education was concurrent with actual practice during the turbulent times of the mother lode.

After passing the bar, DeLong continued his studies, reading state statutes, John Marshall's opinions, the California *Reports*, and various treatises. His education continued amid a flourishing practice in debt collection and criminal defense until 1859, when the Comstock lured him east.[17]

DeLong was not alone on his path to the bar. Robert Henry Fauntleroy Variel was born in the year of the gold rush and went to California in 1852 by oxteam to Camptonville in Yuba County. There he received a public school education and entered the teaching profession at age nineteen. In 1873 he was elected district attorney for Plumas County, even "before he had ever read a page of law." Variel studied law while performing his public duties and was admitted to practice before the district court in 1876 and the supreme court in 1879. He served in the state assembly and practiced law in San Francisco and Los Angeles.[18] Like DeLong, he learned law on the job and read law in his spare time.

The bar examinations of the nineteenth century were less than thorough excursions into legal learning. They were conducted orally and often consisted of a single question, such as What is a deed? or What is a contract? Although simple in form, such an examination, if the issue was thoroughly explored by the examiner, could go to the heart of the practice of the nineteenth century, because the substantive issues raised were the stuff of practice of the period. Other bar examinations were not so exacting. One examination before the California Supreme Court was noteworthy. Justice Edward Norton asked the applicant two questions. First, "What is the purpose of a demurrer?" The student answered, "For the delay." The judge trumpeted, "Young man, that's not the law." The judge asked the second question, "If a man brought you a promissory note past due and wanted it collected by law in the most expeditious manner, what would you do?" The student responded, "I would collect my fee." The judge again declared that that was "not the law," but leaned over his desk to his clerk and ordered, "Mr. Clerk, swear him in." Although the prospective lawyer did not give the "law" answers expected, he did give the judge the practical "lawyering" answers necessary for successful practice in frontier California. As late as 1897, a person was admitted to the Texas bar without answering a single question. The admittee, later Texas Governor James E. Ferguson, observed: "It's not as bad as it sounds, for a lawyer is not like a doctor. When a lawyer starts to practice law, he is really just beginning to learn, regardless of his training. He has other lawyers and the judge to correct his mistakes. If a doctor doesn't know what he is about, he has only the undertaker to cover up his mistakes."[19] Regardless of the nature of the oral examination, the bar's official rite of passage in the nineteenth century was easy compared with the written bar examination of present-day California.

Education patterns of the elite California bar changed substantially during the nineteenth century. In the 1850s, 75 percent of the lawyers read law prior to admission, 6 percent attended law school, and 18 percent graduated from law school. In the decade of the Civil War, 64 percent read law, 4 percent attended law school, and 32 percent graduated from law school. In the remaining three decades of the century, the percentage of those reading law declined steadily to 36 percent in the 1890s. The percentage attending law school and not graduating declined to 3 percent, whereas the percentage graduating from law school soared to 62 percent by the 1890s. Despite this shift, California's bar lagged behind the Massachusetts bar in formal legal education. As Gerard Gawalt has observed, "very few lawyers admitted to practice in Massachusetts between 1870 and 1890 did not take at least one term of study at one of the law schools." Regardless of law school training, the clerkship could prove valuable. As Jackson A. Graves remembered his clerkship in the firm of Eastman and Neuman of San Francisco in 1873, he "acquired knowledge, not only of law but of men, every minute of the day. It was getting practice which the books cannot teach one."[20] The tradition of reading law was declining, but its utility to some was clear.

One reason for the decline of reading law as a path to admission to the bar was that it was a haphazard process, subject to criticism. An observer of the frontier bar commented that Judge Charles N. Creaner, district judge for El Dorado, Amador, Calaveras, Tuolumne, and San Joaquin Counties was "not educated for the law; he was an old army officer. He rarely gave reasons for his decisions; he just decided cases, and almost always decided them right." For light reading, Judge Creaner chose Blackstone's *Commentaries*.[21] Another commentator thought that Francis J. Dunn of the Nevada County bar was "one of the most singular characters at this bar. He was a man of sturdy sense, somewhat uncultivated who had picked up a fair knowledge of law, was pleasant and accommodating when sober, and opinionated and surly when in his cups."[22] Frederick P. Tracy served as San Francisco city attorney in 1857–59 and was a graduate of New England Methodist College, but a contemporary believed that "he was not trained for the bar, and his legal education was defective. He took up the study comparatively late in life."[23] The frontier lawyer came into direct competition with the giants of the bar like Stephen J. Field as well as a growing number of attorneys trained in law schools. Formal education provided a mantle of authority as well as the entrée to the extent that Jackson A. Graves, a successful pioneer of the Los Angeles bar, saw law school training as a requirement by the 1890s.

But the law school–trained attorney did not have the benefit of the circuit experience. DeLong's experience as a frontier lawyer in the mother-lode country evidenced a sense of community similar to that described by Daniel Calhoun of eighteenth-century Tennessee. DeLong's dairies contain numerous entries detailing social and professional occasions. He played cards with his peers and joined them for supper for a "grand howl."[24] In May 1859, DeLong "went up to Sucker's Flat . . . with Judge Bliss." They "had a beautiful time, drank lots of whiskey, saw all the boys and found them all right." He "came home after dark," stopping "at Bridges and had some fun with songs and recitations."[25] The small group of lawyers and judges were a social fraternity as well as the guiding forces of the law on the frontier.

2. Gold-rush clients at Spanish Flats.
Reproduced by permission of The Huntington Library, San Marino, California.

DeLong also found rhetoric as well as learning to be part of the practice of law in the mining camps, just as his antebellum, classically trained counterparts had in their practices. In May 1857, "some negroes, Bules and Todd, came up and retained [him] to defend them in a case against Snyder brought to recover a bill for lumber, labor and goods." With "no chance to win the suit only on defects in pleadings," DeLong retained co-counsel and "studied some on it," finding "several flaws." Two days later DeLong recovered $57.50 for Todd, "by a masterly effort of over 5 hours duration," but lost Bules's case. DeLong reported that he "got great credit for [his] effort." He charged his clients $50 for his services and "got $9 down." [26] On

June 22, 1857, DeLong "started for Brandy City early in the Morning with Judge May and A. J. Batchelder, May [going] to assist [him]." Upon arrival, they "found Judge Smith as opposing counsel." The trial commenced that morning with "a good deal of contrary swearing and more quarreling and pettifogging than [he had] ever [seen]." DeLong "led off throughout and . . . felt that [he did] himself ample justice [in his closing] argument about 2 o'clock at night." The next morning the jury came in for his client "for the full amount." He paid May ten dollars, "started for [the] road and . . . went to bed by dark feeling miserable from too much studying."[27]

On December 14, DeLong was appointed defense attorney for Michael Lyons and Patrick Lynch, who were accused of the murder of Nelson Johnson at Foster's Bar. He made several motions successfully and won adjournment until the afternoon of the fifteenth. The next morning he went "to Foster's" and "saw Johnson['s body, which] . . . was cut up awfully." That afternoon in court, he opened with "several desperate Motions in behalf of prisoners," which were "overruled." In this darkest hour "the whole thing looked mighty bad," so he obtained a compromise to have Lynch discharged. The next day "the Court refused to allow it," so, with "all hope . . . gone," DeLong argued for "four hours . . . until [he] tired out." Rhetoric and knowledge were the stock in trade of the mother-lode attorney just as they had been for the attorneys Robert Ferguson has so ably analyzed. So too, the lawyers of Dodge City described by C. Robert Haywood often relied upon oratorical skills in the courtroom.[28] The short, emotion-packed trials of the mother-lode country forced cogent argument.

Although DeLong strenghthened his practice with experience and long hours of study, Henry K. S. O'Melveny used comparative analysis to hone his practice skills. O'Melveny's 1860 commonplace book contains an extensive comparative analysis of Illinois and California statutes and cases. The subject matter was the stuff of antebellum law practice: contracts, real estate, and debt collection. Real estate law notations include references to homestead exemptions, "Illinois cases in reference to possession," and Mexican titles.[29] Law could be digested and categorized for the practitioner's convenience. O'Melveny's son, Henry, would have the benefit of a college education.

Henry William O'Melveny was educated in the classics. In high school, geometry, rhetoric, history, botany, and chemistry occupied O'Melveny's time. When he entered the University of California at Berkeley at fifteen, he continued the same course of study, concentrating in the classics and Latin. Graduating before his twentieth birthday, Henry accepted a position as tutor on Harry Turton's sugar plantation in Lahaina, Maui. There, like DeLong, he read the classics of the law. He completed volume one of Kent's *Commentaries* on February 6, 1880, and the second volume in July. "Now for Blackstone," he wrote, starting the classic excursion of the nineteenth century legal education. Henry started on September 10, 1880, studying what was relevant and omitting "whatever . . . was useless for an American student to know confining [him]self to what it appeared . . . was applicable." [30] In 1940, when looking back on his educational experience O'Melveny thought that the Berkeley experience, particularly his exposure to Charles Darwin's works, forced him into developing a philosophy of life that carried into a distinguished legal career.[31] O'Melveny, whose lawyering experience started when he joined the family firm, was representative of a new, college-educated breed of California lawyer.

David Murray of Delhi, New York, received a similar education. He graduated from college in 1876. He then read law in the office of a county judge and with his father, who was "one of the Justices of the Supreme Court" of New York. Murray "read thoroughly most of the leading elementary works." To pass the California bar examination, he needed but "a few Months study . . . to become familiar with the practices of the Court." John Dustin Bicknell gave him such an opportunity in 1877 by bringing him in as a law clerk.[32]

T. K. McDowell of Grand Round, Oregon was not prepared well for the bar. Writing in 1872, McDowell told Bicknell:

My education I fear is deficient as I have never studied the Latin nor had that drilling of the mind which is consequent to a collegiate course. At the same time, however, I cannot say that my education is much more limited than many of the lawyers that succeed in the business. As to the qualifications of my mind and heart for the business of the law, I shall leave that for you to say. I should have prepared myself by study— at least on Contracts and Evidence as Blackstone and Kent are about as far as I got when the question would come up whether I should attend law school or not. In studying law again I should prefer your plan explained to me several times in Greenfield (Missouri), to wit, search all the authors on question of law, instead of reading by rote a volume at a time.[33]

Despite his educational disadvantages, McDowell thought "The practice of law and the chances connected with that profession [were] the best plan . . . to make money."[34] In January 1873, he moved to Santa Ana and got a job on a farm. In March he was herding sheep.[35]

With time, the number of attorneys receiving a formal education rose.[36] In the elite bar of the 1850s, only 14 percent of the members were law-school graduates. That percentage increased steadily throughout the fifty-year period studied, with 41 percent of the elite bar admitted in the period 1890–1900 holding law degrees. In addition to the perceived need for a law-school education, the founding of Hastings College of Law in 1878 had a profound impact on the education of the California bar. Although the first graduating class only numbered forty-five, over 10 percent of the total number of lawyers admitted in the period 1890–1900 were Hastings graduates. California's first law school produced much of the young blood that flowed into the elite bar of the last decade of the century. Gerard Gawalt's findings for Massachusetts are similar, with 39 percent of the admittees in 1870–1890 holding law degrees from Harvard or Boston University Law Schools. However, for the same period, virtually all of the Massachusetts lawyers had attended law school for at least one year.[37] The pattern of completing law school before beginning to practice was becoming the norm as the century closed.

The California bar was educated on the circuit, by the glow of oil lamps falling on treatise pages, in collegial moots under the shadow of the mother lode, and in the law schools that became fixtures of the late-nineteenth-century legal education. The generalists, schooled in the classics and through the rigors of the justice courts, were slowly replaced by the specialists. General learning came to be a prologue for the Langdellian method of molding legal reasoning. The society of colleagues traveling on the circuit gave way to the multipractitioner office filled with technicians skilled in the craft of practicing law.

Legal literature, like the study of law, moved from the general to the specific during the half century considered in this book. The education of lawyers in frontier California depended, in part, on the available legal literature, as did the practice of law throughout the nineteenth century. To prepare for the bar, would-be attorneys spent time with Blackstone, Story, Kent, and other sages of the law. For attorneys out on the street practicing their trade, knowledge of the law often depended on the availability of law books. The struggle to learn the law and to keep current was a continuing one for the members of the California bar. As the century closed, the volume of law increased and the challenge expanded.

The treatises used by California's bar were the products of the first third of the nineteenth century. St. George Tucker's five-volume edition of Blackstone's *Commentaries* was published in 1803. Zephaniah Swift's *Digest of the Law of Evidence* (1810) and Simon Greenleaf's *Evidence* (1842) provided practitioners ample material on a specialized matter. Joseph Story's *Commentaries*, published between 1831 and 1845, were scholarly expeditions into areas ranging from the constitution to conflict of laws. James Kent's *Commentaries on American Law*, in four volumes, came out between 1826 and 1830.[38] These treatises gave the bar generalized legal thought from classically-trained men.

The greatest problem for the practicing bar of the 1850s was obtaining law books, whether treatises or official state publications. A July 2, 1850 letter from John Currey of San Francisco to Amos Catlin in Sacramento set out many of the problems. Currey had a collision case in admiralty on his hands. He asked Catlin to "get hold of Cowen's Treatise (Mr. Winans has a copy at Sacramento City) and see what is said under 'Trespass on the case' on this subject." Catlin also was to check "the question of Damages in [the] same book, and in Greenleaf on Evidence (Tarr has my copy)." If that research were to not prove fruitful, Catlin could "find quite a variety of law books at Col Zubriskie's office." Beyond research, Currey also needed books. "I shall want a few of my books again, to wit: Abbott on Shipping, and such Laws of California as you can spare," he wrote. Currey also wanted Greenleaf back because it belonged "to D. R. Wright and he spoke to me about returning it." Finally, Catlin would "find at Mr. Bigelow's office a transcript copy of Halleck's report of land titles in California."[39] Clearly, lawyers had unofficial lending libraries whose books passed from hand to hand.

The opening of the San Francisco Law Library in 1853 eased the problem for the attorneys there. Organized by a committee of the local bar and using private and public funds, the library opened with "25,000 volumes and 1,000 volumes of miscellaneous works." In August, five cases of law books had arrived by sea, with "one thousand volumes of law books, now on the way, . . . shortly [to] be added," the *San Francisco Daily Herald* reported. The courts were the big borrowers. The supreme court drew out 210 volumes in July, the district court 233, superior court 138, county court twenty-eight, and the recorder's court forty-five. The federal district court called for thirty volumes.[40] The resources of such a great collection were a significant advantage for the San Francisco bar. As we will see later, lawyers frequently were founding members of library committees in their communities. The work of many of these local committees often resulted in the construction of a city library or local law library, usually funded by the local tax base. The work of such committees was more urgent in rural California because access to law books was far more limited by transportation facilities.

Outside the instant city, the practicing bar had extreme difficulty knowing what the law was. H. C. Gardiner wrote from Sevett's Bar to James W. Mandeville in 1852:

Necessity in a measure compels me to ask your good offices in my behalf. You know that every justice of the peace is entitled to a copy of our state laws, but as there has been no justice in our township for the last year and a half we are without the necessary books, having nothing to guide us in our proceedings except an old copy of the acts of '49 many of which are now repealed.

He asked Mandeville to "apply to the Controller and provide me a copy of the statutes for the years 1851 & 2."[41] Charles Fernald in Santa Barbara was more fortunate. Charles Huse, then of Benicia, sent Fernald the 1852 Statutes in Spanish. But there were "no copies of the Practice Act in Spanish." Huse told Fernald that he could find the Practice Act "published in the Los Angeles Star," which was "on file in the office of the County Clerk."[42] Huse would better understand conditions in Santa Barbara when he set up practice there in October of 1853.

In Santa Barbara, Huse registered a continuing complaint about the availability of law books. In July 1855 he regretted "very much that [he did] not have a more respectable library."[43] Reflecting upon another attorney one day in 1856, Huse wrote: "It is true that he has a library bigger and better than mine but in time I will purchase more books. All of the knowledge of the law as a science which he has, has been obtained in three years and one cannot learn much in such a short time, let his talents be what they may." The next morning, Huse arose early "and read from a volume of Kent's *Commentaries* until breakfast."[44] Five days later he "read two lectures by Kent on the law of Maritime Insurance and also . . . examined Russell's book on crimes."[45] Two days later he returned to Kent. "I read a chapter today from Kent about incorporated hereditaments. One should have the whole doctrine which refers to this branch clearly established in his mind. All the books of this author are the work of a clear, educated, brilliant, solid, distinguished and certain mind."[46] The treatise-writers clearly helped Huse, and his choice of reading material demonstrated how tenacious the hold of these treatises was on the mind of the antebellum California bar. Huse, like so many others, turned to Blackstone, Story, and Kent for legal insight.

The work of California's lawmakers was apparently not as efficacious. In September 1855 Huse read "a little of the laws of this State. They change these so every year that it is difficult to know sometimes, what this law actually prescribes."[47] In March 1856 Huse recorded an excursion into the decisions of the state's highest court. "Today I read the reports of the Supreme Court of this State in the year 1854, and recently published in a volume. The book has many decisions, but they are very short and do not show the reasoning in the various cases."[48] The nature of state law and the adequacy of a lawyer's library had a direct impact upon practice, as Huse confided in his journal in July 1856. In preparing a case originating in 1846, Huse fretted, "The more I examine it, the more difficulties I find, and I regret that I do not have the books of authorities to satisfactorily resolve the many questions which are presented."[49] But Huse turned to his friend Fernald who loaned him "some books useful in the case of Lorenzana and also looked up . . . the doctrine about the obligations of minors."[50] Although Fernald was helpful, Huse wrote in 1857 that the supreme judiciary was not. "In general they [the opinions] are very short and not elaborated. Sometimes they give the decision without expressing any reasons."[51] The problems of practice in the isolated communities of California were very real in the first quarter century of this study.

One medium that attempted to overcome this lack of communication and information was the newspaper. As Fernald noted in 1853, the *Los Angeles Star* published statutes as a service to the bar and the public. Specialized lawyer's newspapers had a troubled existence in the Bay Area. *The Weekly*

Law Review hit the streets on July 19, 1855, but only lasted fifteen days.[52] The *California Law Journal* came off the presses in 1862, but failed to last one year, which also was the fate of the *Pacific Law Magazine* of 1867. There followed a series of failed attempts by the *Law Bulletin* (1870–71), *Harris and Co's Court and Law Guide* (1873), *Pacific Law Reporter* (1870–78), *California Legal Record* (1878–79), *Pacific Coast Law Journal* (1878–1882), and the *San Francisco Law Journal* (1878–1901). In Los Angeles, the *Daily Journal* (1888 to the present) was born of the boom of the 1880s and survived to serve a rapidly growing legal community.[53] Most of these legal newspapers were started and maintained by lawyers turned legal journalists. Several general newspapers had attorney-editors as well, as we have seen in the previous chapter. Both the specialized and the general press covered legal matters in some detail in the antebellum period. Law was very much a part of frontier life in California.

Despite the increased availability of legal resources in the last quarter of the century, lawyers continued to borrow books from one another. An attorney from the firm of Scott and Montgomery of Anaheim wrote to John D. Bicknell in 1879 regarding a federal mining law question.

> Has there been a decision either in this state, Nevada or Colorado, giving a construction to the latter clause of "Sec. 2324 regulations made by miners." United States Statutes, Act of May 10, A. D., 1892? particularly as to work by copartners, notice by publication, to parties failing to perform labor required, their forfeiture of interest in mines, etc., etc., etc. This is a matter arising in Arizona, about which we have been consulted and not having the authorities at hand to consult, we thought you might be posted."[54]

Bicknell's library was known to be one of Southern California's best. He went to great lengths to keep it maintained, even going to New York in 1874 to obtain a set of the California *Reports*.[55] Charles Fernald had people searching out volumes in San Francisco in the 1870s.[56] As Scott and Montgomery knew of Bicknell's substantial collection, Huse knew that Fernald's library resources were the strongest in Santa Barbara. Whether in urban or rural practice, lawyers believed that library resources were critical for the successful practice of law and constantly searched for the "authorities."

By the 1880s the publishing firm of Bancroft, Whitney and Company of

San Francisco provided the practicing bar with its needs, offering resources ranging from legal forms to multivolume sets. The company proclaimed in Darwinian terms the importance of its law books: "The Survival of the Fittest—A Trinity of Reports Selected and Annotated."[57] The trinity consisted of the *American Decisions and Digest* covering 1760 to 1869 in 103 volumes, the *American Reports, Digest and Index* for 1869–1888 in 63 volumes, and the *American State Reports* issued at the rate of 6 volumes per year. Even with such resources available, in 1889 M. B. Beattie of Los Angeles sent his law clerk to Bicknell's office "to borrow some books from you which we have not."[58] Another Los Angeles attorney, Samuel Wilson, borrowed volume two of Kent's *Commentaries*.

In 1884, in the then quiet diggings of Placer County, the *Argus* ran a story recommending J. F. Lowdery's *Reason's Why: The Citizen's Law Book* consisting of seven hundred pages and containing explanations of statutes and civil procedure as well as legal forms. The newspaper recommended it to justices of the peace, notaries, constables, and citizens. A man from Dutch Flat was selling this gem for $6.50.[59] Whether urban center or rural village, the law in books was not always at hand.

But law books were flowing from the pens of treatise writers, courts, and commentators. By 1885 there were 3,798 volumes of American court reports.[60] Oliver Wendell Holmes, Jr. edited the twelfth edition of Kent's *Commentaries* in 1873.[61] New treatises on new areas of law appeared. Gregory Yale's *Legal Titles to Mining Claims* rolled off the press in 1867, William L. Scott and Milton Jarnagin's *Law of Telegraphs* the same year, and Thomas G. Shearman and Amasa A. Redfield's *Treatise on the Law of Negligence* in 1869.[62] Some notable members of the California bar contributed to this late-century outpouring. John Downey Works had started what was to become a three-volume work entitled *Indiana Practice and Pleading*, when his health dictated a move to San Diego in 1883.[63] On October 1, 1886, Works was appointed judge of the Superior Court of San Diego County.[64] In 1887 he published *Removal of Causes from State Courts to Federal Courts*, and in 1888 was elevated to the state supreme court. Works also published a legal pamphlet entitled *Irrigation Laws and Decisions of California* (1900). His other publications included *Courts and Their Jurisdiction* (1894), *The Speeches of Senator Works* (1917), *Judicial Reform* (1919), and *Man's Duty to Man* (1919).[65] Curtis H. Lindley was the author of *Lindley on Mines*.[66] George H.

Smith contributed *Elements of Private Right, History of Modern English Juris-prudence,* and *Logics and Analytics Theory.*[67] They, along with many others, made the literature of the law voluminous, if not richer, by the close of the century.

The half century in which the bar developed witnessed substantial change, both in the education of lawyers and in the literature they studied and relied on in their practices. The reading of classic law treatises by a flickering lamp in the mother-lode country produced a generation of law-yers, which was replaced by attorneys schooled in law school lectures. Rhe-torical flourish honed by experience and the reading of classical literature diminished, washed down the sluice of practice by a torrent of treatises, reports, and periodical literature. The technically trained attorney emerged, armed with narrowly focused specialties and relying on the increasingly micro-scopic investigations of treatise writers. The antebellum bar had a sure faith in the guidance of Blackstone, Story, and Kent, whereas the bar of 1900 leafed through the pages of thousands of volumes. The subject matter of law in books also mirrored the change in the practice of lawyers. The staples of real property, contract, and debt collection practice sustained the first quar-ter century of this study, but the law emerging from industrialization and modernization gave lawyers of the last quarter century new challenges as well as an explosion in the volume of law.

3

The Conditions of the Practice of Law

In any litigation, no lawyer can be successful if
he has to stop to consider the feelings of the
parties on the other side, and I think this young aspirant for office
would be much improved if we take him across our knees and
give him a good, sound, legal spanking. As far
as I am concerned, I desire to fight that case to a finish.
—John Dustin Bicknell to W. F. Herrin August 8, 1894

California lawyers practiced largely alone in the antebellum period, but increasingly attorneys formed partnerships and moved to specialized legal services within firms. This pattern of organization mirrored national developments as law firms increasingly served business clients who required larger staffs and specialized attention to complex legal problems. Within this movement away from individual practices, lawyers became advisers on a larger range of business questions in addition to being counselors on matters of law. By the turn of the century, the urban California lawyer was part of a growing large-firm structure similar to firms in Chicago or New York. In rural California, the sole practitioner and the small firm continued to offer general legal services to local customers.

Nationally, the period 1870–1915 witnessed the formative years of the large law firm. The transition was one of firm size as well as function. Firms with five or more partners increased in number and persistence across the country. The number of associates in each firm and the size of the clerical staffs grew accordingly. Specialization increased within firms, and partners found that such growth and departmentalization attracted and retained large corporate clients. With growth and specialization, these firms became law factories turning out a corporate product. This new mechanistic image contradicted the old view of the individual, personally involved attorney, but enhanced the new image of lawyer as negotiator, facilitator, and corporate business visionary.[1] The nation's bar, indeed, changed dramatically as America entered World War I.

California's lawyers formed partnerships in the antebellum period, but few survived into the twentieth century. In San Francisco, Frederick Billings and Alexander Carey Peachy formed a partnership in 1849 that soon was joined by Henry Wager Halleck. Halleck, Peachy and Billings was a leading firm there until the Civil War. Halleck, a West Point graduate, returned to the army to serve as general in chief (1862–64) and as a top aide to President Lincoln. Frederick Billings returned to Vermont and later became president of the Northern Pacific Railroad.[2] The Civil War dissolved a thriving partnership. Other lawyers regularly went in and out of partnership with one or two attorneys. Jarrett T. Richards of Santa Barbara had successive partnership practices with John J. Boyce, Charles Fernald, and Charles F. Carrier. Richards arrived in Santa Barbara in 1868. Fernald had been practicing there since 1852 and gave Richards the office of a proven practitioner in which Richards could gain experience and clients. John J. Boyce arrived eight years after Richards and benefited from a similar relationship with Fernald, as did Carrier, who made Santa Barbara his home in 1897.[3] The custom of established lawyers taking in younger partners was not unusual in nineteenth-century California.

In rural California, partnerships were not as common as in the urban, developing areas. Mariposa County, which boomed with mining in the antebellum period and retired to a sleepy agricultural existence thereafter, saw only nine partnerships in the nineteenth century, five of which were only two-men firms.[4] Similarly, Placer County witnessed no more than five partnerships, with one, Hale and Craig, proving hardy enough to persist from the 1870s until the 1890s. This pattern is similar to the one observed by Maxwell Bloomfield for frontier Texas, and by C. Robert Haywood for Dodge City, Kansas. Law practices and law firms were difficult to establish and maintain in frontier communities.[5] Sole practitioners were more common, particularly as boom conditions subsided and lawyers assumed concurrent employment.

The partnership did provide a law firm with the opportunity to specialize and to dominate the law business of a city. In San Diego, the firms of Gatewood and McNealy, and Chase and Leach came in the 1870s to control half the law business of the city as measured by court appearances.[6] Attorneys in successful partnerships tended to continue partnership structures when one partner left the firm. When Chase left Robert Wallace Leach in 1885, Leach formed a new partnership with Edwin Parker. William J. Hunsaker had three different partners, including Chase, during his career. This structural arrangement, which enabled specialization, mirrored the national phenomenon described by Wayne K. Hobson for the period 1870–1915. Maxwell Bloomfield saw the pattern emerging in Galveston, Texas, by 1860.[7] Although some lawyers formed partnerships for colleagueship and others saw partnership as a business necessity, the San Diego bar remained one for sole practitioners and loose partnership relationships until the railroad arrived and industrialization combined with commerce to increase the complexity and demands of practice.

In Los Angeles, Jackson A. Graves formed several partnerships and offered specialized services. In the 1870s he specialized in commercial law and came to dominate the field.[8] In 1878 he heard John S. Chapman make an impressive oral argument before the supreme court and in 1880 he formed a partnership with this skilled litigator.[9] The boom of the 1880s brought new life to the land-title business, and with another partner, Henry O'Melveny, the firm soon dominated the land-title litigation field.[10] O'Melveny, in turn, came to specialize in the creation and management of land companies. His success was due to both timing and longevity. He entered an established practice at a time of rapid business growth and he practiced law for half a century.

Timing and linkages to financial institutions also were factors in the longevity of law firms. Tobin and Tobin of San Francisco, founded in 1852 and continuing on Post Street for over 130 years, forged a link with the financial world that it maintains to this day. Richard Tobin was born in Ireland and went to California by way of Chile. In 1847 he was named secretary to the Most Reverend Sadoe Alemany, the first archbishop of San Francisco. After the gold rush he turned to law, and in 1859, with Robert Tobin, founded the Hibernia Savings and Loan Association. The law firm and the generations that would follow were part of that financial institution.[11] Jackson A. Graves, founding partner of O'Melveny and Meyers of Los Angeles, forged a similar link with the Farmers and Merchants Bank, first as counsel, then as vice-president, 1901–20, then as president, 1920–31, and finally as chairman of the board, 1931–33. Like O'Melveny, Graves also had longevity on his side. Tobin and Graves were very much like their Massachusetts brothers in the bar, who, as Gerard Gawalt observed, moved into the banking industry.[12]

Another centennial-plus firm in San Francisco, Morrison and Foerster, had longevity as well as strong partners that produced durability. Alexander Francis Morrison was born in Weymouth, Massachusetts, in 1856, of Scottish and Irish ancestry. He arrived in California at the age of eight and received a public-school education, a university degree, and a law degree from Hastings. While at Hastings, he clerked with the established firm of Cope and Boyd. Graduating in 1881, he remained associated with Cope and Boyd until 1883, when he joined Thomas O'Brien in partnership. Several partnerships later, Walter B. Cope joined the recently created firm of Morrison and Foerster in 1897. Constantine E. A. Foerster, who joined the firm in 1890, died in 1898, but his son, Roland, joined the firm twenty years later, three years before the death of the founder, Alexander Morrison. In addition to having strong partners, Morrison found a strong and enduring client in the Crocker family of San Francisco. The Crockers gave the firm trust and estate business and also corporate business, which included land and water companies and railroad interests. The firm also specialized in managing sugar businesses.[13]

Another San Francisco law firm that has persisted for over a century, McCutchen, Doyle, Brown, and Enersen, had similar origins. Charles Page and Charles P. Eells established the firm in 1883. Page was born in Chile in 1847 and graduated from Yale in 1868. He studied at the University of Berlin and the University of Brussels before going to San Francisco to read law in the offices of Patterson, Wallace and Stowe. Admitted to the bar in 1872, Page quickly distinguished himself as an admiralty lawyer. He later became the president of the California Title Insurance and Trust Company and a director of the Fireman's Fund Insurance Company, both of which companies did business with the law firm over a long period of time. Charles P. Eells was born in New York in 1854 and went to California in

1866. He returned to New York and graduated from Hamilton College in Clinton, New York, in 1874. Going back to California, Eells entered the law office of E. B. Mastik of San Francisco to read law. After admission to the bar in 1876, Eells practiced in partnership and individually until he entered a partnership with Page in 1883. Eells had become an expert in land-title examination, corporate law, and the issuance of public bonds. Eells brought to the firm expertise that helped it to emerge as one of the most lucrative firms in the late nineteenth century. Edward J. McCutchen was born in San Jose in 1857 and was a Hastings graduate in 1879. He had been a part of several partnerships before joining Page and Eells in 1896, and brought with him the Kern County Land Company as a client. Tenneco, Inc., the successor to the Kern County Land Company, continued as a client of the twentieth-century firm. McCutchen also became counsel to the New York Life Insurance Company. The combination of expertise, long-term clients, and longevity (McCutchen died in 1933) gave the firm the staying power needed for a century of practice.[14]

Athearn, Chandler, Hoffman and Angell of San Francisco had earlier origins than the McCutchen, Doyle firm and a somewhat different path to a century of longevity. The partners discovered each other through their mutual interest in law practice in the mother-lode country and founded the firm of Gray and Haven in 1869. Giles H. Gray was born in 1834 in New York City, and when he arrived in San Francisco in 1853, he had a degree from the Free Academy of New York fresh in hand. He entered the law office of S. N. Bowman and was admitted to the bar in 1856. Gray opened his law practice on the bay, served on the 1856 San Francisco Vigilance Committee, helped found the Savings Union and Trust Company of San Francisco in 1862, and became a member of the City Board of Supervisors in 1863. In 1867 his brother George, an Amherst College graduate, persuaded Giles to join him at their father's mine in Gold Valley. Wintering in Downieville, Giles met James M. Haven, Sierra County's district attorney. Haven had arrived in California from New York in 1850, the same year as Giles's father, Nathaniel. Agreeing that law was more rewarding than mining, the two formed a partnership in San Francisco on January 4, 1869. The firm took on numerous Chinese clients in the early days, but turned to the more specialized field of mining litigation. In 1889 Gray retired. The next year Haven's son, Thomas, joined the firm. When James M. Haven died in 1905, he had completed forty-two years of active law practice. The nineteenth-century partners kept the firm together with family succession and a civil-litigation practice.[15]

The large firms of the 1980s with origins over a century old had several characteristics in common. They had associations with critical economic institutions that also persisted into the twentieth century. Banks were clients that often retained long-term business relationships with law firms. In addition to the firms mentioned above, the San Francisco firm of Orrick, Herrington and Sutcliffe had its origins in 1863, with its founding partner, John R. Jarboe, being the general counsel for the German Savings and Loan Society founded the same year. The firm continued that relationship until 1960. These elite law firms of California were much like the elite law firms of New York City. As Robert W. Gordon has observed, the elite law firms of New York with corporate clients became increasingly specialized to support the legal needs of enterprise.[16] The continuing relationship between law firm and corporate client was mutually beneficial as both symbiotically matured over the decades.

In addition to continuing work from business clients, the aforementioned firms had partners that beat the mortality odds of nineteenth-century California. Many attorneys, like Henry O'Melveny, were notable for their age and their ability to keep active in practice and in the firm's business. Accumulated experience and a mature legal and business insight made many of the senior members of the elite bar valued counselors for corporate clients.

Finally, timing and location were significant. Those firms in place before the boom of the 1880s in Southern California prospered as land-title work expanded. Similarly, those firms in place in San Francisco by the 1880s enjoyed the fruits of industrialization and the expansion of commerical and corporate business. Specialization and a strong firm image helped attract clients, even in smaller cities like San Diego. In rural practice, sole practitioners and small partnerships persisted, following the economics of the times. Many Santa Barbara attorneys could survive business and weather cycles, but Mariposa's bar could not survive the total collapse of the mining industry and the dearth of litigation.

In addition to establishing law firms, the nineteenth-century lawyers formed bar associations for social and utilitarian purposes. The social purpose was central to the formation of the San Francisco bar association in 1872, whereas Los Angeles lawyers created the Los Angeles County Bar

Association in 1878 to establish a law library. These origins were similar to those of bar associations across the country in the same period. The frontier's "scrambling bar" did not encourage strong bar associations, and California's lawyers, although quickly abandoning their frontier heritage in San Francisco and Los Angeles, were still shrewd entrepreneurs on the make.[17]

Social interests were a primary concern of the San Francisco Bar Association (SFBA). Invited by a circular letter proposing such an organization, the founding members held their first meeting on April 27, 1872.[18] By July, the SFBA counted ninety-three members and had the entire second floor of the old Pacific Club and three apartments on the third floor available for use. The second floor was divided into five large contiguous saloons, the central one sporting two billiard tables. Liquor and cold lunch were continuously available, and a hot lunch was served between noon and two. With all these trappings of an exlusive men's club, the SFBA opened its clubhouse doors on July 4, 1872.[19]

The founders of the SFBA were the elite of the city's attorneys. Joseph P. Hoge was its president and Hall McAllister and S. M. Wilson, its vice-president. Hoge was an Illinois attorney who moved with his law partner, Samuel M. Wilson, to California in 1853. Hoge had been a two-term congressman from Illinois and a candidate for the Senate. He and Wilson established law offices in the Montgomery block of San Francisco, the center of the city's legal community, and maintained those offices for thirty-four years. Hoge was an early entrant to the California bar and a survivor. He was elected president of the 1878–79 California Constitutional Convention and to the Superior Court of San Francisco in 1888. He died in 1891 at the age of eighty.[20] Hall McAllister was a forty-niner and perhaps the greatest California trial attorney of the nineteenth century. He was from a family of attorneys. Matthew Hall McAllister arrived in California in 1850 and became the first judge of the United States Circuit Court. His brother, Cutler, was an attorney and served as a clerk in his father's court. Hall also was a survivor, practicing law for thirty-nine years.[21]

The Los Angeles County Bar Association (LABA) was founded in 1878, the same year as the American Bar Association. The purpose of the LABA was the creation of a law library. Bar association dues funded the purchase of law books and members of the association loaned books to the library. In 1886 the library filed articles of incorporation, and among the directors of this institution was George Smith Patton. The library was housed in

Albert A. Stephens' Law Building, at the corner of Temple and High Streets in the center of commerical Los Angeles. Andrew Glassell was the first president of the association and Jackson A. Graves its first treasurer. The bar was reorganized in the 1880s, collapsed, and was again reorganized in 1899.[22] The members of the reorganized bar association of 1888 declared their purpose to be "to promote, through organization, their own interests and to provide an outlet for their group social activities."[23] Originally focusing on the need for a library, the members found that the need for social intercourse was increasingly important as the boom of the 1880s faded and more new attorneys got off the train in Los Angeles.

The leaders and members of the reorganized bar came from the second-generation arrivees who took advantage of opportunity in the 1870s to position themselves for the boom times of the 1880s. Albert Miller Stephens was the forty-two-year old president of the reorganized bar. Stephens arrived from Memphis in 1874, was the president of the Law Library, and was a Los Angeles County judge. John D. Bicknell was the vice-president. Eight charter members of the 1878 bar association also were members of the 1888 reorganized bar association. More significantly, many of the arrivees of the 1870s, the new young men of the lean years, now the pillars of the legal community, were members. Stephen Mallory White, Jackson A. Graves, Reginaldo F. del Valle, George Smith Patton, George H. Smith, Henry W. O'Melveny, and James Shankland were included on the membership rolls.[24] Although not all of these men fit the 1870s cohort, they were the men who survived the seventies and built the infrastructure of law practice that would contribute to their success in the 1880s.

The first reorganized bar did not last long. Brought together for social purposes, the membership was diverted from its original task by the end of the boom of the 1880s and the new scramble for clients in the 1890s, amid industrialization, an economic crash, and depression. As one commentator has aptly phrased it, "During most of the 1890s the Los Angeles Bar Association seems to have been in a state of suspended animation."[25] The business of lawyers in nineteenth century California was the law business. Bar Associations clearly were asides structured for short-term purposes and for social networking. The pursuit of law reform and market control was not perceived by the bar to be a necessity. In this, California's lawyers lagged behind their eastern counterparts, who were working diligently to restrict access to the bar and increase their control of the law business.[26]

What did the attorneys do once they were organized to do the law business? Did they exhibit a tendency to build an ideological scheme or political language of law? Robert W. Gordon suggests that the elite bar of the East, Harvard educated and corporately employed, did rationalize law and enterprise in normative terms favorable to their clients. Law was the ideology of capitalism.[27] In the paragraphs and chapters that follow, we must remember that more members of the California bar were educated in the mother-lode country and by Blackstone than by Harvard and its progeny. We are studying the West, not the East. Although the followers of the Annales school would find the geography of this study overambitious, we also must remember that the private law of California was the business of the state's legislature and courts. The actions of these statewide institutions had an impact on local practice and gave definition to the law that attorneys practiced. Given these caveats, we must look further into the conditions of law practice before venturing into the substantive areas of practice.

What lawyers did in their practices followed the socioeconomic activities of the state. Awash with forty-niners and witnessing the disintegration of the great ranchos, the pioneer bar collected debt, dealt with crime, and transferred property at a feverish pace amid the urban turmoil of the instant cities. With vast lands open to title questions and invaded by squatters, lawyers supported the process of quieting title to land through litigation and the land-claims commission. With the coming of the railroad and industrialization, lawyers increasingly became involved with personal injury litigation and advising corporate clients on a wide range of business as well as legal matters. As the nature of law practice changed from a litigation-advocacy function to a preventive-counseling function by the turn of the century, lawyers increasingly mobilized resources to accommodate client demands. This changed law office was an urban phenomenon. The rural practitioner at the century's end was still practicing law alone or in partnership with one or two colleagues. He was handling real estate and tort matters largely because corporate clients kept their business in the urban centers of the state. Regardless of their locus of practice, lawyers had to deal with the frontier environment, the nature of communications, and each other in law practice.

In the 1850s, lawyers like Charles E. DeLong traveled on circuit with the judge. Clients walked in on the day the court personnel arrived at the seat of justice, and lawyers litigated the next. Trials were had on Saturday, if necessary, to clear the docket. One Saturday at Foster's Bar, DeLong noted, the "Trial progressed with every appearance of success, closed the evidence at half past eleven at night and by agreement submitted the case . . . without argument. Jury retired and after deliberation of about half an hour returned with a verdict for full amount for Plaintiffs; never more disappointed in my life; still storming furious."[28] Given the unfortunate result, DeLong spent Sunday "making out appeal bonds."[29] The work was where the judge was, and general practice included all imaginable types of cases.

By the 1870s the practice in urban areas had taken on a more stable nature. San Francisco lawyers could travel by train to selected outposts of the law, but some found that inconvenient. Samuel Wilson, a San Francisco attorney, wrote to Albert Dibblee in 1877 that he had "always found that cases out of the city [were] sources of great annoyance to [him]. With constant demands upon [him in the city], the inconvenience of going to a neighboring county [was] very great."[30] When business was good, having an office close to home was the most efficient way to practice.

California lawyers involved in confirming land titles often had both distance and communication problems. Material, documents, and briefs often were prepared in California, but the process largely was effected in Washington, D.C., John B. Clark wrote from Washington to John Dustin Bicknell in Los Angeles in 1873 regarding the Bronson case Bicknell had worked on for a year.

> That long looked for (B's original application) I found in the Department carefully filed away with the other papers in the case. I had it forwarded to the Los Angeles office, by mail, yesterday.
>
> It would require a longer story than I care to write, or you would care to read, to give a detailed account of the mismanagement on the part of the attorney, and the gross negligence on the part of the clerks in the Land Office in connection with this case. The latter, of course, was a necessary and inevitable consequence of the former. Herron, whether for good cause or not, I cannot say, is not permitted, and has not been for some time past, to practice as an attorney with the General Land Office. This being the case, he turned your business over to one J. Nance Lewis. . . . Lewis is an entire stranger to me—but I learned privately from friends in the Land Office that his standing therein, as an attorney, is not good.[31]

Many California attorneys maintained liasons with Washington attorneys to pursue land-title litigation, but, as Bicknell learned, the ability of the West Coast attorney to control the conduct of the East Coast attorney was limited. As we will see in a subsequent chapter, this problem of control existed but was not the normal situation.

Lawyers negotiated at great distance and the problem of communications complicated the process. George Hayford, an Orange County attorney, and John D. Bicknell of Los Angeles negotiated a settlement transaction gone sour. James Stewart, a banker in Tilbury Centre, Ontario, Canada, had an unpaid and overdue note secured by twenty acres in the heart of the city of Orange. W. B. Forsyth occupied the land but was unable to pay for it. George Hayford, representing Mr. Forsyth, wanted to resolve the situation with a proposal sent to Bicknell in May 1889.

Notwithstanding our hard times the property is very valuable yet and with the prospects of county division it is still more valuable.

We have not got the money and therefore actually cannot pay up on the place and while we greatly regret the tremendous loss we wish to be fair and not deprive Mr. Stewart of his right. . . .

[We] therefore offer to quit claim the property back to Mr. Stewart on payment to us of a reasonable amount. . . . Surely $1500 is a fair basis of settlement. While he might possibly perhaps do a *little* better after a long and expensive contest in the Courts, during which time the property will depress, run down, and go to waste for a possible term of two years contesting in courts during which time he not only looses the opportunity of first class sales during our coming Boom on county division but [also] the property will be gradually going backward instead of forward.[32]

Stewart did not find the proposal reasonable, in that he had a $7,500 note still outstanding at 10 percent interest per year. The prospect of having to pay a person owing money to vacate land, dramatically increasing the loss, was not satisfactory to Stewart.[33]

Hayford's proposal was a counteroffer to an April offer of $200 to settle the matter. Hayford had rejected that offer with the observation "Somehow I have the idea that Canadian Bankers as a rule are laboring under a general policy to take anything, return nothing." Further, Hayford doubted that "his acceptance of anything but cash and no matter what color that may be" would settle the affair.[34]

By September, Stewart was looking for "a compromise." He suggested that the exchange of a quitclaim deed as Hayford offered in June and the notes and some cash would avoid a showdown in court.[35] But by December, Hayford still stood like Liberty Valance threatening a shoot-out at the bar of justice. Stewart wrote to Bicknell, summing up his position: "In short, for the $200 cost to me, I desire to have my title to the 20ac in Orange made perfect, and am willing to dismiss further action against Forsyth on his releasing to me all his claims to said 20ac."[36] Hayford wrote to Bicknell rejecting the offer and demanding that Stewart pay the 1889 taxes. One week later, Hayford wrote to Stewart directly, accepting the $200 offer if the taxes were paid and the notes returned immediately.[37]

The matter reached settlement in February 1890. Stewart did not hesitate in his response to Hayford's rejection. "I am not anxious to even pay the $200," he wrote Bicknell, "as I consider Forsyth entitled to nothing whatever, but am anxious to get the matter out of my mind."[38] Forsyth was of a similar mind, wanting only the note before signing the settlement agreement.[39] The process, at long distance, took a year. Orange was in Orange County rather than Los Angeles County as now, and the expected boom had not materialized. Bicknell was not like John Wayne with a Winchester ensuring that right prevailed when guns blazed. Rather, Bicknell's law suits were the wedge that kept the slow process of settlement open and finally fruitful.

Delay was very much part of the legal process. Patrick Reddy established a perfect record defending the criminally accused of Bodie. Despite incontrovertible evidence in two cases and strong evidence in four others, Reddy received verdicts of not guilty. His chief weapon was delay. Transient populations made witnesses hard to retain, and juries hard to obtain.[40] On the civil side, delay was a tactic in negotiations and an obstruction for competing enterprise. W. G. Curtis, the assistant to the general manager of the Southern Pacific Company, wrote to John D. Bicknell in 1889 telling him:

> In case Ainsworth persists in his attempts to cross our line without a proper arrangement for the construction of safety appliances, will you please take the necessary action on behalf of our Company, instructing Messrs. Hewitt and Hawgood to carry out whatever you may require

them to do and proceed, if necessary until every obstacle known to the law had been interposed to defeat Captain Ainsworth's design.[41]

The law was clearly a weapon in the corporate arsenal to mold behavior. It also was a device to retain a competitive advantage if possible. A. N. Towne, third vice-president and general manager of the Southern Pacific Company, told Bicknell in 1889 that the "motor line" was negotiating for a privilege to "land freight and passengers in the center of the city." Bicknell was to

> keep this matter a little in mind with a view of obstructing in the city council any movement in this direction if it can be done with any hope of success and without too much exposure, as I believe it would be detrimental to our interests if they were permitted to receive and deliver freight at a more advantageous point than that enjoyed by our Company.[42]

The forum for delay ranged from the courtroom to the council room. The tactic was an important tool used by clients and lawyers to obtain advantage.

The use of delay had legal consequences inherent in civil procedure. As O'Brien, Morrison and Daingerfield of San Francisco explained in 1890, opposing counsel had no patience for the tactic. "Our design was to wait until enough delay elapsed to support a motion to dismiss for lack of prosecution, and as nothing whatever was done we had hopes that we could do so; but from the paper served on us to-day we infer that an awakening has taken place, and that we will shortly receive notice to argue the demurrer."[43] Beyond a motion to dismiss, other motions could provide advantage when the passage of time presented procedural opportunity. Creed Haymond, the general counsel for the Southern Pacific Company, told John D. Bicknell: "It has not been our policy to make the point that the proper party has not been made defendant in suits against SPRR Co. & C. unless the statute of limitations had run or unless there was some great object to be gained. In ordinary cases, we do not raise the question."[44] Delay to postpone reaching the merits of a case was not always useful.

Laywers also worked to eliminate delay by providing one another with information about court proceedings and accommodating one another in scheduling appearances or making motions. Problems of communication and transportation caused difficulty to the end of the century. Attorneys in the remoter areas of California would stand in for counsel from another area. Information about court dates and the progress of a suit was frequently a part of nineteenth-century letters and telegrams. Charles H. Larrabee in San Francisco wrote to John D. Bicknell in Los Angeles in 1873, trying to locate five defendants in a breach of contract case.[45] Juan M. Luco of San Francisco also sought Bicknell's aid in 1880.

> It is my intention to move the Court to strike out a portion of the complaint, that is, the new court.
>
> But fearing to trust to the motion alone, I wish also to demur and even answer perhaps and would like you to obtain an extension of five days to plead.
>
> Please let me know by telegraph if the extension is granted. If it should not be I will write you immediately.[46]

Railroad and telegraph technology substantially improved communications, eased travel burdens, and sped intelligence on litigation.

Regardless of the professional exchanges of services and information, some attorneys played civil procedure by the book. Victor Montgomery of Santa Ana opposed Bicknell in a suit and Bicknell inquired of a colleague regarding Montgomery's reputation. E. E. Keech thought that Montgomery was "extremely technical in his practice and never waive[d] a right, however worthless even to accommodate his brother attorneys."[47] Keech seemingly was on the mark; Bicknell's proposed accommodation failed to receive Montgomery's approval. Montgomery wrote:

> While I am a great believer in professional courtesy, and would like exceedingly well to accommodate you, still I cannot consent to the arrangement suggested in your letter.
>
> I shall not under any circumstances agree to a settlement of a state-ment on motion or new trial at this late day; nor do I care to submit the motion for a new trial on briefs. I am aware that the stay of execution expires on the 23rd inst, and I shall strenuously [sic] object to any further stay of execution in this case, for the reason that I think sufficient time has already elapsed to enable you to bring your motion for new trial on for hearing, and for the further reason that I think the interest of my client requires that I do not consent to further delay.[48]

The delay inherent in the accommodation was not in the best interest of Montgomery's client. Additionally, by forcing Bicknell to trial in the dusty outpost of Santa Ana, Montgomery could put Bicknell's preparation in disarray. From Bicknell's perspective, as a thriving, busy practitioner, accommodation was a means of juggling increasingly crowded appointment books. Delay had many masks.

Although delay could be in the interest of a lawyer or the client, counsel error was contrary to client interest and nineteenth-century practice was far from being error-free. Correspondence showed some of the problems of practice and judges were the most outspoken critics of craftsmanship. In 1876, San Luis Obispo District Court Judge Eugene Fawcett chided Santa Barbara attorney Charles Fernald for an error of interpretation.

> The term "findings of fact—all that we filed" certainly does not embrace "proposed findings" which were rejected by me. The phrase "findings of fact—all that were filed" means such as were *signed* and *filed by me.* I believe there were two sets of these—the general findings, and the special findings. . . . It is only those findings that are adopted and signed by the Judge that the clerk has any right to file at all. The others are so much waste paper—they have no place in the files, and I did not suppose they had been placed there. I presume you will be able to correct the mistake without embarassment to yourself.[49]

Such problems were more easily remedied than others and held only the potential for disastrous results.

The finality of error before the California Supreme Court was certain for the nineteenth-century bar and the justices were more than willing to point out attorney error. In 1876, Charles Huse, a Santa Barbara attorney, received a stinging rebuke from the high court. The justices gave Huse short shrift in *Brewster* v. *Johnson* (1876): "There was no oral argument of the cause, nor has either party filed points and authorities. We decline to perform the duty of counsel by examining the record to ascertain if possibly error may not have intervened in the court below."[50] When counsel did appear before the court, the justices demanded clarity. Justice John D. Works in *Poindexter Dunn* v. *C . E. Mackey* raised numerous objections to counsel's language because the court did "not understand what [was] meant sufficiently to attempt to state their point."[51] The court in *Stephens* v. *Loule* was equally mystified because the justices were "unable to ascertain from the complaint that the contract made by the brokers was within their authority. Whatever the word 'net' may mean, it was incumbent upon the pleader to show that the condition imposed by it was fulfilled."[52] Justice Works was equally upset with counsel in *Bailey* v. *Fox*, finding that there was "nothing in the complaint to show that the plaintiff was in any way injured."[53] In *Dale* v. *Purvis*, Works was a bit more gentle.

> The only commendable feature of such a mode of attack is its extreme brevity; and although brevity in the argument of counsel is pleasing to the court, we think in the present instance, it has been a little overdone. We respectfully suggest to counsel that, in order to call upon us to review the action of the court below, they should point out in what respect the instruction attempted to be brought in question is erroneous.[54]

The court in *Wainwright* v. *Weske* was more pointed. The justices noted, "the words 'damage' and 'damages' [could not] be found in the complaint." Worse yet, "the complaint, in legal effect, [showed] that the plaintiff exchanged property of no value for valueless stock and two thousand five hundred dollars. It [was] thus made to appear that the plaintiff, instead of being damaged, was benefitted to the amount above stated." Given these circumstances, the court concluded that "the complaint . . . [was] insufficient in any view that can be taken of it."[55] The sloppy draftsmanship of counsel in filing law suits cost clients consideration of their claims, and appellate scrutiny made the malady even clearer.[56]

Failure to bring a good record to the supreme court was another judicial complaint. In *Baldwin* v. *Morgan* the plaintiff's name was neither on the summons nor in the complaint, and no decree was ever entered or put on the judgment roll.[57] In *Schurtz* v. *Romer*, the court criticized counsel for failure to provide "a proper index to the testimony and exceptions."[58] The court reminded counsel of specific duties in *Vassault* v. *Edwards*, specifically, "the duty of counsel to have clerical and typographical errors in the transcript, which are material, corrected, and they must see to it that the corrections are made in all the copies filed with the clerk."[59] The court was critical because sloppy appellate practice and a poorly constructed record created an additional time burden for the justices. Alternatively, the justices, particularly Works, demanded skilled professional presentations worthy of the learned profession.

The judicial pen sometimes slashed with venom at legal and procedural errors by attorneys in appellate practice. In *Buckingham* v. *Waters*, Justice

Joseph G. Baldwin caustically commented on Caleb Burbank's craftsmanship. Concerning the legal claim, Baldwin acerbically observed, "Upon what theory of the law of contracts this pretension is based, the argument of the learned counsel for the Appellant fails to inform us." Baldwin went on to write, "The second count is as bad as the first." Then he struck at the noxious procedural elements:

> Though we have recognized the use of the common courts, as proper in the practice in this State under our statute, we have never gone so far as to recognize such a jumble of all the causes of action in one count, as here illustrated; besides, the count itself seems to predicate the defendant's liability upon his own loan and expenditure of money. If this were a clerical error it ought to have been corrected when a demurrer was interposed to the court. But the fatal error is in uniting one count, as one cause of action, all these matters, without any specification of the sums due upon each several cause.[60]

Baldwin, as did Works thirty years later, took civil and appellate procedure seriously, because both men saw a relationship between rights and remedies. The rights-remedies view assumed that procedure allowed a judge to fashion an optimal remedy to make parties whole. Further, as jurists, both men exhibited a belief that procedural pragmatism could resolve real conflicts through the law. The failure of counsel to follow the rules put theory and application into confict. Property or contract rights could not be restored if counsel failed to follow the procedure to properly place the dispute before the judge.

Judges could, given some procedural room to maneuver, find a way to understand the substance of an appeal. Justice Lorenzo Sawyer was a bit gentler on counsel in *Calderwood* v. *Pyser*. He observed, "Much of the argument of appellant [related] to points in no way arising on this record." Further, he noted that "the statement [was] very artificially drawn, and all of the papers filed on the part of the plaintiff [were] far from being precedents to be followed." Despite all these problems, Sawyer thought that "the question sought to be raised by the plaintiff [was] substantially presented."[61] In the rarified air of appellate practice, the burden on counsel was substantial.

The conditions of practice in nineteenth-century California present more than one version of how lawyers organized to do the law business and how they behaved in fact. The formation of firms and bar associations could indicate a structured system of legal support for the business clients of the state. Counsel error and inefficiency in communications and negotiations present a blemished portrait. Even issues of behavioral causation have more than one possible interpretation. Those who approach the operation of the bar as a capitalistic conspiracy elevate ideology in historical writing.[62] As we continue to investigate the words and deeds of California's bar and their clients, we must remember both that we are attempting to view their legal world in their terms, and that, for the people, laws were their learned and accepted customs. As John Phillip Reid has so brilliantly stated the point, law in the nineteenth century "was the expression of an agrestic, community-centered world we have lost, a custom bottomed on the sovereign's law, learned by living in a coercive state, and instilled into the marrow of social behavior."[63] It was this law that Charles E. DeLong knew before he opened Blackstone and it was this same law that entrepreneur David Jacks put into action without the benefit of counsel.

4

Collecting Debt

I should deem it wise that this note be placed in the
hands of some person who makes it his particular business to
collect money, as in the rush and whirl of affairs in
my office I am unable to give the particular attention to individual
cases that is required to be a successful collector.
—John D. Bicknell to F. B. Lane, May 5, 1898

Debt collection was the central part of law practice for the antebellum bar and remained a key part of private practice throughout the century. California attracted gold seekers and absconding debtors. The boom-and-bust economy made men wealthy and created work for lawyers and their creditor clients. Debt collection flowed from broken contracts, overdue promissory notes, unpaid bills, and delinquent mortgage payments. Both creditor and debtor were armed with the law and all the ingenuity of humankind.

For creditors, the problem was collection. California was known as a haven for debtors. The legislature made bankruptcy easy, and many a debtor used it to avoid being ruined "by paying his debts."[1] The 1855 statute of limitations provided a two-year period from the date of the accrual of an action for the commencement of a lawsuit.[2] Others who "came to the United States as absconding debtors" and "assumed fictitious names for the purpose of more successfully eluding the vigilance of their creditors" found a haven in the California Civil Code, which barred attachment unless the

underlying debt was incurred in California or contained an express stipula-
tion that it be paid in California.[3] The Golden State was truly a land of
opportunity and a place for another economic chance with a clean slate.

Creditors seldom thought that the public policy of allowing debtors a fresh
start was in their own best interest. Rather, they called upon their attorneys
to wage war against the debt-ridden hordes. Daniel E. Waldron, a San Francisco attorney, asked J. M. Rothchild, a Los Angeles lawyer, to collect a
particular account, instructing, "If this old Bilk don't pay on demand, sue
and attach him at once."[4] George A. Davis and Company, a San Francisco
implement manufacturer, was equally insistent, telling John D. Goodwin,
a Quincy attorney:

> If you can squeeze this money out of Mr. Mitchell do so. If we can
> make it by suit-attachment or any way do it. If he is not good for it, we
> do not wish to waste any more paper and time upon it. But if he is—
> we want our money and must have it. If there is anything in it, go for
> everything in sight—collect attorneys fees' expenses if possible.[5]

In this instance, business necessity required the collection of debt. Others
found timing to be important in collection. Charles H. Larrobee, a San
Francisco attorney, told John D. Bicknell of Los Angeles to strike immediately. "I enclose you [a] note against M. D. Hare, who is candidate for election as constable, and I think you can squeeze the amount out of him by
threatening attachment & [on account of the] pending election."[6] Other
creditors believed in a nobler form of persuasion: the moral duty to pay.
James T. Jenkins of Spanish Ranch wrote to D. W. Jenks in 1884, "I have
earned my money and it is due me by Law, if not by a moral disposition to
do what is Equitable and fair."[7] Occasionally, debtors found holy writ to
support their lack of duty to repay loans. C. D. Cushman reminded David
Jacks in 1890, "Our blessed Savior said" in Luke 6:35 that we should "do
good, and lend, hoping for nothing again, and your reward shall be great,
etc." He guaranteed repayment of the loan in one paragraph, and told Jacks
in another paragraph that if Jacks were to grant the loan, he should "let it be
done with the assurance given by the Saviour of a great and heavenly reward."[8] Third-party nonsignators did not provide much assurance of return
on a loan, regardless of their lofty station.

The first problem for a lawyer trying to collect a client's debt was finding the debtor. The large and changing population of California made locating people problematic. The law firm of Graves and O'Melveny told the Merchants Protective and Collection Agency in 1885 that the man they sought was not in the "great register of the city and county of Los Angeles nor in the city directory." That was not surprising, because "this town and county attract[ed] a large immigration, much of it floating and it [was] simply impossible to find strangers." Further, the law firm asserted, we are "constantly in receipt of claims of the character of those last mentioned [out-of-state] and it is rare that we ever find the parties and *never* do we succeed in making a collection."[9] On other occasions, the debtor could be located. Jackson A. Graves found Mr. Smart of Downey City, but reported to Lilienthal and Company in 1881 that prospects for collections were not good. "He will promise payment," Graves observed, "with the same good grace that a worthy Friar does absolution and fail to pay on time with equal grace. To sue him comes to folly, if we can even catch him."[10] On other occasions, Graves tracked his man down only to report, "He will not pay a cent. He is also busted."[11] Creditors also wrote to John D. Bicknell looking for debtors and were "willing to pay for this information."[12] For Bicknell, Los Angeles was as much of a puzzle as it was for Graves in the search for urban debtors.

In rural California, debtors became lost in the transient economy of the mines. J. M. Richards of Donner Lake had the promissory note of W. and J. Dickenson but told the sheriff of Plumas County, "John Dickenson was with McDouglas pack train the last I knew of Him." Dickenson had told Richards in the winter of 1864 that he would "pay . . . all he could," but with snow a real prospect in 1865, Richards needed action to "get anything." He pleaded urgently, writing, "They are trying to Swindle me out of my Money."[13] Some of the debtors that departed the diggings turned up in Los Angeles. Z. Reed of Bodie wrote to John D. Bicknell in 1880 regarding his hoped-for recovery. "I wish you would write and let me know how you ar gitten along with White and Denna and if you ar likley to make Enything out of them. Watch them close an Don't loose a point. Make them pay if you can." Bicknell responded to Reed, but the news was not as good as the Bodie creditor had hoped for. Reed replied, "It is hard for me to loose so much money on them scamps but I lef it to you to do the Best you could. Tell White I not forget him. You can send me the money thrue the Post Office."[14] In rural California it was often not the financial institutions that suffered when creditors were left holding the empty bag. It was the Richardses and the Reeds of the frontier economy, who loaned money at interest on the promise of repayment.

Merchants also were aware that the transient nature of early California entrepreneurs made collecting on accounts imperative. Ah Jake of Downieville told Hai Loe of North San Juan, "The lawyer can collect that bill easy." [15] Other merchants used more informal collection agencies. Tie Yuen of Downieville wrote to Kong Yuen and Company of San Francisco in 1874 and requested help collecting $110 owed him on account by Wo Tong, who was about "to start for China." [16] A Grass Valley liquor store proprietor, Dan Collins, sold general merchandise on a cash and on a credit basis. Collins kept ledgers with daily notations of credit extended to the consumers of California's mining frontier. [17] L. B. Clark of Smartsville ran his store in a similar fashion. Customers could work off their tabs at $3.50 per day in 1864 and 1865. High-volume corporate customers gave Clark promissory notes for provisions. In the mines, cash was scarce and credit a necessity, but the problems of collection were the business of the frontier attorney. In San Francisco, the commercial center of the state, Albert Dibblee had similar problems in the boom-and-bust cycles of the 1850s. When the supply of goods exceeded demand and prices fell, some merchants were slow to pay their own debts. Commission merchants Crosby and Dibblee constricted credit and moved to cash transactions when merchants were slow to pay. When negotiation failed, they turned their creditor woes over to the famed trial attorney Hall McAllister for collection or litigation. [18]

Collecting was, of course, the attorney's bread and butter. Charles Chapelain of Rich Bar sent "the note due to A. L. Clark" and the accounts to "others for $530.42" to John D. Goodwin of Quincey for collection. He directed Goodwin "to Commence suit and attachments." [19] Whereas Chapelain instructed his attorney to take action, Stella Carpenter of Ukiah entered a plea for help to John D. Bicknell in 1878.

> Dear Sir,
> Have not received the money due the 12th of March. The interest against Biles yet—nor the receipt that taxes were paid. When money is due the 12th of December and not paid 'till the 22nd of March and the note expressly states "to be compounded if not so paid" and the Lawyer don't take compound interest, or any interest in it anyway, why should

the delinquent care if he don't pay at all till the end of the three years. Now I wish that you would see to it that it is all right for you know just how I am situated with two little helpless children and no one to help me at all. I am living very quiet and entirely alone doing my own work. Imagine your wife so placed. I spent a good deal for children, both have been very sick. The remainder is interest and of that I endeavor to live. Can't get principal nor interest—will you help me.[20]

For creditors the challenge was sometimes engaging the services of attorneys. The size of the account, the ease in locating the debtor, and the obviousness of assets were all factors in turning a lawyer's attention to debt collection. All of these features were a part of business-to-business accounts, for example. Lawyers in such cases became negotiators rather than litigators. John D. Bicknell handled one such case in 1876, an account of approximately one thousand dollars against Asbestine Stone Manufacturing Company by Davis and Crowell of San Francisco. The creditors thought Asbestine or its members were good for the account and did not "wish to put them to any expense." Bicknell was to negotiate a security agreement for the account with "a reasonable time to pay it."[21] Often the negotiation or litigation options were available, unless the debtor was judgment-proof or nowhere to be found.

Lawyers frequently wrote letters on behalf of clients, requesting or demanding payment. Jackson A. Graves attempted to collect three promissory notes totaling $651. In July 1879 he wrote to the debtor, Soto, requesting, "Can you pay them now. I don't want to sue."[22] Soto was certainly not flush in the hard times of 1879. In September, Graves wrote to his client, Dinkelspiel and Company, that the notes were uncollectable. Graves had taken the account "in the hope that [he] could find something floating about . . . belonging to Soto." Unfortunately, Soto's assets were "so tied up that [they could] not be gotten at" by legal process.[23] Negotiation took time, and when a financial house of cards collapsed, the race to the courthouse could shut some creditors out.

Negotiation could create ill-will as well as results that were mutually advantageous. John B. Ellisons and Company of Philadelphia had a long-range negotiation with H. J. Crow and Company. Having refused a one-third settlement of the account in 1874, Ellisons and Company engaged the services of John D. Bicknell of Los Angeles. The credit department told Bicknell in the spring of 1875, "We want you to feel that you are fully authorized to make any settlement you can with this most miserable case—Crow lied, cheated and swindled us in every manner he could."[24] Negotiation became litigation, and as the leaves turned their autumnal shades, Ellisons and Company were still in court, requesting that Bicknell "offer a compromise in this case."[25] Crow, like Soto, was in debt to multiple creditors, who flocked to court. Simultaneously, Bicknell was representing Henry C. Biddle of Santa Barbara, who wanted to pluck Crow for new notes "payable in [gold] coin."[26] The lengthy process of law was frustrating to creditors who faced unpaid bills and cash requirements.

As creditors saw others circling over the assets of debtors, it stirred them to seek legal advice. A letter from John W. Forbes of Monserrate to H. S. Ledyard of Los Angeles, regarding the condition of Stewart and McKenzie of Julian in 1875, got Forbes through John D. Bicknell's office door in a hurry. Forbes wrote that Stewart and McKenzie's affairs were "in very bad order." Further, he added,

> They have not a cent of cash and their debts amount to nearly $1300.
>
> Various attachments have been served on them and their stock is now reduced to 3000 head, 600 of which were to have been delivered to a man named Anderson. I advise you to make an attachment of their whole stock at *once* as people there are tired of waiting and many talk of attaching.[27]

Cave Johnson Couts sounded the same alarm to Juan B. Bandini a decade earlier when he saw the debtor's cattle being attached by the sheriff on behalf of Abel Stearns. Couts urged, "You must get your lawyer to attend this immediately. We have no lawyer in San Diego."[28]

When all was lost, creditors asked their lawyers to return outstanding notes to avoid continuing legal expenses. In 1854, Sitler, Price and Company of Philadelphia wrote to Wells and Haight, a San Francisco law firm, calling back notes they had forwarded for collection. They did "not wish to be put into any unreasonable expense." The situation was hopeless because "Knorr and Fuller had dissolved, and E. M. Seller and Company [were] out of business." "They would get worse than nothing," they wrote, because "the expense would therefore fall on us."[29] The best lawyers could not squeeze assets out of the victims of faulty judgment, collapsing markets, or business cycles.

Lawyers and creditors throughout the nineteenth century were very aware of the danger of boom-and-bust economics. The phenomenon was national, statewide, and occasionally local. San Francisco's gold-rush boom collapsed in 1855. In the 1850s, the San Francisco economy was linked to national and world business structures and was partly independent.[30] Though San Francisco's financial institutions had early origins, the problems of exchange were chronic in the 1850s and 1860s. In 1852, Crosby and Dibblee, San Francisco commission merchants, reported to C and Y Belden of New York that there was a "great scarcity of [gold] dust. More of the Bankers are having great difficulty in making up their remittances." As late as 1877, Albert Dibblee had to explain to Salem, Massachusetts, clients that the term "local currency" meant "Mexican dollars clean, bright, and full weight." Recovering from the collapse of its banks, San Francisco emerged as a western financial center between 1868 and 1887.[31] The booming range-cattle industry of Southern California began to decline in 1855 and collapsed in the drought of 1863–64.[32] National economic calamity visited the state in the late 1870s, but the boom in Southern California set off feverish speculation.[33] Despite at least a rudimentary knowledge of economics there, the desire to profit was strong.

Although San Francisco developed a strong banking industry by the 1870s, other regions were not as fortunate. In 1878 the *San Francisco Evening Bulletin* observed, San Francisco "has been measurably fortunate in her Savings Banks. Some of the earliest established still continue, notwithstanding all the violent fluctuations in values to which they have been exposed, and the senseless runs which have been made upon them on two or three occasions."[34] In Los Angeles, the Farmers and Merchants Bank weathered the financial panic of 1875 and enabled enterprise in the area to grow.[35] Matthew Keller was able to restructure debt in Los Angeles at lower interest than was available in San Francisco.[36] But in the remote areas of the state, gold or silver coin as well as paper money was physically difficult to obtain.[37] In 1874, Heimann and George of Anaheim wrote to John D. Bicknell explaining their difficulties.

It has proven impossible to raise that balance due at once and we are compelled to ask you leniency for a few days more. The taxes, payable during the past week have nearly clean out our town and we might as well have undertaken to press "blood out of a turnip" than to raise

money yesterday and today. We have no banks or moneyed establish-
ments to fall back on in our place and we are perfectly lost in a emer-
gency of this sort.[38]

Money-supply problems as well as asset-identification problems were very
real for creditors and their attorneys.

The existence of a banking industry, combined with the arrival of the
Santa Fe Railroad in Los Angeles in 1885, set off a real estate boom. The
competition between the Santa Fe and Southern Pacific lowered fares and
brought a flood of people to the area.[39] William Warner wrote from Sweet-
land to George, Allice, and Elsie Warner in 1887, "The people are getting
the Los Angeles fever—Billy Minner was down 3 or 4 weeks in that short
time. He made $5000.00 speculating in property."[40] Jackson A. Graves ex-
pressed confidence in the boom in November 1887.

> Don't you be afraid of the boom letting go. I send you one of our daily
> real estate reports, which is a fair average of our daily doings. You will
> see that sales run up to over $200,000 per day with few mortgages.
> Some of the wildcat outside schemes, to wit: lots in the desert have
> fallen through, and it is good that they have. Good property, City and
> County, is stiff and in demand. People are flocking here from every-
> where, and things move right along.
>
> The five acres on Seventh Street will subdivide into 22 lots, which
> in my judgment are worth and will bring $2000 each. The demand in
> that direction is beyond comprehension.
>
> As high as it is now, it will *double in value* in 12 months.[41]

But as quickly as it came, the boom was over when the banks withdrew easy
credit in 1888. The lawyers like Graves who participated in the legal
paperwork of the boom were part of the processing of the paperwork of
financial ruin.

When the joy of buying real estate turned to the pain of selling, lawyers
were a necessary part of liquidation. Attorneys handled the sales, gave
advice, and processed the paperwork. Bad deals in real estate speculation
gave many anxiety attacks. John Mohler Studebaker of South Bend, Indiana,
relished carriage making all the more when his California speculation was
derailed. He wrote to John D. Bicknell in 1888,

I am extremely anxious that we close up our claim against Boyce. That is a deal that Monroe got Case and I into. There was nothing in it for us and it was a very foolish deal for him to make. We paid $8000, cash, on the property, and then he sold it for $3000, cash down, to Boyce. Now what we want is to make Boyce pay up the paper that is due, or make him give security if he has anything. I do not consider the property worth the amount he owes us.[42]

The firm of Graves, O'Melveny and Shankland of Los Angeles had to give Mrs. Abbie R. Bartlett similar bad news in 1889.

Property in the neighborhood in which your property is located had depreciated in value fully fifty per cent within the last year.

The depreciation in outstanding properties has been more than you can understand. All outside properties were inflated to prices ten fold their values, and when the crash came they had to seek their natural levels.[43]

When the speculative bubble burst, investors joined Henry D. Bacon's lament, "How soon I am fast coming to grief."[44] Lawyers were able to structure transactions in and out of the real estate market, but for creditors, timing actions in coordination with the economic realities of market values was difficult at best.

Lawyers regularly collected debt through litigation or negotiation in hard times. The law firm of Holladay, Saunders and Cary of San Francisco gleefully reported successful collection of "money on the note in the suit" in 1855. The "amount [was] now in [the] Bank awaiting orders."[45] In 1882, H. B. Coffman of Princeton instructed Ebin O. Darling in Bear Valley to "go after [Eligio Arrollee] red hot and make him pay." Three weeks later the matter was settled.[46] The *Los Angeles Star* daily told tales of promissory note cases in which creditor judgments had been rendered.[47]

Lawyers dealing in transcontinental collections faced problems made manifest by distance. The law firm of Sweeney, Jackson and Walker of Rock Island, Illinois, responded to John D. Bicknell's request for help in 1881. "[The debtor,] in the employ of B. D. Buford and Co., . . . has nothing. He is considered here as execution proof. Would like to help you if we knew how we could."[48] California lawyers were mostly on the receiving end of such inquiries. Bradstreet and Son of Dubuque, Iowa, was looking for Thomas Mercer of Marshalltown, who had "run away" with their client's money.[49] A Cincinnati attorney by the name of W. Cornell was seeking David E. Adams, a brother at bar, who had left without paying him on a note.[50] Creditors from Illinois and collection agencies from New York wrote to John D. Goodwin in Quincey about debtors who drifted into the darkling crevices of the mother-lode country.[51] James H. Shankland corresponded regularly with New York attorneys and collection agencies regarding Los Angeles debtors.[52] Most letters contained bad news rather than good. But the same was largely true of incoming mail from out-of-state lawyers. J. V. Beach of Portland, Oregon, told a typical Pacific coast tale to John D. Bicknell in 1880.

> Our code makes attorneys for non-resident clients liable for costs; it also requires a non-resident plaintiff to give security for costs in advance if demanded by defendant. If Young has faith enough in the justice of his claim to send twenty dollars for costs we would feel justified in suing on the note and risk the fee. I do not think Farwell is worth much now but a judgment could probably be collected off him in a month or two.
>
> Quite a number of Los Angeleans here. We have several collections against Cal. breakdowns, in fact, this seems to be a sort of asylum for "busted" men.[53]

Oregon, like California, had statutory provisions that made the collection of debt a legal challenge and the state a place of repose from the ravages of prior economic indiscretion.

The most imposing statutory bar to collecting debt was the statute of limitations. Graves, O'Melveny and Shankland of Los Angeles explained the problem to a client in 1889.

> The Wilber note is undoubtedly barred by the statute of limitations. You do not give the date of the judgment against Ford; if it was rendered more than two years ago, it is also barred.
>
> Under the statutes of our state, we cannot maintain an action in this state on any note made in another state, or any judgment rendered in

another state, two years after the maturity of the note or the entry of the judgment.[54]

Harriet E. Cain of Warsaw, Missouri, did not know that patience was not a virtue with respect to the law when she wrote to John D. Bicknell in 1887.

> I have written Mr. Parkinson several times that I wished he would pay me the balance due on that note I hold against him, but receive no reply. I understand he is waiting to settle some business affairs with yourself. It is nearly 20 years since the money was loaned. I think I have been quite patient over the matter. Can you do anything?[55]

Frank O. Day of Cook Creek, California, wrote to Joseph B. Wells, a San Francisco attorney, about a "debt made in St. Louis some four years since for over $300." He wanted to know if it was "worth a dime."[56]

A lawyer's laconic letter conveying the law's public policy gave little solace to creditors who waited too long. The law firm of Thompson and Davis of Marion, Iowa, thought they might salvage a promissory note that was worthless in California by having it returned "to get it into a Judgment before outlawed—ten years in [their] State."[57] Others thought federal court an alternative and questioned the constitutionality of California's statutes.[58] But all the schemes and questions could not reverse the simple statutory fact that California's fleet-footed failures and miscreants had time and the law on their side.

Rather than questioning the statutes, most of California's attorneys kept clients aware of the consequences of delay and used negotiotion to preserve creditors' interests. John D. Bicknell renewed promissory notes before the running of the statute of limitations or obtained real estate or personalty as security for debt.[59] David Jacks of Monterey had his attorneys renew notes and write new mortgages prior to the date of legal limitation.[60] If the date slipped by, negotiation was in order. James H. Shankland wrote to the law firm of Ulman and Remington in New York City in 1877, "Deft is unable to pay at present. Is employed at salary $90 per month and lives up all the salary. He promises however to pay $20 on 1st of September which is the best we can do, particularly as the claim [is] outlawed and a suit would in all probability fail."[61] Promises were better than lawsuits when the statute had run, but some debtors knew the game as well as the attorneys.

Graves, O'Melveny and Shankland ran into one such debtor in 1888, a brother attorney. They wrote to Samuel S. Parks,

> Judge Carpenter . . . here acknowledges the debt, (but we think, from the way he acts, that he will plead the Statute of Limitations, if he gets a chance).
>
> Under the statute of this state, the owner of these notes could not maintain an action on them, should Judge Carpenter plead the Statute of Limitations, if the action to put the same into judgment is brought two years after Carpenter arrived in this state. In other words, an action must be brought within two years, in this state on a note made in another state.
>
> Since starting to write the above letter, Judge Carpenter returned and asked us to have the holder of the notes make a proposition for settlement, and said that if he would take any sum that he could possibly raise by any means, he would try and clear the matter up.

A month later they were "vainly endeavoring to get a proposition from Judge Carpenter." But, they complained, "he talks all right, pleads other engagements, says that he will be in to see us and is figuring on what he can do, etc., etc."[62] Negotiation could be lengthy and, in some cases, unfruitful.

For some debtors, negotiation, delay, and excuses were a course of conduct. In 1883 H. Goodman of Taylorville wrote to his lawyer, John D. Goodwin, with a problem.

> I also send you Bill of H. Ganser, you will please collect it. He owns a team which you can atach [sic]. He is trying to keep me out of my money. First he gave me an order on Green Mountain Mining Co., and he had no money there. . . . After that he promised to pay me when he was working, but did not do so. He is now Teaming for Bransford and McIntire in Greenville. If you let him off this time, you may not catch him again.[63]

Other debtors sought additional time to pay, for a variety of reasons. Jesse B. Graham needed time to "sell some land."[64] Dr. E. K. Abbott of Salinas needed time because his "cash from sales [was] scarcely sufficient to meet [his] wants in [his] mercantile business."[65] Edward Albon of San Jose needed time to sell "a part of this lot."[66] W. C. Fairchild needed time because of "an attack of fever and ague."[67] Ellen Callahan needed to "see [her] cattle" before she could consider paying.[68] J. Bates of Sierra Valley thought he might be able to pay "as soon as the weather [got] cooler."[69] A. F. Ford of Taylorville had nothing "until after harvest."[70] John Chase Hall, a San Francisco attorney, could not pay John D. Goodwin until he ran down one of his debtors, who was all "tied up and tangled up in mining schemes" in Arizona.[71] Excuses for not paying debts expanded with the imagination of the mind and times.

Some would bear the whips and scorns of delay; others would not. General William S. Rosecrans of San Rafael wrote to his lawyer, John D. Bicknell wondering what went wrong. "While in Nevada last autumn, I received your note conveying A. Cottle's request for a little time on his note for $1300 due me Oct. . . . I [told you that I] would let it stand a short time to oblige him. Since then I have heard nothing from him."[72] Harry Fiske of Woodland had no patience. He wrote in 1883 that he thought "it better to push Hambly. Sickness [was] no excuse for failing to pay a just claim."[73] Others made softer demands on debtors in a state of dalliance. John D. Bicknell wrote to John Cadman about a note of $825 Cadman owed to W. H. Shinn that had been assigned to Bicknell's client, Mrs. Brandt. "I expect from the conversation we had," Bicknell wrote, "that it would be paid when due. The necessities of my client are such that I am compelled to demand the immediate payment of his note."[74] Bicknell was not going to stand by to receive the debtor's swift kick.[75] Other creditors and their lawyers could not be as aggressive.

Circumstances, court costs, and lawyers' fees limited the reach of small creditors in particular. Francisco Butler of Santa Ana wrote to John D. Bicknell in 1876 that he could not "possibly advance the necessary costs to litigate, and need[ed] money *so badly* that rather than the delay [he was] compelled to accept what [he could] get."[76] Often debtors would pay interest only, and creditors would carry them for another year.[77] In contrast, banks, like the Farmers and Merchants Bank of Los Angeles, eschewed litigation to avoid "Court Notoriety."[78] These financial institutions could afford the luxury of moral suasion only in good times, and in bad were forced to sue.[79]

Regardless of the reasons for debtor-delay in paying or creditor-delay in filing suit, timing was important, as some creditors learned. C. T. Hopkins, president of the California Insurance Company of San Francisco, wrote to John D. Bicknell in 1879:

I hope your complaint is not demurrable for [delay is ruinous to us] and
the other side, out of spite, will be apt to fight for delay. The moment
we get the receiver appointed, we shall get to work as quick as possible
to redeem the property from neglect. But how are your Courts as to the
prospect for dispatch? Are the dockets [crowded]?[80]

Hopkins could see the asset value depreciating, and delay reducing recovery's efficacy. Graves, O'Melveny and Shankland reported in 1888 to
their client, Asa Ellis, that the debtor's fleeter foot had thwarted the client's
interests. "About one hour before attachment was levied, Wright recorded a
deed of these last two sets of Lots to his wife. It is probably a fraud, but will
take a lawsuit to find it out, so you see you are not in a very good position to
pursue the Wrights first."[81]

The legal system afforded both debtor and creditor leverage in their
economic parrying. The game for the creditor was to obtain a quiet settlement of debts without creating an atmosphere that had other creditors
smothering the assets in an avalanche of attachments. Debtors, on the other
hand, could play the game with excuses, conveyances, hiding assets, and,
finally, bankruptcy.

The universal complaint of the early 1850s was that the state bankruptcy
laws made it ludicrously easy to defraud creditors and still come out rich.[82]
The financial panic of 1855 and the fall of the major financial institutions of
San Francisco made it clear that statutes protected few creditors and jeop-
ardized the financial partnership structure. In the midst of the panic, Alvin
Adams, one of its victims, received a letter from his lawyers telling him of

the suspension of the house of Adams and Co., San Francisco, in the
midst of a general and unheard of financial disaster.

Your friends here understood your peculiar position as a partner of
the house. They were aware of your apprehension lest under the law
of California while designing to be a special partner, you had in fact
rendered yourself liable as a general partner, and of your anxiety often
expressed to be relieved of a risk so serious.

Upon close examination of the case there seemed to be too much
ground for these apprehensions on your part. A failure of the house
must consequently make you liable for its debts.

After as thorough and anxious a consideration of the whole matter as the urgency of the occasion allowed it was decided to adopt a course of action which should make the assets of the house most available for the payment of creditors and at the same time for the protection of the partners.

A suit has been commenced in your name as plaintiff against Messrs. Haskell and Wood as defendants for a dissoulution of the partnership, the settlement of its accounts and the liquidation of its debts.[83]

The fall of Adams and Company indicated both the financial fragility of the San Francisco market and the problems of partnership business organizations.[84] Further, the financial and mercantile communities came to realize that sound business practice was a necessity.[85] Lawyers would play an important part in the transition.

For attorneys the insolvency process was a legal as well as a business judgment. There was no federal bankruptcy law between 1841 and 1867. The 1867 federal bankruptcy act was "cumbersome, badly administered, and corruptly applied."[86] It left minimal assets for creditors after others had procedurally plundered a debtor's assets. Congress repealed it in 1878, and not until 1898 was another federal bankruptcy act made law.[87] California did provide for insolvency proceedings through assignments for the benefit of creditors. This process involved a general assignment of all or substantially all of the debtor's property to a trustee, who would marshall assets, distribute them to creditors, and return the surplus to the debtor.

The assignment for the benefit of creditors was an alternative allowed under state law that was attractive to debtors. John B. McGee of the Tybo Consolidated Mining Company of San Francisco put it very well in an 1875 letter to his lawyer, John D. Goodwin: "My friends urged me to go into Bankruptcy. I declined from the fact it would place the friends whom I was trying to protect in [a] bad position."[88] J. S. Bransford, a Taylorsville merchant, saw the other obvious advantage: "I think it best to assign all partnership property for benefit of creditors rather than bankruptcy. It will be better for us and much better for the creditors as much expense will be avoided."[89]

There were problems, however, with the procedure. Graves and O'Melveny set out some of them in an 1885 letter to James H. Shankland:

The machinery for discharge of an assignee for the benefit of creditors can call him to a/c [account]. Then he can give notice and be discharged just as an assignee in involency. We doubt whether he can free himself of his liability to creditors in any other manner unless in an action in Equity. This would be too expensive a course to pursue in so small an estate.

The only reason that we do not seek the recovery now is that we are afraid that you would go to distributing and getting signatures [releasing assignee & debtor] at the same time and that some few might object to signing and we would be in the same position as in Starises case where all have received their money and one had not released the assignee.[90]

These were legal as well as logistical problems, but lawyers were in the business of solving them.

Debtors also created legal and logistical problems by making arrangements with certain creditors just ahead of other creditors, pushing themselves involuntarily into insolvency proceedings. George Roberts, a Lompoc real estate agent, presented John D. Bicknell with such a transaction in 1881:

Buell came down with a lot of leases and wanted to assign them over to Mrs. Banning. The net proceeds to go to her, he, Buell to collect the rents and be to all trouble, costs, etc., etc. in the matter. His reason for the assignment of the rents was that he had to make a payment to Mrs. Banning on his note to her and that he did not know what might happen & that he wanted to secure the payment to her by the net proceeds of the rents in those leases. I notified the renters that Buell had assigned the proceeds over to Mrs. Banning. Heacock lately was appointed Receiver for the Bank and he claims the rents & has got the proportion that has been threshed so far. Buell has commenced suit against one of the parties for the value of the grain that they turned over to Heacock. Buell made the assignment in good faith months before the Receiver was appointed and he wants those rents to go to Mrs. Banning.[91]

Phineas Banning, Mrs. Banning's husband and a well-known Southern California developer, also wrote to Bicknell, offering that he was "under the impression [that] Mrs. Banning should hav[e] nothing to do with this affair."[92] When debtors made such arrangements which in turn became known to other creditors, these out-of-favor creditors turned to the law for protection. Eugene Fawcett of San Luis Obispo discovered such a ploy and wrote his Santa Barbara attorney, Charles Fernald, in 1877:

> We are thus left to look out for ourselves. I recommend that on the 17th . . . (or as soon as Mr. Huse's obligation to us is due), we sue, and attach all the property, and every vestige of property, he has. I propose to make the war savage, and to prolong it until we have received some sort of satisfaction. That H. should have made E. a preferred creditor over us certainly relieves us from any and all obligation to forbear.[93]

The lawyer had to be aggressive in his client's interests as well as creative in solving practical problems.

Lawyers also had to be discreet in pursuing debtors. Too much publicity could trigger that avalanche of attachments from anxious creditors. Charles H. Larrobee of San Francisco gave John D. Bicknell some practical advice in 1873 regarding collection of the Harris and Company account.

> You will have to proceed with the utmost caution—prepare all your papers in your own office up to the time of procuring the writ, and then endeavor to have that fact quiet until you can have opportunity to serve it. Unless you exercise such caution you will likely be defeated by a sale—for the two partners are at loggerheads, and neither of them intend to run the saloon after election.[94]

When the process was successful and recovery could be realized before insolvency proceedings, the fleet of foot to the courthouse door were rewarded. On other occasions the notice of bankruptcy was not good news to creditors.[95]

The petition for bankruptcy was an important tool of negotiation. The law firm of Graves, O'Melveny and Shankland reported to their client that thirty-two cents on the dollar was the best they could do in 1889 because the debtor "had his petition in insolvency prepared to file."[96] The threat was enough to compromise a claim because, as attorneys commonly advised, less money was available to the creditor in insolvency proceedings, although more than 32 percent was sometimes available.[97]

Although the challenges faced by attorneys in insolvency proceedings seemed formidable, some of the involuntary proceedings were relatively simple. Graves and O'Melveny handled one such case, instructing the firm of Hendricks and Youmans on the procedure.

> Enclosed please find original petition in insolvency by creditors of W. P. Robinson, property verified, together with copy of the petition, bond on the part of the creditors, order to show cause why debtor should not be adjudicated an insolvent, and a copy therof. Please file the same and get from one of the judges of your court the order to show cause. Fill in, in the order, the day in March on which the hearing will be set, and ascertain, if you can, where Robinson is. We understand he is in the mountains. You will have to give time enough to allow proper service of the copy of petition and copy of the order upon him. If we remember rightly, service must be had ten days before the hearing. Sign your names in conjunction with ours as attorneys of petitioning creditors. Please report to us the date at which the matter is set for. We do not anticipate that there will be any opposition. We will forward to you proofs of claim after we hear from you as to when the matter will come up. We think that under the case of Luhrs v. Kelley, 7 West Coast Reporter, page 252, that as soon as the Court has made an order adjudicating Robinson an insolvent, it can order the election of an assignee by the creditors without further notice. Please look into Luhrs v. Kelley, and see if you agree with us. This has always been our practice up here. We do not know what other attorneys have done throughout the State.[98]

The form of proceeding was straightforward, but in actual practice, uncertainty was very evident. In fact, even as late as 1888, practice was not uniform due to the inefficient communications network in the bar.

Another part of debt collection practice was filling in the blanks, as Graves and O'Melveny directed. Some attorneys had difficulties with this aspect of practice. Creed Hammond's letter from Sacramento to John D. Goodwin in Quincey in 1869 was one such instance:

> When I received the papers in Madden v. Reynolds I felt like murdering you—how did you expect the sheriff of this county to make an arrest on an order directed to the Shff of Plumas County. You must be more careful my boy when you proceed under "the statute." See sec. 77

Pr. Act for form of order [the 1851 Statute provided a civil remedy of arrest and bail]. We of course could do nothing in the premises. You may tell your client that we raised heaven and earth pursued the defendant with a vigilance worthy of the cause, charged you $100 for expenses but could not capture him.[99]

The Oroville law firm of Gray and Sexton wrote to Goodwin in 1882 with a problem with the case of S. C. Buss, insolvent: "You will see by the blanks which I send that your clerk has used the *wrong one*. The blank he used is the one where the *Creditors petition*. The one I send you is where the *Insolvent himself* petitions."[100] The advent of preprinted forms in the 1870s and 1880s enabled a more regularized practice, but the right forms and blanks had to be filled in by skilled counsel.

Lawyers also helped creditors collect on mortgages. The practice was simpler than collecting on other notes because real property was held as security for the promissory note. The problems of collecting, however, were similar. Depreciated real estate reduced recovery. Delay dogged the process. Statutory defenses, such as the homestead exemption, virtually barred recovery in certain circumstances. Bankruptcy also existed as a possible refuge for the debtor.[101]

Debtors tried to delay the payment of the underlying mortgage principle in some instances. They commonly paid interest at a high rate in return for a renewal of the mortgage transaction rather than suffer a foreclosure.[102] In hard economic times such an arrangement was potentially beneficial to both parties because the interest payments arrived on time.

The major problems for lawyers in collecting on a mortgage were the original paperwork and the foreclosure proceedings. When made, the mortgage instrument had to describe the property mortgaged with precision. Lawyers had to check the homestead books, because five thousand dollars of a property's value was exempt from execution. If a married woman was involved, statutes required precise and proper acknowledgment of the making of the instrument. Finally, foreclosure was statutory, and the steps had to be taken with care.[103] Foreclosure, like attachment, could set off a wave of creditor actions against the assets and possibly precipitate bankruptcy. Once awash with these statutory proceedings, lawyers had to be careful of their clients' interests.[104] As with other collection problems, settlement prior to bankruptcy was an ever-present option.[105]

Lawyers did collect, however, and made their clients happy. This success flowed from negotiation and lawsuits.[106] Another means of collection was turning the note over to a third party, as William Hickman suggested to John D. Bicknell in 1879. Hickman wanted an uncollected note turned over to Mrs. Ferguson. He wrote, "she has done *so well* with the Backman note that I feel inclined to give her a *chance* at the . . . parties. The *Ladies* you know have '*God given*' Gifts for collecting bad debts."[107] With equal tenacity Nellie M. White of the Hamilton and Heath firm tracked down a debtor on the streets of San Francisco. She wrote Bicknell in 1879, "I can get hold of him here as he is known to have means and Mr. Heath requests me to write to you and have you send me a execution for balance of judgment directed to Sheriff of City and County of San Francisco."[108] Collection agencies were another mechanism available to creditors, but they were competition for lawyers.

The long arm of the criminal-justice system also was a means to the end. After hounding a debtor to ground, the firm of Graves, O'Melveny and Shankland found their subject, Sly, in jail. On February 29, 1892, the law firm wrote to W. H. Damsel, the manager of the Adams Express Company, and asked whether Damsel could end the creditor's distress by "getting [Sly] to give [Damsel] a check for the money in the First National Bank" and a "bill of sale" for the "saloon property" that the law firm had attached. Graves advised cunning in the transaction because "this money [was] on deposit in the name of Denton" and Sly would have "to sign the check A. S. Denton." Further, a cash inducement to Sly might be necessary. If he signed the check and bill of sale in return for cash, Damsel was to "leave with the prison officials whatever you are going to give him, to be turned over to him as soon as the check [was] paid."[109] Otherwise, Sly could outfox Damsel by stopping payment on the check. Just having a check in hand should not cause a creditor to leap to the conclusion that it was good.

Debt collection in the nineteenth century was the bread and butter for the frontier bar. Lawyers confronted numerous problems in this area of practice but solved most of them. Creditors and their lawyers did express an ideology, whether they were of the lending or the legal elite. They believed that the payment of money at interest for value received was to be performed. The law reflected that belief, but other aspects of the law limited the ability of those creditors and attorneys to enforce the promise. Lawyers, better than some creditors, understood the reach of the law and attempted to explain the ways of legislators and judges. Although debt collection was very much a part of early practice, by the close of the century it had diminished in significance. Attorneys like Bicknell had turned to the more complex world of real estate titles.

5

Real Estate Practice

*The title insurance business . . . making abstracts and
certificates of title, & insuring titles. The latter branch of the business
is going to be remunerative. . . . The searching business . . .
is a science in itself. . . . The old system of abstracting and searching
titles cannot be said to pay in these modern times.*
—Jackson A. Graves to B. Reinstein, December 26, 1895

Real estate practice was another central feature of nineteenth-century law
practice that also received public attention. As with debt collection practice,
lawyers and clients maintained a dialogue about expectations, frustrations,
and the law. Both areas of practice involved gaps between expectations based
on law, and applications. In that property was central to nineteenth-century
values, both lawyers and clients communicated frequently about it.

Property had been the source of wealth for Americans since the seven-
teenth century, and nineteenth century lawyers supported the land transactions that continued the entrepreneurial expansion of land use in California. California's land use was hampered by two related phenomena: Mexican
land-grant claims of title and squatters. The ambiguity of Mexican land
grants and the absence of land surveys prepared prior to or even contem-
poraneous with settlement of the land created uncertainty. The hordes of
settlers of the first quarter century swarmed onto available lands, staking
claims regardless of earlier conflicting titles. It was left up to California's

legal community to help sort out the titles, quiet titles to land, and facilitate the transactions that would enable the economic growth of the state.

Congress handled the problem of Mexican titles in 1851 by passing an act creating a commission to hear and decide private land claims. The commission heard 813 claims, confirming 521.[1] For claimants and their lawyers the job of "proving up" a claim was substantial. Henry Halleck, a San Francisco attorney, explained some of the problems to a client in 1852.

> From the imperfection of the records and the peculiar character of Spanish and Mexican grants, it will be found necessary to take a large amount of parole evidence, respecting occupation, boundaries, &c. . . . Let me add to this, the fact that all the proceedings of the legislative body & decisions of the courts of California under the former Gov't are in manuscript in the Spanish language, [to give you] some idea of the labor [involved].[2]

The problem of ascertaining title was not limited to Mexican or private claims. Claims to public land often involved the same kind of inquiry. A title memorandum of Chipman and Dwinelle chronicled a series of rapid transactions affecting title.

> A man named Kinse Kinsmill was first occupant to 1862. He built a house but did not preempt. He sold to Meloon; no record of sale. Meloon fenced and set out vines. In 1862 Meloon sold to Harrison: sale recorded. Meloon having pre-empted previous to sale a man named Schmidt being on the premises at this time as tenant of Meloon who owed him labor some $300. Schmidt in March 1865 sold possession to Darling and Morris and they sold to present occupant.
>
> The present owner Powell holds the title from Harrison and will sue for possession and damages, rents and profits—several thousand dollars unless he sells to the man in possession.[3]

The rapidity of frontier transactions and the inexactitude of the description of these transactions contributed to the difficulty of real estate practice.

The rapidity of transactions and property description errors made title uncertain enough to decrease the value of land and to increase the amount of legal attention given to deeds. Thomas B. Dibblee described typical concerns to John D. Bicknell in 1880.

It is a very unsafe and unwise thing for us all to be passing these conveyances after the hasty manner in which they were written—without
careful examination.

There might be tracts duplicated or conveyed twice, and this is certain to bring us to trouble at some future time when it might be very
difficult to correct the error, and when perhaps the property may have
become very valuable. . . .

As we have gone along I have made note of errors. I am sorry to say
that I find the Deeds very defective, so much so that contrary to my
hope, I think that any Deed of correction would hardly be practicable,
or at least it would be a very complex and confused instrument at least,
and would not prevent the errors in the original Deeds causing mistakes
to persons hereafter examining these titles.[4]

Beyond the problems inherent in deeds, lenders were very wary of land
with title problems, and rightfully so, given the extensive litigation that land
titles generated. George Smith Patton wrote to Arthur J. Hutchinson in
1889 regarding the same problem, but with a legislative solution.

Mr. Glassell, Col. Smith, and I had a full discussion this morning regarding the title to the Hays Tract. We do not think it advisable to
submit the Abstract as it stands, to a possible lender, at least until we
have made further effort to discover the facts regarding the original
locators. We suggest that between now and our coming up, you make
further inquiry from all possible sources as to this matter. Examine the
records of the Recorder's office for deeds, mortgages or other instruments by any of these parties, as well as the records of the Clerk's office
for any possible suits to which they may have been parties. In regard to
inquiry from Henry Hunsaker, we think it would be well to risk any
suspicions that might be excited in him as a last resort. We can only
leave the method of making such inquiries to you, so as to run as little
risk as possible. . . . In case we can show that the original locators were
adults at the time the Statute commenced to run, then, according to the
opinion both of Judge Anderson and of Stanley, Stoney, and Hayes, the
title is good. In the meantime, Col. Smith has prepared a bill to be
presented to the Legislature, following the suggestions of Justice Field
of the Supreme Court, to cover just such a case as ours. . . . The bill is

one which is approved by all lawyers, and is really necessary under the present state of our law.[5]

Patton was well aware of the problems, from both the standpoint of law practice and that of property management.

Colonel George H. Smith told him of a possible solution six months earlier in a letter composed while Smith was on vacation in British Columbia.

The system of registering deeds would I think work very well in a new country like British Columbia, where the titles are simple, but I don't see how it could work here with our complicated titles. The system we need is for the state or rather the County to have made and printed an abstract of all the deeds, mortgages, &c in the Recorders Office, and a printed alphabetical index to each class of instruments, and to impose upon the Recorder the duty of furnishing abstacts or certificates as required. Certainly something should be done to excape from the grinding monopoly and extortionate charges we are now suffering from.[6]

Colonel Smith's observation articulated another obvious problem for investors and their lawyers: costs. In addition to legal fees for title searches, the transaction fees added to cash-flow burdens.

But these classic problems of real estate practice were minor when compared with those created by the horde of squatters that peopled early California. Archibald Peachy reported in 1852 that "many of the [Mexican] Grants are covered with Squatters and it is feared by some that they may be difficult to remove on the titles being confirmed." But Peachy had greater faith in California's pioneers. He wrote "They will [go] quietly .... if they cannot purchase from the owners of the land."[7] As executors of the Joseph L. Folsom will, Halleck, Peachy, and Van Winkle would see a different side of humanity. When Folsom died hundreds of "miners" jumped his land. James Wilson wrote to the law firm in 1855, demanding that "some immediate steps [be] taken to put a stop to this wholesale squatterism."[8] But squatters were a part of San Francisco life, from the city's birth until the enforcement of the Van Ness Ordinance and the extinguishment of Jose Y. Limantour's claim in 1856.[9]

In rural California, squatters found vacant land equally appealing. In

Monterey, landowner David Jacks used litigation and leases to stem the tide of squatters. William Irvine of Patterson, Wallace, and Stow of San Francisco advised Jacks in 1869: "I do not believe forcible entry and detainer can be maintained against your squatters. Take the necessary pains to get their true names, so far as they can be ascertained and bring ejectment and enjoin them. Probably they cannot be enjoined from anything excepting what the law regards as waste."[10] Jacks found leases more effective. By leasing at low cash rents or for improvements only, Jacks was able to bar his tenants from legally questioning his title.[11]

John D. Bicknell used the lease as a tactic to preserve interests in land. One of his early clients, General William S. Rosecrans of Chickamauga fame, approved Bicknell's 1874 "plan of precluding title by giving leases for one year to squatters on favorable terms to them."[12] Michael J. O'Connor purchased Rosecrans's land and retained Bicknell to obtain a patent for the land and to deal with "the hoard [sic] of squatters."[13] Bicknell filed ejectment suits, but the law dragged slowly; within four years of litigation and negotiation leasing became a more common solution. The litigation and "squatterism" reduced land values. O'Connor complained in 1878 that "buyers . . . expect us to make great sacrifices; but . . . [the land] will bring 25 to 33 1/3 p. ct. more as soon as we get the squatter cases settled."[14] As time went on, some squatters wanted out. W. R. Farris offered to sell his claim for the $350 he supposedly had invested in improvements. O'Connor took a dim view of the offer.

> Please say to Mr. Farris that I decline his proposition. He has enjoyed the use of that land free of rent long enough to pay for his improvements and the least compensation he can make me for the injury he has done is to deed them to me for a nominal consideration. He threatens to fight it out if I don't buy him out, and adds in a P.S. that he has a small place in Oregon which he wishes to improve and desires to go there this summer.
>
> There is an ancient belief that rats desert a house that is about to fall. I have a suspicion that Mr. Farris is conscious of the approaching destruction of all his hopes of getting a title to the land he squatted on. Hence, it would be a brilliant piece of diplomacy to get me to pay the cost of his improvements.[15]

Squatters had the costs of litigation to bear as they harvested their crops in the heat of the Los Angeles sun, but their business costs did not include rents.

O'Connor's faith in the legal system ebbed with time. In June 1880 he wrote, "[I] hoped the Supreme Court would give us the right of possession before the Squatters harvested their crops—in which case we could have gotten some rent out of them, but now I fear it will come too late." [16] By September, O'Connor was hoping for leases.

> As to leasing—will you not be able to get better terms after a favorable decision than before it? I am, of course, very anxious to get some income from the property, yet in view of the probable settlement of the cases before the court within a month, I would suggest that no leases be granted until that time *provided* you have reason to believe you can then make better terms. [17]

As O'Connor correctly observed, the cloud upon title also reduced the rental value of the property.

By 1881 O'Connor's faith in the law had slipped further. He instructed Bicknell that

> leases . . . should contain a clause obliging the lessee to notify the lessor of the time when he will reap and sack the grain, in order that he may have an opportunity of seeing that he gets his fair share of the crop. You see that I have a poor opinion of the honesty of the squatter class. . . .
>
> I suppose that some of those who went on the land in 1876 and have continued on it to the present time, raising crops every year, could be made to pay costs and damages for their occupation, to the extent of a fair rental. But you should know best and I must submit.
>
> That the land is now largely occupied by jumpers is further evidence to my mind of the error made in judgment by suing so many persons, when the principals involved could as well be tried and settled by one suit, against a few persons, at comparatively small expense. I urged this view upon you when I was in Los Angeles, and now when you tell me, that not one cent of the costs can be collected, I am forcibly reminded of my original opinion of the useless expense of the proceedings. [18]

Costs mounted. Squatters harvested. Five years had passed.

As Thanksgiving neared in 1882, O' Connor was "willing to go on selling at from $25 to $20 per acre."[19] O'Connor was now paying litigation costs at the expense of the land he had been fighting to retain.

But a new day dawned in 1885, nine years after it all began. The United States Supreme Court upheld O'Connor's claim.[20] He wrote to Bicknell in 1885 from Marnaroneck, New York.

> The reading of Judge Field's decisions of our cases gave me great pleasure. It seems to me we are now secure from attack from any quarter. It has been a long contest and the result has been just as you predicted from the first.
>
> Use your discretion in settling with the squatters. I approve of your method of taking what you can amicably rather than by judgment. Los Angeles juries never looked with any favor upon my title, and though [Judge] Sepulveda may not be on the Bench, I have no desire to go before judge or jury, when it can be avoided.[21]

The litigation system had triumphed, but at great expense.

Bicknell also had lands in his portfolio of investments. Interestingly, J. T. Thornton of Winchester wrote Bicknell in 1888 regarding those lands.

> I am afraid that at the price at which you hold your land, you will have to wait some time before you sell, as there is so much cheap land yet on the market. But if you don't care to lease, I will do my utmost to sell it. However, I am inclined to the opinion that it might prove to be a good plan to lease, as you get the land cleaned and in condition for cultivation, with one year's rent, even if the lessor did not purchase it. But the greatest advantage would be in keeping off settlers who are squatting on the land under U. S. settlement laws, and therby obviate that trouble.[22]

Bicknell knew the advice to be sound and far more economical than ejectment suits.

The element of cost in litigation and the uncertainty of juries and appeals hampered real estate development. As O'Connor's travail forced him to spend a great deal, so too did twelve hundred squatters on the San Fernando Rancho force the Los Angeles Farming and Milling Company to pay out over fifty thousand dollars in legal expenses starting in 1890. Jackson A.

Graves won every case, but such "unjust litigation" was costly. The story of squatters was repeated all over the state in every decade. It was a lawyer's challenge of the first magnitude and a claimant's cash-flow nightmare. It also was a psychological trauma that landowners had to endure more than once for the same piece of land. Albert Dibblee of San Francisco wrote to his brother Thomas in Santa Barbara:

> Today on consulting Mullan & Hyde, I learn with surprise and disgust that we have to go into the case seriously and show pretty near our whole title and what it rests upon over again. This thing, so far as it affects our land, is a miserable outrage—but Capt. Mullan says that to fail in appearing at this examination and in establishing our boundaries that are threatened, would be to incur the danger of having an over-lapping patent issue and thereafter a contest in the courts.
>
> I am almost sick of my life to think that I shall be compelled to go into this confounded contest again, when I thought the grant was laid forever. It will be a hard task to educate Mullan & Hyde in this case and I ought to begin at once.[23]

Litigation was an ever-present yet distasteful part of nineteenth-century life for landowners and their lawyers.

A lawyer's work with landowners and squatters also extended to disputes among squatters. One such case came to John D. Bicknell in 1879. Joel H. Turner of Newhall wrote on behalf of a Mr. O'Neal, who had bought a "squatters claim" from a party that had occupied the land for a year. O'Neal moved in for three months, but had "to leave with his sheep to find feed." When he returned he found a "Dutch man . . . in . . . possession of his cabin, land and everything else" and the Dutchman refused "to give possession" to O'Neal. The land was unsurveyed and O'Neal wanted an attorney to help him regain possession. In that O'Neal was "a sheep man," he could "pay his fee to his attorney."[24] Given the rapidity of transactions and the transient nature of the early California population, conflicts of this nature were certain to arise and find their way into a law office.

Lawyers also represented landowners in sales and leases with title issues put aside. In their sales functions, they were brokers and promoters. Bicknell's representation of William Rosecrans and Michael O'Connor included land sales and rentals.[25] Bicknell also performed land-brokerage services for numerous other clients.[26] As a land promoter, Bicknell's reputation grew.

T. K. McDowell of Anaheim saw a potential boom in his area and wrote Bicknell to encourage his participation. "What we need is some live energetic capitalist like you . . . to take hold of this matter and push things. As it is the Kraemer boys hold back & do nothing and nobody else seems moving at present."[27] But, in the real estate business, there were good times and bad. As Bicknell told W. N. Monroe in 1891, after the boom was over: "It is very different from the times when we were booming Monrovia, and since the collapse most all of our enterprising citizens have found it necessary to go though the process of settlement and liquidation which has hindered very materially the growth of the country."[28] Whether broker, promoter, negotiator or litigator, the lawyer played an important role in the real estate enterprise of California.[29]

Lawyers dealing with California real estate problems had to be both prompt and thorough in their legal actions. Whether using the lease to defeat a possessor questioning title, ejectment litigation to dispossess a squatter, or negotiation to clear title, the Statute of limitations prompted action.[30] As in actions on debt, time was of the essence. Because of vast acreages and hordes of squatters, the statutory provisions of adverse possession and limitations on actions favored action rather than sitting on rights. In both cases, the legislative intent was to quiet title in a short period of time. Michael Burke of San Francisco inelegantly stated the intent in an 1868 letter.

> So far as the Statue of Limation being known to me or any of us . . . I undertake to say such a law was not known to 8 tenths of the working Class and perhaps is not now known to the same class of people. Such Law was only know to Legislatures, Lawyers, opperatives and Black Mailers.
>
> The Statue of Limitations . . . has not been tested before the Legal Trybunals as to its Constitutionallity which there is may Dishonest Cheemers in this state. The honest Intention of the Legislature [was] to quiet the titles to Land.[31]

To determine whether the statute of limitations could remedy certain situations was a matter for a lawyer specializing in real property law. Michael J. O'Connor recognized this need for specialization as early as 1875 in a letter to John D. Bicknell.

They may have a legal but not equitable claim to the land and I hope you will be able to get the legal title without much expense. If [Caleb] Ferris has left the country we may have to rely on the Statute of Limitations to cure the defect in his case. He deeded to [William] Rosecrans in March, 1868, but the Patent is dated from the 21st April 1874. The State recognized his right to the land from the time of the approval of the Location, as appears by W. L. Ranson's book, on the 1st March, 1872 and I believe General R[osecrans] has been in possession, or has claimed to be in possession since 1868. I am not lawyer enough to know from which of these dates the Statute of Limitations commences to run.[32]

Although property law was the stuff of nineteenth century law practice, the interests at stake as well as the increasing complexity of law gave many the perception that specialized knowledge was essential to the successful pursuit of any legal conclusion.

Clients also paid close attention to legal developments. David Jacks was in court so frequently over the title to Monterey County lands that he bought a law library and subscribed to advance-sheet services. He occasionally wrote his lawyer, S. O. Houghton, in San Jose to tell him about the cases he thought relevant.

In Department 2 of the Supreme Court filed March 23rd, 1886 Martin vs. Ward n. 9262. In the latter part of the opinion "The sixth finding of the jury, to the effect the Defendant repudiated the agreements and claimed to hold the premises as his own, on or about three years ago, coupled with the fact that he himself testified that for two or three years before suit was brought, he had not paid the taxes on the property as required by Section 325 of the Code of Civil Procedure, to make out an adverse possession are conclusive on the defendants pleas of the Statute of Limitations."

This discussion with regard to failure to pay taxes, may possibly be of some use to you in the Leary Case. And it may be well to make a note of it and put amoungst the papers, in the Correy suits.[33]

Jacks wrote eleven days after the supreme court rendered its decision. Law was important to the client and not exclusively the domain of attorneys even in 1886. Whether the statute of limitations was involved or not, time represented money in the real estate business because a lawsuit, a cloud on a title, or a squatter reduced the value for immediate sale.[34]

Lawyers performed numerous functions in regard to California real estate. Title searches and abstracts of title supported the public policy of quieting title rapidly in order to facilitate transactions. These property-law experts became the founders of title insurance companies, and title insurance quickly came to replace abstracts and lawsuits. Lawyers also transacted real estate business for their clients. They were part of the transactional society that moved property into productive action. Litigation was very much a part of early real estate practice and in it lawyers helped to speed the process of patenting land and quieting title. This necessary process moved land into a commodity status, which enabled the dynamic economic growth that California experienced.

In forming title companies, men like Jackson A. Graves created competition for the lawyers that continued the task of title searching. But business clients and investors wanted the certainty and cost control that title insurance afforded. This was not a California phenomenon; New York moved to title insurance in the 1880s for the same reasons.[35] As Graves had observed in 1895, the old ways of searching and abstracting could not be maintained in modern times.

Modern times brought the ebb of real estate title practice and debt collection, but created new opportunities for lawyers. The railroad and industrialization spawned new legal challenges for lawyers in terms of business structure and management while at the same time generating legal business because of its human costs. Lawyers and their clients exhibited a closely held belief in the significance of private property as wealth and as right. The legal system was to remedy wrongs done to those who held title and to provide a process for quieting title. Again, law and application did not always converge as lawyers or as clients thought it should. With modern times, the costs of change would be in human terms, and the law of torts was to address rights and remedies.

6

Tort Practice

The jury has rendered a verdict, and . . . they
gave the plaintiff one dollar. . . . Col. Wellborn . . . shook hands,
congratulated me, and asked if I was satisfied;
I told him, by no means; that "the judgment was excessive."
—Jackson A. Graves to E.S. Pillsbury, September 28, 1894

Modern times brought new personal injury problems to California's lawyers. The nature of communications between lawyers and clients changed. Clients were more frequently corporate entities like the Southern Pacific Company or an injured individual. The questions about what juries would do became increasingly hard for the practicing bar to answer and both corporate defendants and their lawyers looked for ways of rationalizing the costs of industrialization to make the costs more predictable. The communications of John D. Bicknell are particularly helpful in illustrating the local knowledge of the law.

California lawyers faced tort litigation late in the nineteenth century. Early practitioners handled infrequent tort claims, but with the coming of the railroad, tort practice exploded in volume and value. The sheer volume of cases pushed the profession to settle rather than litigate, but debt collection practice had also habituated lawyers to settle cases. Finally, lawyers began to transcend the litigation-settlement role to assume a modern risk-management role. Corporate defense attorneys had to look to risk in the insurance sense of corporate policy as well as the legal liability sense, which all lawyers were trained to recognize. It was the railroad lawyers like John D. Bicknell who led the profession from the courtroom to the boardroom in the analysis of risk.

Lawyers handled a variety of tort cases prior to the advent of industrial accidents. Defamation cases hit lawyers' desks as did nuisance claims, blasting injuries, and transportation accidents.[1] Mining generated personal injury cases when timbers fell, elevators failed, or fatigue caused the hand to falter.[2] Mines also generated tailings that destroyed adjacent lands and poisoned streams.[3] Lawyers moved to protect clients' interests with traditional common-law causes of action and broader legislative remedies.

The railroad defense lawyer quickly found that the locomotive generated a great deal of power to haul freight and passengers, but it also drove claimants into court. The train killed cattle along the tracks, started fires, and injured employees, passengers, and the public. The lawyer looked first to liabilities as a matter of law, then to the facts to assess the clients' chances in trial, and finally to the possible economic impact to determine whether settlement or litigation was the best business policy.

Railroads had a statutory duty to fence their track. This imposed an expense upon the railroad but provided a defense when cattle were killed on the track. The legal duty to fence was part of the western heritage because of the open range and the cattleman's desire to impose the expense of protecting his property upon the railroad. However, when cattle prices fell below statutory recovery limits, it became profitable to drive them onto the tracks and collect the damages. The Southern Pacific, after years of unfortunate experience, developed an incident report for cattle kills. On the top of the form, in bold letters, the company instructed: "Great care should be taken to prevent the killing of stock. Come to a full stop, if necessary, to avoid the accident." The company also warned, "If an engineer kills stock when it is apparent that he might avoid doing so, the value to the stock so killed will be deducted from his pay."[4] The form certainly contained incentives for safety, but cattle died nonetheless.

On August 17, 1889, sixteen beeves died on the Southern Pacific's cowcatcher in a single incident. The report read, "They were driven on[to the tracks] by owners."[5] John D. Bicknell received the report and analyzed the issues in a lawyerly fashion when writing to J. A. Muir, Southern Pacific's assistant division superintendent for Los Angeles.

To form an opinion as to the liability of the Company it becomes very important to know whether the right of way of the railroad is within the public highway or not. That is to say, under Sec. 485 of the Civil Code "Railroads are required to maintain good and sufficient fences on either or both sides of their track and property." "In case they do not make and maintain such fences, etc. the Company is liable," as provided in the section. How if it is true that our right of way is within the public highway where we cannot make and maintain fences without destroying the highway the rule would be quite different, I think, as to our liability than it would be if our right of way belonged to us and the public road ran parallel to it as you state in your letter. If we occupy the highway, our use of it being lawful, Sentous Bros. have also a right to occupy the highway in the driving of their cattle, and with that condition of things if we could show that the owner of the cattle was guilty of negligence which proximately contributed to the injury or killing of his cattle he could not recover therefor. Any question as to whether he was guilty of such contributory negligence is generally one to be determined by the jury in view of the circumstances. There is no doubt that if a person wantonly or carelessly drives stock upon the track of a railroad he is guilty of contributory negligence and if the stock is injured or killed he cannot recover.[6]

When the factual dust cleared, Bicknell's legal judgment was that going to trial was worthwhile, since liability was not clear.

The jury did not support the contentions of the railroad and found for the cattlemen. Bicknell analyzed the situation for Creed Haymond, the general counsel for the Southern Pacific, in March, 1890.

Taking the whole case together it is evident that it was an unavoidable accident and that we are not liable and that we ought not to pay. but there is just enough in it to make it difficult about setting aside the verdict. That is to say, there is proof going to show that a large amount of dust was raised by the travelling cattle; that the cattle were strung out on both sides of the track and in a position to be easily seen by the engineer upon the approaching train. If we are liable for this beef, it is cheap beef on the verdict ($300 + $100 costs). I think I have a fighting chance on appeal, but like all cases of this class it is doubtful about our ever getting a verdict. Upon the whole I consider it the best business policy to pay the judgment.[7]

Five days later Haymond returned Bicknell's letter, congratulating him despite the defeat in trial. "I think that under the circumstances you did pretty well in the cattle case. The verdict was a small one, if we had to lose, anyhow, I have found it almost impossible to defend any of these cases successfully and have generally advised settling them."[8] The elements of company policy were clear: litigate when liability was not clear, settle the small claims whenever possible. Bicknell's advice and Haymond's experience converged regarding the desireability of settling such cases. By 1890 the modern inclination of looking to the settlement conference rather than the jury trial was clearly a part of tort practice.

The locomotives also started grass fires from time to time, particularly in Southern California, where dry grass was a common condition along the right of way. As in the cattle cases company policy looked first to liability and then to settlement. Bicknell also looked to risk management to reduce claims and litigation, recommending that the "section men . . . put the right of way in the very best condition . . . to prevent fires."[9] Bicknell's risk-management approach came after years of experience with small claims and hostile local juries.

Personal injury litigation mushroomed with the penetration of the railroad into more and more California communities. People in wagons met loco-motives at crossings with dire consequences for the wagon passengers.[10] Others crossed the tracks at places of their convenience but to their detri-ment.[11] Locomotive starts and stops caused passengers to fall and passen-gers hurt themselves getting on and off the train. Injuries multiplied for passengers, the public, and employees. Lawyers had to represent their cli-ents and make the litigation-settlement system work. The Southern Pacific Company adopted, after years of hard lessons, a policy of settling whenever liability was established. When facts were in dispute, a similar position emerged, as John D. Bicknell expressed it to William T. Rankin, the assis-tant general counsel of the Pullman Palace Car Company of Chicago, in 1889. "I have been an attorney for the Southern Pacific Railroad for some years and tried too many damage cases not to be alarmed at a case where there is controversy between the person injured and the employees of the road as to the facts of the case. My advice in this case is if we can get a reasonable settlement to adjust them." [12] The case involved a Pullman porter who allegedly struck a passenger who refused to pay the sleeping car fare of twenty-five cents. Rankin thought the company was "not liable" for an act by the porter committed outside the scope of his employment. [13]

With the facts in conflict, Rankin had "a man interviewing witnesses in Alabama and Florida" who were on the Pullman when the incident took place in Pasadena. [14] But "the investigations [were] not encouraging," particularly because the porter was "surly, unaccommodating," and may have been drunk when the incident occurred. Rankin thought an offer of $250 would settle the case, but noted "that to procure a settlement we might raise these figures a little." [15] Bicknell found that the plaintiffs were willing to settle for $500, although they had demanded $1,200.

> I am constrained to do this as there is no doubt but what the plaintiffs in these cases would obtain a judgment, and while the actual damages sustained by both would not be that much yet we take the chances of a jury running away in their verdict and the judgment would probably be affirmed by the Supreme Court to that amount. . . . I have had too much experience in this class of cases to expect much favor at the hands of a jury. [16]

Rankin agreed that the settlement was "excellent." [17] The resolution of many cases was clearly controlled more by counsel than by Los Angeles juries in 1889. Here the lawyer's skill in negotiation was critical to settlement.

Even when settlement failed and trial progressed to a verdict, settlement after trial was always possible. George C. Fabens, Southern Pacific's claims adjuster, and Bicknell agreed that there was "no liability in the Schram case," but, Fabens believed, "It would be [the] charitable thing to contribute something to the family" in return for "a full legal release." [18] The settlement offer of $150 was not agreed to and the case went to trial, with a jury verdict for the railroad. The Supreme Court ordered a new trial and Bicknell evaluated the case for settlement in 1891.

> It is a case in which a new trial is very dangerous. If the plaintiffs are entitled to anything a judgment for a much larger amount would be sustained. Upon this trial there were two witnesses of several years experience as engineers in the employ of the California Southern Railway who testified that a train consisting of nine cars made up of five

freight cars, three passenger cars and a baggage car and a ten wheel locomotive could be stopped within one hundred feet. I met this with the evidence of our master mechanic, a master mechanic of the California Southern and four engineers that it could not possibly be stopped in less than three hundred feet, and they considered a stop at 350 feet a good one. It is barely possible that if our engineer could have stopped the train within one hundred feet we were negligent. The case is a dangerous one as there is just enough conflict in the evidence to send it to the jury. As a matter of fact the accident was occasioned by the negligence and carelessness of the deceased. He drove directly upon the track in the face of an approaching train. The wheels of the wagon by some accident got stuck in the track, and the only question is whether the engineer did or should have discovered Schram in the position that he was upon the track and did all that he could to stop the train. . . . We were running at a higher rate of speed than the ordinance of this city permitted. . . . I . . . recommend that this case be compromised if possible.[19]

The failure of settlement resulted in trial and Bicknell did not want to risk facing another jury. This was wrongful death and, in Bicknell's experience, widows were known to tug at the hearts of jurors.

On some occasions it was necessary to try a case before a jury more than once and to pursue legal issues to the state supreme court. John D. Bicknell tried a case involving a Santa Ana boy who had lost his leg in a railroad turntable. Bicknell recommended that the verdict of $300 with $113 costs be paid to avoid the possibility of a new trial. Given the verdict and the developing railroad law of the state, he also made a risk-management recommendation. He advised that "locking turntables . . . located out in country towns and places like this turntable at Santa Ana where children are in the habit of playing would save a great deal of vexatious difficulty."[20] A little over a year later the boy's guardian brought a $50,000 lawsuit on the same facts (the mother had brought the first suit). Bicknell again went to court "to fight that case over again."[21] A month later Bicknell reported a "serious defeat." He had "always considered the case a dangerous one but did not deem it possible that a jury would award so high a verdict as they did, to-wit, the sum of $12,500."[22] Bicknell again recommended the use of locking devices on turntables. He also appealed the decision in order to "settle the law in this state as to the rights of children to play upon turntables." [23] One year later the California Supreme Court established that it was "the duty of the company to protect its turntables from trespassing children." Bicknell observed in the midst of another defeat, "If this is the law, the sooner we know it the better." [24] With the law clearly in place, Bicknell advised corporate risk management in accordance with the supreme court decision. [25]

In cases involving small claims or verdicts, the pressure to settle was simple economics. Bicknell regularly offered to settle small claims for livestock "to close the matter[s] right up." [26] If the case went to trial in a justice court and the jury gave the plaintiff the verdict, an appeal usually resulted in a settlement. [27] The same was occasionally true for cases involving plaintiffs' verdicts of five thousand dollars to nine thousand dollars. [28] The court costs for the railroad on appeal made settling small claims economical, much as legal fees on appeal made plaintiffs interested in a compromise.

As the railroad business became regional in scope, California lawyers found themselves involved in tort practice at long distance. For example, the Southern Pacific asked Bicknell to settle the claim of a New Orleans woman who had lost her right arm in a train accident near El Paso, Texas. [29] Tort practice, because of the interstate nature of the clients, grew in geographic scope in the late nineteenth century. The railroad's information network provided the details, but it was the California attorney who negotiated or litigated.

The problems for nineteenth-century practitioners were those of a developing law and an expanding volume of cases. Tort law and practice grew with the railroad. Industrial accidents became the engine that drove lawyers to argue facts to juries and law to judges. In the process the legal profession contributed both to the settlements that kept the courts from being overburdened and the litigation that gave foundation to the developing law of torts.

These lawyer-client communications about business and law must be measured against legal change. Tort law was the most rapidly changing branch of the law in the period of this study. In the 1850s tort law cases constituted only 9.7 percent of the docket of the California Supreme Court. The cases decided during 1860–79 equaled 38.6 percent of the sum, and the cases of the 1880s were 51.7 percent of the whole. In the period 1850–1900, the appellate reports reveal 248 decisions for plaintiffs and 26 for defendants.[30] The sheer volume of cases in a new field of law was staggering for its time.

The California Supreme Court developed law in a way that at times gave the practicing bar mixed signals. The court on numerous occasions decided cases, used doctrines, or interpreted fact situations favorably to enterprise and against plaintiff employees. The fact that the supreme court did develop employer defenses to tort liability and did apply those defenses to fact situations incontrovertibly relieved enterprise of some of the costs of industrialization. That the application of the defenses was not universal does not imply a judicial desire to burden enterprise. Subsidizing industry was not the goal or the result of judicial lawmaking. The victims' welfare was not the goal or the result of appellate craftsmanship. Rather, the California law of torts involved both the subsidizing of industry and victims' welfare. A tension existed between the decisions of juries, which were based on circumstances rather than judicial pronouncement, and the law declared by courts. What the supreme court could give in the fellow-servant rule, a common employers' defense against liability in cases brought by injured employees, the local jury could take away with awards unprofitable to appeal. As the supreme court developed exceptions to the fellow-servant rule and the legislature crafted a workers' compensation program, the social cost-spreading and the social consciousness of employer liability slowly changed so as to more closely approximate the victim-welfare ideas that have come to dominate twentieth-century tort practice.[31]

Given the facts of legal change and the evidence in attorney-client communications, what was the ideology of the bar? Perhaps Bicknell understood it best when he faced defeat in his turntable case. Even though the law was changing, he knew what the law was and could operate within it. He could then advise business leaders from a position of knowing the parameters of corporate conduct in the field of tort law.

7

Corporations

I think you had better take some legal advice.
—Crosby and Dibblee,
San Francisco Commission Merchants, July 3, 1857

Many California lawyers grew with their corporate clients to face the legal, financial, economic, and public relations problems of corporate development. California's rich and diverse economy produced a wide range of corporations working to develop the land, its mines, and its industrial vitality. Lawyers helped to form these corporations, to manage them, and to represent them in many forums. These roles in corporate life and law practice furthered the designs of entrepreneurs to release the productive energy of California's many resources.

Law firms that worked with corporate clients often expanded their scope of representation with corporate activities. Henry W. O'Melveny began working for Southern California electric power companies in 1891 and spent much of his professional life working for the utilities.[1] O'Melveny also represented Henry T. Oxnard's Chino Valley Beet Sugar Company, which led him into corporate restructuring, water litigation, labor law, antitrust law, and condemnation litigation.[2] His partner, Jackson A. Graves, founded the Oil Storage and Transportation Company, which led the firm into oil leases and the incorporation of oil companies.[3] James Norris Gillette's political and legal activities also led him into oil representation. Gillette was a Wisconsin lawyer who came to California in 1884 to establish a practice in Eureka. He turned from his practice to politics, winning election as city attorney in 1890, as a state senator in 1896, a U.S. Congressman in 1902 and 1904, and as state governor in 1906. Gillette returned to practice in San Francisco and the combination of practice and politics turned him to oil industry lobbying in the nation's capital from 1916 until 1920.[4] These examples were typical of lawyers who, through law practice or industrial relationships, grew close to their corporate clients.

More important to an understanding of lawyers and their corporate clients is knowing what attorneys did for corporations. An attorney's representation of a corporate client or employment as house counsel set out a relationship, but function portrays the lawyer's role in a clearer brush stroke. Sources for analysis are not comprehensive, with the exception of Henry W. O'Melveny's fifty-one-volume daily record of law practice and John D. Bicknell's nineteen-volume letter book. From these records some general roles emerge. The national experience was one of increasing involvement beyond representation in litigation. William Henry Moore of Chicago assisted the Diamond Match Company in increasing its capitalization in 1889.[5] Standard Oil's S.C.T. Dodd devised a new trust form of organization to enable the consolidation of the oil business' assets and management.[6] The legal arrangement permitted Standard Oil to become a fully integrated enterprise by the early 1890s. Lawyers created new business structures and developed new patterns of commerce.[7] The advice of counsel went far beyond litigation to the essence of business by the close of the century.

In California, a state with an agricultural base, extractive enterprises, and industrial ventures, lawyers faced a variety of problems born of the economy and the rapidity of growth following the advent of the railroad. The railroad made a dramatic impact on the last quarter century of California history, speeding the development of market-oriented agribusiness and enabling the expansion of industrialization.[8]

In the corporate world, lawyers performed many functions. Attorneys were creators of relationships, drafting corporate articles, contracts, and various other legal devices of business. They were facilitators of enterprise, buying and selling land as agents, negotiating contracts, and mediating differences of perspective.[9] Some lawyers, like Jackson A. Graves, were bankers' lawyers who became bankers. They smoothed the financial transactions that greased the wheels of industry. The law was in books but lawyers on the street put the dynamics of law into action.

An important benefit to clients was that lawyers were problem solvers. They sorted out the clutter of enterprise when needed. John D. Bicknell put it well in a letter to E. L. Mayberry of Hemet in 1896: "The affairs of the Bear Valley Company are in such an interminable complication and confusion that no attorney can safely undertake to advise without a thorough examination of the whole history of the transactions of this corporation." [10] Solving problems sometimes involved an attorney's immersion in the business of a corporation to bring business and legal sense to the client's transactions. When an attorney had an ongoing relationship with a company, knowledge of the business made providing legal and business advice easier.

Lawyers also sorted out understandings, intent, and meaning in transactions for corporations. Henry W. O'Melveny's journal entry for Saturday, February 4, 1899, recorded one such session among lawyers.

> Bicknell & Wood, Balch & Kerckhoff & I met at Bicknell's office. Wood had drafted sec. 12 again [contract of the San Gabriel Electric Co.]. Much discussion over what it meant. We all seemed agreed on what we were trying to say but Kerckhoff was afraid that its literal interpretation would not be what was intended. It was understood by all parties and it was our construction of the contract that we pay for our deficiency of the 35 months service. The difference between $35.00 per HP and the actual cost to them.
>
> Wood gave an example and it was satisfactory to Balch & Kerckhoff. I can not remember the example. [11]

The obligation of attorneys also was to decide upon the law's commands concerning corporate practice. An O'Melveny entry four years later was representative of this situation.

> Kerckhoff . . . show[ed] me Variel's proposed articles of incorporation. Novel scheme to avoid stockholders liability and right to vote.
>
> Went to Variel's office. He said it was merely an idea, not based on decisions or precedents or amendments.
>
> Trask and I were of the opinion, there was no doing what Variel proposed. Met Dolge this afternoon told him I thought plan illegal. [12]

The drafting of corporate instruments always had to be within the framework of the law and the facts. Both were the province of the lawyer, who
was, along with his entrepreneurial clients, limited by the rule of law.

Lawyers also advised their corporate clients on the developing law that
had an impact on the clients' interests. These law reviews were both to inform and to guide clients to policy positions. As shown already in tort law,
John D. Bicknell advised that certain safety devices be installed on railroad
turntables to prevent accidents and liability exposure for the company. He
also reviewed the license-tax cases for the Southern Pacific, noting, "There
is considerable doubt as to what the attitude of [the United States Supreme]
Court is upon the questions." [13] When the Interstate Commerce Commission filed restraint of trade charges against the Southern Pacific, Bicknell
was ready with legal analysis. [14] Frequent statutory changes that affected
common carriers required Bicknell to advise his client on a broad range of
issues. "I will call your attention," he wrote in 1894 to John M. Crawley,
assistant general freight and passenger agent of the Southern Pacific Company, "to certain sections of our Code which occasion so much uncertainty
at times as to the law governing the rights of the common carrier as between
the consignor and the consignee." [15] Despite the ambiguity, Bicknell advised
a corporate action most clearly in line with legislative direction. The rule of
law rather than corporate convenience and profit prevailed.

In other instances, case law directed business decisions. Bicknell, in re-
viewing the planned reorganization of the Rialto Irrigation District, called
"the plan . . . visionary and impracticable." The reason for his opinion was
a "recent decision of the Supreme Court of the United States" that "would
certainly render the bondholders less willing to enter into the proposed
plan of manipulating bonds." [16] The law had an impact that had to be judged
in its immediate business context, whereas corporate planning had to be
brought into accord with the rule of law.

Law and business sense would merge in advice to clients, as would be
expected. The firm of Graves, O'Melveny and Shankland of Los Angeles
gave such advice in 1890.

> As a matter of strict business, justified by the decisions on the subject—
> and also as a matter of policy, to prevent hardship to debtors, which
> you would not like to see occur, we would advise you in all cases when
> you take promissory notes, whether secured by mortgage or not, as

collateral security, to notify the makers of said notes in writing that you hold them as security, and that you look to them for payment. You will by such means put an end to all dealing between the maker and payee of such paper; or at least put the maker in such a position, that any dealing had by him with the original payee will be with full notice of your rights, and at his, the maker's risk and peril; and he cannot, if seeking clemency at your hands, say that he did not have knowledge of your rights.[17]

The law and bank practices came together to make advice simple and direct. Hence, legal advice to business clients often commingled law and business practice with the obvious goal of facilitating business transactions with the least liability exposure.

When the issue was before a court, lawyers were loath to advise action until the pending issue was given legal certainty. One of Bicknell's clients, the New Bear Valley Irrigation Company, was involved in a lawsuit and Bicknell advised maintaining the status quo. "As a rule of business," he wrote F. P. Morris of Redlands in 1896, "when I [do] not know what to do I generally find it safe to do nothing." When the court ruled, giving "an intimation . . . of the law," then they would "know better how to proceed."[18] Certainty in legal affairs allowed reasoned direction for business policies.

On other occasions, lawyers had to tell their clients that the law forebade a certain arrangement. Bicknell wrote to William Banning in 1896 that Banning's proposed contract for the construction of a wagon road from Avalon to Eagle Camp on Catalina Island would not evade the state mechanic's lien law and suggested an alternative transaction that would accomplish the same objective.[19] George H. Smith informed George Smith Patton in 1889 that a contract was binding and there was "no escape." The case law was clear.[20] Wilson Crittenden had to give Benjamin D. Wilson the bad news that he was liable for certain debts. Quick maneuvering of assets and of the law could not avoid the legal consequences of some prior structural transactions.[21]

Prudently structured corporate transactions avoided legal problems as well as business headaches. Here, lawyers explored alternative business plans within the framework of the law. Bicknell's advice to Henry E. Huntington regarding the San Gabriel Valley Rapid Transit Railway Company involved such planning. Huntington was to purchase the railroad but not the "old corporation" stock to avoid outstanding claims and problems. Bicknell also helped Huntington with property and eminent domain matters to facilitate the creation of a railroad.[22] Bicknell also structured corporate transactions and financing for the Los Angeles Consolidated Electric Railway Company. Bonds and stockholder liability were topics of concern and they required careful legal craftsmanship.[23]

Counsel also had to deal with issues of competition and corporate cooperation. When another railway company took advantage of a statutory opportunity to operate on Bicknell's client's tracks, Bicknell advised his client to "enter into negotiations . . . and make the arrangements amicable."[24] But clients did not always follow the considered advice of counsel. Rather, the Los Angeles Railway Company declared litigation war on the Los Angeles Traction Company despite advice and a precedent that disposed of all the defenses Bicknell could think of after research.[25] The decision to litigate rather than negotiate bothered Bicknell and he wrote to Henry C. Campbell, a San Francisco attorney, in 1885: "I find myself in the embarrassing position of a lawyer when his client urges aggressive measures, and his better judgment is that we will suffer defeat. . . . Under my view of the law governing this case and the business situation here . . . , I would not litigate."[26] Bicknell filed a law suit at his client's direction and concluded: "I might as well open the campaign and educate them up to an understanding that we had some interests in this city and some rights that they were bound to respect. We intend to force them to come to our terms or fight it out to a finish."[27] The lawyer's job was certain under the circumstances and litigation was a tool of business policy. Interestingly, the lawyer did not advise litigation because of the certainty of legal defeat, but saw that the suit could not encourage an environment that recognized the interests of the parties.

Lawsuits also came from other states to lawyers representing major corporations in California. Corporate creditors filed against the Pacific Railway Company in Chicago. Bicknell decided not to have the California defendant appear in Chicago, but rather to raise defenses in a California court when the creditors came to collect their judgments. He told Isaias Hellman in 1891, "[I] very much prefer to do our fighting upon our own 'dung hill' in the State of California."[28] However, Bicknell favored New Jersey incorporation statutes to California's because the "corporation has the power to issue three kinds of stock."[29] Federal law guided Bicknell's advice on freight rates and were his defense in Kentucky litigation.[30] As corporate practice grew, the California lawyer had to be proficient in federal statutes and regulations as well as state law.[31]

Because legal advice and business practice advice tended to merge as a lawyer grew closer to his corporate client, the distinctions were harder to make. In 1893, Bicknell ran into one such problem, regarding the removal of telegraph poles from land on which the Southern Pacific wanted to build a spur. An injunction had already been issued and it left Bicknell in a quandry that he resolved, with part, in a letter to W. G. Curtis.

> As a matter of law I cannot advise the removal of the telephone poles, as it would be a violation of the restarting order. In short, I cannot put myself in the position, as an attorney, advising a violation of the order of the Court, but would not feel much anxiety if some of our people had moved that pole four or five feet, being entirely ignorant of the order to the Court.
>
> Technically, we are now in contempt by taking out of the spurtrack.
>
> Technically we will be in contempt if we remove the telegraph pole.[32]

In other cases, even though business practice did not run afoul of law, Bicknell advised against them. In one instance, Bicknell advised that a freighting contract with Karl's Fruit Company was "not ... unlawful," but that the terms were "impracticable" from a business operations standpoint.[33] In practice, the latter type of case was more common than the situation involving ethical conflict. However, the subject matter of Bicknell's 1891–96 correspondence with the street railroads of Southern California and the Southern Pacific make clear that business practice and legal considerations were not always easily separated.[34]

John D. Bicknell's career moved from the debt collection–property law practice of the 1870s to the heady corporate practice of the 1890s because of his railroad clients. Instead of the periodic cases of debt or transactions taken one at a time, Bicknell grew close to the business policy interests of the corporate and railroad clients he represented. In the process he handled the usual troublesome cases that afflicted big and small clients alike. But corporate structure, finance, and operations also became a part of his practice. These aspects of practice at the juncture of rural California's urbanization and agricultural California's industrialization moved law practice to new and more diverse problems than simple legal advice and action.[35] An attorney's knowledge of the law and business practice had to merge so that he could provide the services his clients needed to succeed in the late-nineteenth-century environment.[36] The complexity of the body of law converged with the increasing intricacy of business arrangements in the last quarter of the century.[37] The business attorney had a counterpart practicing criminal law who also operated in the law's rapid movement from mother-lode justice to its formal complexity at the close of the century.

8

Practicing Criminal Law

---

*If we are to be governed by laws erected under
the Constitution, then let the action of those laws be general.
Let there not be statute law for one man and
lynch law for another. If we are to have anarchy and confusion prevail,
let the announcement be made, so that all may take warning.*
—Los Angeles Star, December 4, 1858

The history of criminal justice administration on the far western frontier has been a comingling of vigilante tales and episodic glimpses of the formal system. The two modes of criminal justice administration have numerous similarities, despite the fact that vigilante actions were outside the realm of the formal legal system. To see the law in action in California, we must explore the relationships of these two systems of frontier justice.

Vigilantism in America has received a great deal of attention, which has benefited recent historical analysis. The analysis of various vigilante movements has yielded useful typologies. Generally, vigilantism consisted "of acts or threats of coercion in violation of the formal boundaries of an established sociopolitical order which, however, [were] intended by the violators to defend that order from some form of subversion."[1] "Crime-control" vigilantism was "directed against people believed to be committing acts proscribed by the formal legal system. Such acts [harmed] private persons or property, but the perpetrators escape[d] justice due to governmental inefficiency, corruption, or leniency of the system of due process."[2] "Social-group control" vigilantism targets minority groups and has as its goal keeping those groups in their place.[3] "Regime-control" vigilantism has as it goal the alteration of the government to make the system more effective in guarding the majority's values.[4] For the purpose of analyzing the structural and procedural similarities of the frontier criminal justice system, crime-control vigilantism will be the primary focus of this chapter.

Pioneer vigilantes took the administration of justice into their own hands, primarily for the purpose of establishing order and stability in newly settled areas.[5] These pioneers closely held legal and cultural values regarding the sanctity of the person and of private property.[6] Vigilantism was a violent sanctification of the deeply cherished values of life and property.[7] On the far western frontier, vigilante movements were concerned mainly with the disorder in mining camps, cattle towns, and the open range.[8] San Francisco's vigilance committees of 1851 and 1856 confronted the social dislocation of a gold-rush instant city. Montana's Bannack and Virginia City movements of 1863–65 and Granville Stuart's crusade against cattle and horse thieves in 1884 proved to be the deadliest for enemy deviants. These were notable among the hundreds nationally.

To many in the legal profession, vigilante justice was supportive of the formal legal system. The nineteenth-century lawyer was a vigorous exponent of law and order and he supported the system's goals of crime repression, but he tolerated due process violations to increase the effectiveness of the vigilante system. At the same time, these supporters within the legal community worked to modify the formal system to provide what vigilante justice offered: simplicity, certainty, and severity of punishment.[9]

We must look at the relationship of these systems in behavioral terms. The vigilance committee characteristically organized itself under a constitution, articles, or declaration of purposes. Members signed the creation document, subscribing to its contents as if to a contract. The committee then went about its business of catching miscreants. Once apprehended, the criminally accused was afforded a trial by his peers with an appointed judge who presided over appointed counsel for both the accused and the people. The trial took place the day of arrest or very soon thereafter. Witnesses were sworn, testimony received, arguments made, and a verdict rendered. All the trappings of due process were had, and, as Richard Maxwell Brown has found, most of the guilty were executed.[10]

In the 1850s a transition from whipping and banishment, common in the gold fields, to hanging took place. California's gold-rush pioneers started to face enemy deviants by the summer of 1849. Local miners used the forms of criminal procedure, and if the accused was found guilty, the sentence of whipping, banishment, or hanging was carried out immediately. Many of the early mining districts were in remote areas, and even in the more settled areas jails were not common.[11] Whipping, banishment from the diggings, and death were practical punishments that were culturally acceptable.

Whipping was both punishment and persuasiveness in the hands of frontier justices in the California mother-lode country. Alcalde Stephen J. Field used the whip to recover some stolen property in 1850. After trial, Field ordered:

> [The defendant shall] be taken from this place [Marysville] to Johnson's ranch [the scene of the crime], and there receive on his bare back within twenty-four hours from this time fifty lashes well laid on; and within forty-eight hours from this time fifty additional lashes well laid on; and within three days from this time fifty additional lashes well laid on; and within four days from this date fifty additional lashes well laid on; and within five days from this date fifty additional lashes well laid on. But it is ordered that the four last punishments be remitted provided the said defendant make in the meantime restitution of the said gold dust bag and its contents. The Sheriff is ordered to execute this judgment.

The next day the punishment was levied and the defendant produced the bags and the gold dust contained therein, thus avoiding the remainder of the sentence.[12] Field's sentence was not one provided by statute, but one designed to give both punishment to the criminal and restitution to victims.

One "lynch trial," reported to have taken place in Nevada City in April 1851, had all the trappings of frontier due process. The butcher shop on Broad Street had been robbed of gold dust and three persons had been apprehended and incarcerated. A crowd, assembled to consider the consequences of using the mother-lode justice system, concluded that "to let them go to Marysville was to let them go unpunished," and formed a committee of safety, electing a president and sheriff. The committee sent the sheriff and a posse to the local jail and used "gentle force" to obtain the accused. Returning to the assembled committee, the prisoners were tried before an elected judge and jury of six. Counsel for both sides was selected and a collection taken up to pay one hundred dollars to each for legal services. Witnesses were sworn, testimony taken, and after two days of trial, a verdict of guilty rendered. The sentence was thirty-nine lashes. After sentence had been passed, one prisoner confessed and another made partial restitution. They both had their sentences reduced and all three of the convicted men were whipped by "Butcher Bill" and a teamster. One prisoner died as a result.[13] The process was very much like the formal law system, as were the results.

What lawyers did in the mother-lode country to defend the criminally accused varied little regardless of the forum. Lawyers of California's mining frontier were very much a part of the profession's eighteenth-century heritage. The eighteenth-century bar, as Robert Furgeson has so ably observed, was a "company of men of letters" schooled in general learning, not case law, statutes, and treatises.[14] In the generation of lawyers and judges from Hamilton to Webster, general learning and rhetorical ability rather than technical expertise, distinguished the lawyer from the other professions. On May 10, 1819, John Quincy Adams wrote in his diary that "to live without having a Cicero and a Tacitus at hand seems to me as if it was a privation of one of my limbs."[15] The rhetorical abilities of lawyers like Daniel Webster were legendary to the extent that they could overcome legal technicalities and send a man to the gallows. In 1830 Webster gave an eight-hour summation to a jury, describing a bloody crime in detail and reminding the jurors that "though he take the wings of the morning and fly to the utter most part of the seas, human murder to human vision will be known. A thousand eyes, a thousand ears are marking and listening, and [a] thousand of excited beings are watching his bloodstained step."[16] The jury, like Webster, saw those steps leading to hemp, despite substantial technical error by Webster. But in 1830 "moral justice was done."[17] The nineteenth-century attorney was a true gentleman of the bar, learned in letters and defending cultural ideals.[18] As we have seen with Charles E. DeLong, the mother-lode education of lawyers and their use of rhetoric and lengthy argument were very much a part of this heritage.[19]

The rhetoric at trial was more than just a cultural manifestation of the antebellum bar, it was the best form of advertisement for an attorney in a society where crowds gathered in the courthouse on the day of trial. California's criminal lawyers, Lawrence Friedman has written, were hunters and gatherers. They were men who wanted publicity and needed a courtroom or newspaper reputation. In the 1850s California lawyers distinguished themselves by bringing order to law and structure to the legal system in the frenzied instant cities and scrambling mining camps. In a period mostly remembered for vigilance committees, the bar worked to bring security to the streets and regularity to the criminal proceedings. The California bar, like the Dodge City bar analyzed by C. Robert Haywood, "kept as a clear goal the vision and reality of the justice system as a bulwark of fairness, order, and community conscience."[20] The story of William Higby in this chapter shows one such struggle amid the popular justice of the mother-lode country.

A final factor, that of a national crime rate in decline, also helps to form a context for this chapter. As Kermit Hall has so insightfully observed, "The criminal justice system probably became more effective, as professionalization took hold, and, at the same time, urbanization and industrialization imposed a social discipline that slowed the rate of crime."[21] As for California's crime rate, Lawrence Friedman and Robert Percival have demonstrated the same decline in Alameda County in the period 1870–1910.[22] What needs to be added to our understanding of this decline is the hard work of many lawyers like William Higby to bring the vision of justice into accord with the institutional justice system and the cultural setting for the struggle.

Culturally, the rule of law was very much a part of the ingrained social principles of California's pioneers.[23] Criminal law protected interests in property and reinforced American values having to do with private property.[24] This faith in the rule of law was tested in the gold fields and on the streets of San Francisco by a criminal element.[25] One response to crime was the formation of vigilante committees, the San Francisco committees of 1851 and 1856 being the most notable. The reason for vigilante action was the subject of Henry Haight's August 29, 1851 letter to Samuel Haight.

The insufficiency of the courts, the imperfections of the laws, and the corruption of public officers have heretofore rendered the punishment of crime very uncertain, sin frequent, and hence the organization of this committee to administer summary justice (so called after the code of Judge Lynch). It will dissolve soon probably as the worst criminals have been hung or imprisoned or have fled.[26]

The certainty of law enforcement and the stability of the community went hand in hand. Many other vigilance committees made their sporadic appearances but largely yielded to the criminal justice administration system by the Civil War.[27] Lawyers played a major role in moving that society from an informal to a formal criminal justice system.

The most obvious movement to a formal justice system was the establishment of institutions. Pursuant to California's 1849 constitution, the first legislature created a court system wherein the state supreme court did appellate work and nine district courts conducted mostly trial work.[28] Justice courts operated in townships handling petty crimes and misdemeanors.[29] District attorneys prosecuted criminals on a part-time basis and the local bar acted in defense, often by appointment, without compensation. But in criminal work, the notorious case was the thing. Patrick Reddy, for example, made a substantial reputation in Bodie and Bridgeport, never losing a case, before he moved on to San Francisco.[30] The courtroom enabled a formalized display of talent to a community of potential customers. In addition to having the opportunity to perform, lawyers were also participating in institution building in the social sense.

William Higby's experience in the mother-lode country was an example of this process. Higby was an attorney who became Calaveras County district attorney in 1853. By the time he left the position in 1859, he had earned the title "Bloody Bill" for his effectiveness as a prosecutor.[31] From 1869 to 1877 Higby went on to the state senate, to the House of Representatives, and to private practice in San Francisco. He also developed a substantial lumber business and a water company amid his public service enterprises.[32] But before we look at Higby's letters, we must see something of the times and places of popular justice.

The California that Higby observed in those heady days of fortunes found and lost had vigilantes, lynch mobs, and the formal criminal justice institutions concurrently struggling to give the society stability. One of the first examples of popular justice occurred in Placerville, then called Hangtown, in February 1849. A group of men seized a miscreant and held a trial with a judge, jury, and representatives. Oscar T. Shuck observed more than fifty years later that "the regard for law [was] illustrated in the adherence, imperfect and prejudiced though it was, to those forms and methods of procedure with which the citizens were already acquainted."[33] Hangtown's residents provided the due process with which they were familiar. Shuck also commented that the greatest "weakness of lynch law proceedings" was "the haste and lack of deliberation." However, in 1901, he thought that "the modern evil of procrastination in dealing with criminals" was equally shameful.[34] The "lynch mob," rightfully characterized, did not give the criminally accused any of the trappings of due process.[35] Other popular justice groups, like that in San Andreas, observed a much more formal procedure. Hours after Charley Woodruff shot the coat button off one Mr. Brown, Brown killed his assailant. The people took "the matter into their own hands" that fateful December day in 1851. The next day they chose a judge, jury, prosecutor, and defense representative. The jury heard both sides and delivered a verdict of not guilty of murder, whereupon they turned Brown over to the constable. Brown was brought before Justice Porter, who bound him over in the county jail to await the action of the next grand jury.[36]

A similar event occurred in the Monterey-Salinas area when ranch owners organized a company in 1850 to combat horse thieves that the military was unable to apprehend. The ranchers were successful in rounding up suspects and "immediately upon their arrival at Swan's ranch; a court was formed and a judge appointed." The leader of the gang confessed. Two other suspects were determined to be mere travelers and released. The company then took the rustlers to Monterey where they were tried, found guilty, sent to jail, and then escaped. The escape convinced the minority that they had been right when they had called for immediate execution after the trial at Swan's ranch.[37] The theme of lost opportunities to enforce the law would run through most of the popular justice movements of the century.

This theme coincided with the concern that punishment be swift and certain. In 1850, at Beal's Bar on the American River, the resident miners arrested a thief, conducted a trial "with great deliberation and order," and immediately administered thirty lashes and banishment.[38] In 1853 in Sacramento, Joseph Lamson reported that "a miserable fellow" had been found guilty of a "horrible crime, for which, however, no punishment had been prescribed by law, and he [was] discharged after legal examination." A mob seized the once-tried soul, constituted itself into a court, held a trial, found him guilty, and immediately had one hundred stripes laid on his back.[39] The Sacramento example, of course, demonstrated that popular justice went beyond statutory limits and punished crime by community definitions.

William Higby's first observations of popular justice came from San Francisco. In February 1851 Higby wrote to his father that lynching was "such

[a] speedy and dreadful punishment" that it should strike terror into evil minded men and put a check on crime."[40] But the rope did not crush the flagitious spirit of malefactors. In June, Higby wrote another letter. "The people have become dissatisfied with the public authorities of the city," he told his father, "because criminals are not brought to justice and punished as their deeds merit." That was not always true, however, as one burglar was caught red-handed at nine o'clock one evening. San Francisco's citizens whisked the villain before a judge and a jury that brought in a verdict at midnight. At two-thirty in the morning the defendant was executed by hanging, which was "a fearful retribution inflicted by an indignant and outraged people."[41] Some caught stealing were publicly whipped, whereas others were "threatened [with] a hempen cravat."[42] The work of San Francisco's vigilance committee had begun.

A month later Higby believed that vigilance was working. On the last day of July, he wrote his father that "more security is felt for life and property. Less crime is committed and the laws are more vigorously enforced." One reason for the calm was that many of the criminals were in jail. Another was the wisdom of the legislators in allowing the death penalty "in the discretion of the jury" for grand larceny. But vigilance committees continued "to find out and punish crime."[43]

In 1852 Higby was in the mother-lode country plying his trade. The events of the summer moved him to write his father. A Mexican who had murdered a Frenchmen had been brought to preliminary hearing, with Higby as prosecutor. But before the process of law could be completed the residents of Jackson broke into the jail and hung the accused. Higby "tried hard to pacify the people all through the examination and inspire respect for the authorities and allow the prisoner to have a trial by the legal tribunals." The crowd would not hear of it because they had "lost all confidence [in the legal system] and charge[d] the authorities with letting murderers escape."[44] This complaint of pervious jails and corruptible jailkeepers was a familiar one. It was the administration of the law, rather than law itself, that the Argonauts did not trust.

In another case, Higby was defending. One Jackson resident shot another for his use of abusive language. The vigilance committee took the shootist to trial. Higby argued that the defendant was entitled to counsel and the committee agreed. Higby defended and "the Committee concluded to let him go."[45] Fights and shootings over affronts, insults, challenges, and feuds were not uncommon in the 1850s.[46] The fact that a shooting occurred was not unusual either because the population was well armed. In 1850 Philip T. Southworth observed that "guns and pistols [were] manufactured cheeper [*sic*] at Liege, Belgium than any other place in the world," but he did not think California was a good market because "almost every person goes armed to the teeth."[47] What was important in the episode was that, despite the popular forum, the people afforded the criminally accused counsel. Further, counsel was able to persuade the vigilance committee of the innocence of the accused and they acted upon their belief to set the accused free. Again, armed and aroused citizen-vigilantes displayed an ingrained sense of due process.

Later in June, Higby reported continuing crime and the justice system in operation. With a degree of resignation, he observed that "crimes of some degree [were] an almost daily occurrence in this country." To Higby, it seemed "as though men tried to act as bad as they know how." But one Jackson jury returned a guilty verdict in one murder trial while another jury was undecided.[48] Despite the existence of the formal mechanisms of the criminal justice system, the Jackson vigilance committee also pursued culprits.[49] Higby's observation must be understood in this context of concurrent systems working to suppress deviants. The official system maintained the faith in law and the jury to do justice and the vigilance committee operated, with Higby participating, to retain some semblance of the rule of law.

Mexican bandits also gave the vigilantes someone to chase. In February 1853, Higby reported a gang "robbing and murdering for two or three weeks." One Mexican was apprehended and dispatched with hemp. Citizens in a posse had pursued the Mexican band to ground. With flourish, Higby wrote, "They have to be hunted like wild beasts that endanger the lives of men, and no mercy should be shown them."[50] Chinese miners captured another Mexican who had murdered one of their number. The Chinese brought the accused to Jackson to stand trial before "Judge Lynch."[51] Amid this brush-fire war against crime, Higby became county district attorney located in Mokelumne Hill, the home of a midsized vigilance committee that operated from 1852 until 1856.

Firmly settled in his new position, Higby set out to establish the legal system as the sole institution of criminal justice administration. Two weeks before Christmas in 1853, Higby reported to his father that the "people are becoming more civilized or stand in greater fear of the law, for crimes are not so frequent as they were, although 12 persons are now in jail."[52] Civilization, fear of the law, and a diminished crime rate were all related. Higby was the instrument of civilization and law to suppress those who would threaten community stability. The challenge often came from outside the community, as it had before. In August 1854 he reported "gangs of thieves and robbers . . . lurking about again." But, he wrote, "the people have no mercy for such. Law is too tardy in many instances, except Lynch Law, which is extremely unsafe and uncertain though courts are succeeding much better than once, in detecting and punishing crime."[53] The value of speedy justice was great and the regularly constituted authorities were best. Popular sentiment and institutional process seemed to be converging.

The success of this convergence was evident in a crisis situation. On August 20, 1854, Mokelumne Hill burned to the ground. Although "much property was stolen and some persons were detected [looting,] . . . they were attended to immediately by the authorities," Higby wrote with satisfaction, "and *no lynching was done* [Higby's italics]."[54] Despite a stable crime rate and continued "drinking and gambling" in Mokelumne Hill, Higby saw cause for some optimism, writing, "Those who commit crime are in a hurry to get out of this country. This is an indication that they fear prosecution."[55] The battle against the criminal element was constant, as was the struggle to gain the people's confidence in the institution of criminal justice.

That struggle received a setback in Jackson in 1854. The Jackson vigilance committee had taken a horse thief into custody and administered summary hempen justice. Higby was shocked. He went to Jackson and "talked plainly." The result was that "some of the most active [vigilantes] left suddenly." But this was clearly a defeat. Higby wrote: "I was possessed with mixed emotions to find such a total disregard of law, of right, of justice of humanity, of public decency and morality, in the village where I had resided so long and when too I had done so much to punish crime as was admitted generally."[56] The efforts to bring civilization with law had suffered. This meant that Higby had to redouble his efforts.

With the challenge before him, "Bloody Bill" attacked the problem. "Criminal offenses are attended to as soon as heard of," he wrote in January 1855. He did "not hesitate, day or night, week day or Sunday." He was "always ready to act" and left "no room for escape." Higby acted in this manner "so that the people [might] have confidence in the authorities and to avoid or keep down mob law or lynching." With some satisfaction, he declared, "Our county is as free from mob law as any other county in the state." But there was a menace from outside of town still within the official system. "One thing has encouraged lynching more of late," he lamented. "Our Governor has commuted the punishment of several under sentence of death to imprisonment. Much dissatisfaction has been caused by it."[57] The greater the challenge, the more forthright his efforts needed to be. In Jackson, Bill "obtained 13 convictions before magistrates [in March, which was] . . . far more than usual." The result was that the town was "usually quiet and peaceful."[58]

Higby's toil was bearing fruit. In May 1856 he had few criminal cases pending, which to him was "the best indication that crime is decreasing."[59] A year later the crime rate seemed stable but had not decreased.[60] The vigilance committees of Jackson and Mokelumne Hill had retired. The institutions of justice were fully operating and that degree of civilization that Higby glimpsed in the mother-lode country was there in no small part because of his efforts to give legitimacy to law and the institutions of criminal law.

Other members of the bar across the state carried on efforts to suppress criminals. John Hume reported a situation similar to Higby's in Placerville in 1852. "The constant excitement of life here is wearing and tiresome, and the country is full of crime and bloody tragedies," he lamented. In fact, "within the past week two men were hung for stealing by a mob at Coloma." But his resolve was not deterred. "Today I have obtained warrants for two men, on a charge of larceny, and when I close this letter shall go straight to a Justice office to prosecute them."[61] While Higby and Hume were prosecuting, other lawyers assumed the bench to try cases,[62] and others defended the criminally accused.

Charles E. DeLong contributed to the stability of Marysville in the 1850s in a variety of ways. He joined the local residents to "hunt robbers." In 1856 they "took two Indians for robbing Chinamen" and "brought them to Foster's Bar" for trial.[63] In addition to catching criminals, Delong also defended many of the criminally accused in the camps. On September 8 and 9, 1856, he defended Michael Purcell on a charge of assault and battery. The jury heard the case and balloted eleven for acquittal and one for guilty. The judge sent them back for further deliberations. When they emerged, they were unanimously in favor of conviction. DeLong observed that it was "a proof of what one obstinate man can do."[64] Other cases took on more significance.

3. Charles E. DeLong, veteran of gold-rush law practice.
From Men of the Pacific, *published in 1903 by the Pacific Art Co. of San Francisco.*
Courtesy of the California State Library.

One 1857 case gave DeLong a challenge and provided important insight into the legal process in the mother-lode country. In December a crowd brought to the courthouse Michael Lyons and Patrick Lynch, who had been accused of the murder of Nelson Johnson at Foster's Bar. The court appointed DeLong to defend. He agreed after Lyons promised to pay him twenty-five dollars. The case was called for a preliminary hearing and then adjourned until four o'clock the next day. DeLong's motion for separate trials was granted, which "presented the novel appearance of trying an accessory before the conviction of the principal." With little time to waste to prepare a defense, DeLong rode over to Foster's Bar to view the scene of the crime. There he examined Johnson's remains, which had been "cut up awfully." He galloped back to court and "made several desperate [*sic*] motions." The judge overruled all of his motions and "the whole thing looked mighty bad." Then he turned "to compromise" and "obtained the discharge of Lynch." The next day, DeLong had a plea-bargain agreement but "the Court refused to allow it" and the cases went to trial, DeLong observing that "all hope was gone." Despite this, he argued for "four hours and spoke until [he] tired out."[65] Lyons and Lynch lost, but the process of institutional procedure won. The crowd had brought the prisoners to the system, not to a popular tribunal. A judge had ruled on legal motions, decided to reject a bargain, and conducted a trial. DeLong had argued the cases as best he could as he had done on the civil side of the docket, with about as much preparation time. Justice was swift and rhetoric, within the institutional process, still the lawyer's tool of advocacy.[66]

The rough-and-tumble period of the gold rush passed and formal criminal justice institutions took the place of frontier practices. Lawyers took positions of district attorney, judge, and defense lawyer. The process became more formal, trials longer. John J. Carey, the district attorney of Sacramento County, lamented to John D. Goodwin of Quincey in 1884 about the problems of office. "You as an attorney can understand," he wrote, "our inability to controll [*sic*] our time, and that most of the time we ought to be in different places and attending to different matters at the same time yet being human we cannot do impossible things."[67] Trials lengthened. In 1885 Carey wrote that "I expect we could try the Burns case in 4 or 5 days. We have already been 9 days and the prosecution is not in yet. I will finish tomorrow." The reason for delay was "the XXamination of witnesses."[68] The system was maturing, but, as Robert H. Tillman has demonstrated for Sacramento County in 1853–1900, the formalized legal system did not change the conviction rate. The problems of transient witnesses and jurors of the gold rush era changed. In the 1850s instant trial and judgment short-circuited any witness problem or juror absence. In the period after the Civil War, Patrick Reddy's tactic of delay allowed witnesses to wander from the diggings before trial. As Tillman found in Sacramento County, the same kind of delay put a limitation upon obtaining convictions.[69] His observation in 1986 was similar to Oscar T. Shuck's in 1901 that the delay inherent in criminal proceedings was becoming an obvious problem.

The evidence used in this chapter to illustrate the nature of the criminal justice system has differed from that used in previous chapters. Rather than discussing the mechanics of the practice of criminal law, our historical observers have told us of the system they witnessed in action. Importantly, lawyers like Higby worked hard to give the institutions of the law legitimacy in the eyes of the people. He wanted the criminally accused to have due process in the courts rather than in popular tribunals. The gold-rush lawyers were like the Dodge City lawyers C. Robert Haywood has written into history.

> They kept as a clear goal the vision and reality of the justice system as a bulwark of fairness, order, and community conscience—a goal well within the grasp of the frontier settlement. Deviation was never uncontested, perfect alignment rarely achieved. But there was always within the court system, the most rational governmental structure in town, an ongoing testing of what pragmatically the community would tolerate.[70]

Our observer-participants in this ongoing struggle were living the role of the bar as civilizers and as institution builders.

Another issue emerges from both observations and actions regarding the death penalty, calling into question the underlying assumptions of Thomas L. Dumm and Louis P. Masur that coalitions of capitalists engineered the punishment into law.[71] Although the evidence in this chapter is limited, the observers as well as the participants in the gold rush agreed that the death penalty was appropriate even for crimes against property. Despite all of the nineteenth-century reforms before 1849, the cultural expectations of the participants in mother-lode justice were contrary to Eastern limitations on the death penalty. The death penalty for robbery, public executions, and the lash were very much a part of life in the 1850s. In fact, the California legislature made the penalty of death in robbery cases available to juries in 1851 and the California Supreme Court upheld this statute.[72] A cultural lag? Perhaps. Or a cultural value of protecting private property? Our observers did not say. They only acted upon their values. Their situation was different from the East of Dumm and Masur. We remember the words of "Bloody

Bill" Higby that they were dealing with wild animals that endangered the lives of men. In the mother-lode country or any frontier society, the participants were not under the control of a centralized government, but cultural norms were at work without a government-declared public policy. Perhaps the cultural norms they expressed in their actions were the cultural values they acted out on John Phillip Reid's overland trail.[73]

9

A Lawyer's Stock in Trade

*This country in the past has afforded more litigation
than its share. Whether it will keep in the same ratio I cannot tell you.
I can only state that there are more men here today
in the profession by long odds, than are necessary to do the work.*
—Jackson A. Graves to Charles M. Dodd, June 4, 1897

Legal services and how lawyers received compensation for their time evolved
with California's robust and dynamic economy. As the economy moved from
the gold rush to agribusiness and industrialization, lawyers changed from
individualized fees for service to cultivating regular clients who would become a source of monthly harvests. In the process of change, the concept of
what a lawyer did and how that service could be valued shifted slightly.

Daniel H. Calhoun described how eighteenth century lawyers on circuit
would carry a branding iron to collect their fees.[1] Fees paid in kind were not
unusual in California in the 1850s and early 1860s. Money was dear and
often unavailable. Gold coin arrived in Los Angeles by steamer from San
Francisco.[2] Montgomery Martin warned Benjamin D. Wilson in 1850 that
money was "very scarce" in San Francisco.[3] Thomas A. Hereford reported
that money was "as scarce as in any country in the world" in San Pedro in
1851.[4] As a result of the physical scarcity of money, barter became a part of
the transactional process. Adolph Eberhart of San Francisco proposed the

exchange of a wine press for wine in 1863.[5] Three years later Eberhart was exchanging wine for groceries.[6] In Los Angeles, a furniture dealer was settling a debt with lumber, not coin.[7] Matthew Keller's general store sold merchandise for money, labor, lumber, a bay horse, and chickens and eggs until the mid-1870s.[8] Another medium of exchange was, of course, gold dust. In fact, when Joseph Lancaster Brent, a pioneer Los Angeles attorney, negotiated a fee for the defense of an accused criminal suspect, he asked for "two ounces." Surprisingly for the 1850s, the defendant "drew out some coins from his pocket and gave me one ounce."[9] In the period of extensive land-title litigation, the money to pay legal fees was scarce and land plentiful. The branding iron was useful, but the quitclaim deed was needed more by California's frontier bar.

Californians were land rich in the 1850s and 1860s, which resulted in attorney fees being paid in this commodity. J. F. Dye of Antelope Rancho was one such client of Halleck, Peachy and Billings of San Francisco. Writing in October 1854, Dye found his land "covered with Squatters" and sought counsel to "attend to [his] claims." Dye saw "no way to get [his claim] through unless [he could] pay in land." Naturally, the fee in land or money should not be excessive.[10] Jose Antonio Castro signed a contract with the law firm of Hepburn and Dwinelle in 1862 agreeing to deed one half-league of Rancho Sanjo de Santa Rita to the firm in return for legal services to establish his title to the rancho.[11] Not surprisingly, lawyers accumulated a great deal of land in the antebellum period.[12]

At times, lawyers and their clients saw the value of counsel differently. A lawyer's time was his stock in trade. The profession generally viewed its time as the currency of the business. Clients sometimes thought the dollar value of that time to be less than their counsel's valuation. William Hickman of Mammoth City wrote to John D. Bicknell in Los Angeles in 1879 that he "was glad . . . to learn that [Bicknell was] kept busy for that means "*Cash*."[13] Time was money, but like many clients, Mrs. Helen Clark of Santa Ana believed there were limitations.

> There is a lawyer in Santa Ana. I went to him along with Mr. Peters and it took him 20, or 30 minutes and he charged $5.00. Can he oblige me to pay that much? I tell you that gave me the blues to think such a few minutes and make me pay five dollars when I did not know how to

get a dollar. I will try and get it just as soon as I can if money was not so hard to get I should not feel so but our crops are pretty much all dried up." [14]

Mrs. Clark knew that time was money, but thought ten dollars per hour for advice was unreasonable. Archibald A. Ritchie of San Francisco registered a similar complaint with Halleck, Peachy and Billings in 1853. "You charge me more than I think is right," he moaned. Further, he "did not expect to be hurried for the payment." [15] Clients were, like Ritchie, sometimes tardy in payment.

Some clients argued that fees should relate directly to results. Michael J. O'Connor, a client of John D. Bicknell, was one of the many land claimants under seige by squatters. In 1876, the squatters had dispossessed O'Connor's tenants and he wanted action. "Please take the most economical means of getting rid of the squatters," he wrote in September. "When they find you are in earnest about the business, I expect that very few will wait for the Sheriff to eject them." [16] Six months later, he was not as optimistic. "It is very unfortunate that those squatters interfere with the renting, but I hope you will soon get them in a position where they will not be able to prevent your getting rent for this year." [17] Bicknell went after the squatters with the strong arm of the law in ejectment suits, but the December rains also brought a loss in the trial court. O'Connor's concern turned to cynicism when it came to paying the legal fees. The day after Christmas, O'Connor wrote:

> You ask me to express myself freely on the matter of the charges etc. in your letter. It would not be candid in me to remain silent or to say that I am satisfied with your management of the suits. You made a mistake in your haste to commence those ejectment suits; to which you may remember I was very slow to consent. The result of that haste has been very disastrous, and is likely to cost me a larger sum before the ground you have lost can be recovered—assuming that it will be finally recovered. If you have not thought of this estimating the value of your services in these cases, I submit it for your consideration. [18]

For O'Connor, a lawyer's fee should reflect a downward adjustment if there were unfavorable results. Even if the results were favorable, some clients grumbled. Jackson A. Graves made the case to his client for a $30 fee for a

$536.00 debt collection made by another attorney, arguing, "he has earned every cent I have paid him, as all of this money came by the hardest of licks and only after constant and continued dunning."[19] Graves believed that time and effort justified the fee.

The nature of the services came into question when John D. Bicknell charged San Francisco attorney Charles H. Larrobee for his time. After receiving the bill, Larrobee fired off a stern letter.

I do feel a lettle sad that you should have charged me $10 for the 'unpleasant talk' with my clients, the Ballona men. But perhaps the service you rendered me is a proper subject of charge simply because it was unpleasant. It was not unpleasant talk—but on the contrary then very pleasant—which resulted in giving you $500 (coin) per year; nor was it unpleasant then of me to give you the business of E. O. Fargo & Co. which netted you some $750.00—a moiety of which I declined to receive from you as my share of the fee. But never mind. I have now spoke it out and shall feel better. I don't mind the money—but it was unexpected and hence the shock.[20]

The reciprocal business relationship, in Larrobee's mind, justified a favor rather than an invoice. James E. Wadham, a San Diego attorney, paid taxes for Bicknell on his properties there and wrote, "My charges for doing a friendly favor are naught." But he added, "Whenever you require assistance from this quarter, I claim it as a privilege to serve you."[21] Reciprocal business and favors had a close relationship at times.

A long-term business relationship with a client frequently resulted in negotiation on fees where a meeting of the minds had not occurred. Graves, O'Melveny and Shankland extended the hand of negotiation to C. A. Hooper in 1897. "In the ten years that this firm has been together," they wrote, "we have never had any trouble with any client on that score [the amount of fees]. And if any charge we ever make should seem to you unreasonable, we will only be too glad to have you say so." Then they assured Hooper, "[The] fees will be adjusted on a basis agreeable to you."[22] John D. Bicknell offered similar advice to Stephen White, a law partner and United States Senator, in 1889. "As Longstreet is still your partner," he wrote, "it may be well to tone down the fee somewhat as he seems to have some feeling in the matter."[23] Under some circumstances, the sensibilities of clients as well as the lawyer's concept of the value of time had to be considered. The problem was, as Bicknell mused to J. D. Pope, a Los Angeles attorney, "Our clients do not always estimate our services to be of as much value as we do ourselves."[24]

Lawyers involved in land-title litigation clearly saw the value of their services in terms of the value of the land. The Washington, D.C., firm of Stanford and King wrote to Bicknell in 1875 regarding their fee in the Bronson case before the U.S. Land Office commissioner. "We think we are entitled to at least $500," they asserted, "and if the land is very valuable, twice that sum would not be too much."[25] John B. Clark, Jr. also tied fees to land values. Writing to Bicknell, he noted that "the amount of compensation asked is not considered here [Washington, D.C.], in view of the value of the land involved, either exhorbitant or unreasonable." In fact, another law firm, Britton, Gray and Drummond, "would have charged not less than one-fourth the value of the land."[26] The value of land seemingly was equivalent to the client's ability to pay, although compromise and negotiation of fees was a normal part practicing.

Fees in certain types of litigation were fixed by the presiding judge, but this only constituted a ceiling. Jackson A. Graves told Isaias W. Hellman in 1893 that he had "a judgment of foreclosure against him for $30,000 in favor of Balfour, Guthrie & Co., in which a fee of $1500 for foreclosing the mortgage was allowed by one of the Superior [Court] Judges of San Bernardino County." Despite the court-approved fee, Graves wrote, "[I do not] propose to charge him the $1500, but at the same time expect to have a reasonable fee, which I propose to fix."[27] An 1874 statute had abolished attorney-fee agreements in mortgage instruments and contracts. All attorneys' fees were "fixed by the court."[28] Judges also fixed fees in probate proceedings. The fees for lawyers, executors, and others normally were paid out when the estate was distributed. As Graves, O'Melveny and Shankland told the Michigan Trust Company in 1896, "the custom in this country is to have attorney's fees charged up when the estate is ready for distribution."[29] When that day came, lawyers had cash to move, as did John D. Bicknell when he bought part of the Titus Ranch in 1894.[30] Albert M. Johnson, however, could not wait. In 1893 he wrote to L. T. Hatfield, the attorney-executor on an estate.

> The prevailing stringency in the money market has materially affected this office during the current month, and as there will be something of a fee coming to me in this estate for services rendered on behalf of

the residuary legatees, which fee will be fixed in due season by the court, I take the liberty of requesting an advance from the executor of $300.00 [31]

The "money market" was, of course, the economic depression, which had hit the recently established practitioners hardest.

Many lawyers structured fees for collecting debts in both good times and bad on a retainer plus percentage, or solely on a percentage of the recovery. John D. Bicknell firmly set forth the former arrangement to M. S. Champlin of Chicago in 1889: "I . . . decline to take any case where the fee is entirely contingent. I have sometimes taken cases upon a small fee in cash and a portion of the fee contingent but decline to take any case where the entire fee depends upon the success of the litigation. There may be attorneys here who will accept your proposition." [32] S. W. Geis, a Merced attorney, gave Ebin Orvis Darling a similar proposition in 1883. Geis "would be willing to take a retainer of $50 and a contingent of 1/3 recovered beside, but would not be willing to take the case otherwise." [33] The retainer at least guaranteed something in return for the time spent.

The contingency fee in the debt collection business was the norm. Time was worth a percentage of the recovery and the times as well as the likelihood of recovery dictated the percentage. In the turbulent times of the antebellum period, creditors frequently left the amount of fees completely to the discretion of the attorney." [34] Other creditors allowed a specific percentage. W. Hoffman of Fort Jones offered P. O. Hundley "one half for collection" in 1862. [35] George W. Gere, a Champaign, Illinois attorney, found Charles Fernald's name in *Hubbell's Legal Dictionary* and offered him "25% for collecting these notes." [36] Daniel E. Waldron, a San Francisco attorney, told John D. Bicknell in 1875 that he was confined to "10 prct in cases of collection." [37] Several of his regular clients, the Haas Brothers, only allowed five per cent on collections. The Haas Brothers "are the closest figures I have yet met in my practice," he groaned, "they seem to think that as there is so small a margin of profit in their business that lawyers' charges to them should be very light." [38] E. O. Fargo, a San Francisco liquor jobber, simply allowed Bicknell to deduct his fee from any collection. The fee was within his discretion. [39] In 1881 the "law and collection department" of John B. Ellison and Son offered graduated percentage rates: 10 percent for claims under one hundred dollars, 5 percent on claims between one hundred dollars and five hundred dollars, and 2 1/2 percent on claims over five hundred dollars.[40] By the 1880s, specialization in debt collections as well as volume business allowed more standardized fees.

When attorneys acted for clients as land agents, the percentage fee was not unusual. In 1875 John D. Bicknell received a 2 1/2 percent "commission" on large land sales.[41] On small transactions the fee was as high as 18 percent.[42] Bicknell's regular clients paid him fifty dollars per month for superintending land sales, mortgage and rent collections, and the like.[43] In 1887, Thomas H. O'Connor, a New York investor in California lands, made Bicknell an alternative offer.

> We would expect to pay you a commission on the sale of (5) percent, the same as we do now on the smaller sales. In return we would expect you to make all collections of interest and notes without further charge to us and that the present charge of legal fees of Fifty Dollars per month should cease. Then in case foreclosure proceedings should have to be taken, we would expect to pay you your regular fees in all such cases.[44]

These types of fee structures were common and related to the marketing of land as well as the legal services associated with maintaining the investor's interests in receipts.

Where money did not change hands in a settlement or in the execution of a judgment, lawyers often charged clients a flat fee for services rendered. Los Angeles land-title opinions garnered $300 to $600 each in the 1850s.[45] Prolonged title litigation involving the dispossession of swarms of squatters could go as high as $10,000 by 1892.[46] Appearances in court in 1851 could be billed at $25 to $500, depending upon the nature of the action.[47] Trial court appearances billed at $100 to $200 per case were common in the nineteenth century.[48] Going to the California Supreme Court could draw $250 to $1,000 per case.[49] Attending to a mortgage bond was worth $200 in 1889;[50] however, recording documents and other clerical tasks were billed at $1 to $10 per transaction.[51] The hierarchy of service fees placed litigation skills at the top until the 1890s when advice and litigation avoidance became highly valued by clients.

The clients that looked for regular advice and services were corporations and land companies. These clients also preferred to pay monthly salaries for most services and fees for extraordinary legal problem solving. General William S. Rosecrans paid John D. Bicknell fifty dollars per month for "all legal and supervisory services necessary to care for the business [a land company] and . . . to . . . pay [for] extraordinary and unforeseen circimstances bring[ing] on more onerous duties."[52] Bicknell also was on salary with the Southern Pacific Company with a provision for fees in certain litigation.[53] Jackson A. Graves had a similar fee structure: "The legal business of the West Los Angeles Water Co. for, outside of its heavy litigation with regard to water rights, we beg to state that we will attend to all your small matters, counseling, advising, drawing documents, etc. for $50.00 a month, the same sum we are charging the San Pedro Lumber Co. and several other corporations here."[54] For the bar of the 1890s the advantages of such agreements were obvious. John D. Bicknell explained it to Thomas B. Owen of Seattle in 1892. "The main part of my work," he wrote, "is in connection with corporations that pay me regular salaries instead of fees." The benefits were manifest; by having a salary, an attorney could avoid "the work and friction of a general practice."[55] A salary provided cash flow and eliminated the hassles of collecting.

Lawyers rendered services and billed them out, but on more than one occasion fees went uncollected. McGay, Holladay and Saunders of San Francisco had 25 percent of their billings for 1851 uncollected.[56] Jose Carillo of Santa Barbara received a bill for one thousand dollars from Halleck, Peachy and Billings of San Francisco for representing him before the Land Commission. On September 27, 1853, he wrote: "I regret that this is not in my power, *today*, to comply with your wishes, but rest assured that no efforts will be lacking on my part to remit to you by the next steamer. A resort to legal measures, as you hinted at in your letter, will be unnecessary."[57] October brought another letter to the law firm, this time from F. G. Blume of Bodega.

> I am very sorry that I have not been able to pay you for your services for the confirmation of my title by the U. S. Commissioners.
>
> Nearly all the land has been taken up by Squatters, who are willing to purchase the land, but refuse to do so, until the time for appeal has expired, and the title to be declared valid, and the lines run out.[58]

Charles Huse of Santa Barbara had a fee of eight hundred dollars due him from Francisco Caballeri, who did not have the cash, but who assigned a judgment to Huse in lieu of coin in 1855.[59] J. R. Scott of Los Angeles sued Jose Sepulveda to get his fee in 1856 and settled for one-half the billed amount.[60] In 1874 one of John D. Bicknell's clients, Cyrus Bellah of Pleasant Valley, wrote regarding fees for representation before the U.S. Land Commission. "I wold have sent more but did not hapen to hav eney more."[61] Other clients did not write, so Bicknell did. Regarding a $1250 fee for a trial and appeal which was unpaid, he wrote a sharp letter to H. L. Armstrong, the president of the Old Settlement Water Company. "We insist that this matter should now be adjusted. We see no good reason for any further delay. We, therefore, by this letter seek to demand of you a settlement of our fees for the services rendered."[62] Promises and excuses were not cash, as Bicknell, who depended more on salary than fees, knew.

Sometimes the nature of the case gave attorneys a dim view of recovering much. Bicknell wrote to R. B. Canfield of Santa Barbara in 1890 about one such case. "While the whole matter is not a character that is very inviting to an attorney who loves to get fees, yet as we are to some extent I suppose it is out of duty to either throw the matter up or to assert the legal rights of the Howards as against Mesick."[63] Jackson A. Graves thought a similar case to be minimally rewarding when he wrote to Curtis, Oster and Curtis of San Bernardino in 1893. "We think the only chance of any of us ever getting a fee out of it (Hanley v. Osborne) is to bet a settlement, as Haley, I am afraid, is almost as bad off financially as Osborne."[64] Some cases and clients simply did not have much potential for fees.

Attorneys also took on cases without compensation, particularly for those in need. Jackson A. Graves wrote to Dr. Rebecca Lee Dorsey in 1897 about one such case.

> Your bill for $150.00, which was forwarded to the relatives of Tilda Swanson of Denver, was returned to me. Herewith find proof of claim for $75.00. I wish you would cut your bill to that amount. I know it is not adequate compensation, but there is but little in this estate, and the girl has a poor old mother in Sweden whom she was supporting, and I would like to see as much of the money she has left go back to her as possible. This is one of the cases where you can afford to be magnanimous, and I will try and see that it is made up to you in some other way. I am attending to the legal business of the estate without charge.[65]

Because of the unfortunate circumstances of the client, the lawyer's time was contributed.[66]

The range of fees for California's nineteenth-century bar was great. Litigation skill was of a high value until the corporate needs of the 1890s increased the value of advice and litigation avoidance. The lawyer in general practice depended upon the fee system throughout the period. Counsel who had salary arrangements with corporations had the certainty of cash flow in their practice. The Southern Pacific Railroad started this practice, with its movement into all areas of land acquisition, torts practice, and corporate affairs, as we have seen in previous chapters. The railroad also created a law department with lawyers on staff drawing a salary. With Creed Haymond as general counsel, the law department provided continuing transaction-processing as well as litigation support for the corporation. Further, by having salaried attorneys within the corporation, the railroad started a cost-containment program to rationalize the legal costs of doing business. As the century closed, the elements of the modern fee structures were emerging. Salaried professionals on corporate staffs and litigation specialists collecting contingency fees operated together by the turn of the century.

10

The Public Image

*The rock that the legal profession is in most danger of
coming to wreck on is that of excessive charges. There is a continuing
low growling in the community on this subject.*
Santa Barbara Daily Press, June 6, 1882

The underside of the bar's history was its public image, not always a flatter-
ing one, but one that lawyers worked to overcome with civic activity and
usually tasteful advertising. The public attitude toward the bar in its negative
aspects was of colonial origins, but the democratization of the bar in the age
of Jackson gave rise to criticisms of poor professional preparation at the
same time that it became dramatically easier to gain access to the bar. Economic downturns in the business cycle gave lawyers "clean-up work" in
collections, forclosures, bankruptcies, and corporate reorganizations. Personal economic tragedy and global economic dislocation required whipping
boys. Although the public found the banks, the railroads, and the corporations at fault, lawyers also were convenient targets of reproach.[1] California
had its share of economic adventures, making its bar equally blameworthy
and giving rise to popular demands for relief and barbs.

Hinton Helper's *Dreadful California*, published in 1855, mirrored negative
national attitudes, but also described the plight of attorneys in hard times.
Successful attorneys, "disciples of Blackstone, Coke and Story," fed off the

"unsettled state of public affairs." Those who were most successful molded business "almost exclusively to their own interest, and everybody [knew] it would be a very unlawful thing in a lawyer to neglect himself." Yet those same "unsettled times" drove other lawyers "to the necessity of engaging in the most menial and humiliating employments." Some, "to save themselves from the severe pangs of actual want, [were] compelled to fish around the wharves for crabs."[2] Despite Helper's negative implications, he did establish the dichotomous nature of the pioneer bar.

Criticisms of professional preparation were a two-edged sword in the hands of journalists. Judge Jeremiah Burckhalter completed his first term on the Mariposa County Court of Sessions in 1862. Some in the community questioned his ability because he was "not . . . a lawyer by profession." The *Mariposa Gazette* replied to the critics that he "worked well."[3] The *Contra Costa County Gazette*, on the other hand, poked fun at professional standards in 1865. "A young candidate for the legal profession was asked [at his bar examination] what he should do when first employed to bring an action," the paper reported. "Ask him for ten dollars on account," was the prompt reply. The young man was admitted to practice.[4] Thirty years later the paper ran a telling one-liner: "There is an old legal maxim which holds that "ignorance of the law excuses no one (except lawyers and judges)."[5] At the turn of the century, even sympathetic authors chronicled the rough-hewn learning of early lawyers and judges. M. M. Estee wrote in 1901 that Judge Charles N. Creaner, the district judge of El Dorado, Amador, Calaveras, Tuolumne, and San Joaquin counties, "was not educated for the law; he was an old army officer. He rarely gave reasons for his decisions; he just decided cases, and almost always decided them right."[6] Despite his educational handicap, Creaner learned on the job, reading Blackstone when time permitted. Frederick P. Tracy, San Francisco's city attorney from 1857–59, was a forty-niner but "was not trained for the bar, and his legal education was defective." The criticism of professional preparation was focused on the antebellum bar in particular, but despite the increased educational attainment of lawyers by the turn of the century, the press still spilled negative ink.

An alternative strain heard from clients went to professional performance issues. Albert Dibblee, a San Francisco commission merchant, wrote to his brother Thomas in 1879 to help him through the litigation hoops.

I think you will find Pringle a rather weak man in court. He is nervous & fidgetty in trying a case. . . . In talking with W. Barber be sure you bring out your points clearly & see that he comprehends the exact point. He is not chain lightning, like Hall McAllister, to seize a point fully before you have half stated it. I have been vexed and annoyed at finding him slow to take in the essential point in some cases where I have obtained his opinion in other matters. But he is a good, sound, safe lawyer & is regarded as strong in law.

Another client complaint zeroed in on personal attention to the client's case. As Elwood Cooper explained to Albert Dibblee in 1880, personal attention from the attorney was more valuable than the attorney's good reputation.

Our lawsuit has been going on pretty much all week, Judge Spencer presiding. I believe the Attorneys have settled their pleadings and the judge will return to San Jose. The court will terminate the cause there, probably 60 days hence. We have the matter in such shape as we wanted it. Highton deserted us but sent P. Galpin. The latter has given the subject more attention than all the other Lawyers. He did nobly. Fernald has improved wonderfully and is twice the man he was before this suit commenced. I would rather employ Galpin today in a case than either Wilson, McAllister or Highton. They have so much to do that they are practically worthless.[7]

To clients, the personal attention to litigation was key. Hall McAllister was California's most gifted trial lawyer, but when he was so burdened with clients, even he could not give an individual client complete and undivided attention. This, however, did not temper the criticism. Even though the press and authors like Estee did see that law and common sense were related, they frequently lauded the latter.

That relationship of law and common sense was explicit in a *Contra Costa County Gazette* story in 1865. The paper reported that Judge Regan of Buffalo had been criticized for one of his rulings. The judge replied: "I have no law for it. I give it as the opinion of the court, based upon common sense. I am no lawyer. I never read a law book in my life, and I never will, for the reason I see so many d——d fools who have read the law that I dare not venture the experiment." The *Gazette* then ran this one-liner: "It is a fact that among the statutes of Georgia there is a law which fixes a tax of ten dollars a year on all jackasses, doctors, and lawyers."[8] The "judge" in this case, like others lauded in the press, was a justice of the peace, a local citizen schooled in survival. Law was in books and wisdom somehow emerged from the soil. Such Jacksonian anti-intellectualism dogged the bar of many counties in the early years.

A second strain of criticism was the costs of legal assistance. In the popular mind, costs were legal fees, but court costs were also a part of legal expenses. The *Los Angeles Star* poked fun at the profession in an 1852 story entitled "Humerous Story About a Lawyer Taking Silver from Client." The paper asserted that Sergeant Davy, the lawyer, "was once accused of having disgraced the bar by taking silver from a client." Davy responded to the charge, the *Star* reported, by saying, "I took silver because I could not get gold, but I took every farthing the poor fellow had in the world, and I hope you don't call that disgracing the profession."[9] This theme of money-grubbing behavior became one of the most popular.

Another theme, the costs of litigation, received some journalistic play. The *Contra Costa County Gazette* sounded this note in an 1861 story entitled the "Cost of Law." The *Gazette* told of a "suit ... recently decided in Nevada County, which was orginally commenced before a Justice of the Peace for two hundred dollars." The problem was that the suit had been "in the hands of courts and lawyers for a long time." The result was that, when decided, "the judgment amounted to about eight hundred dollars, exclusive of lawyers' fees and other outside expenses."[10] The popular impression was that litigation expanded the real costs of justice. The *Gazette* ran a story four years later about a New York will involving five hundred thousand dollars, observing that "the lawyers will get the lions share." In the opinion of some, the costs of justice should not include a lawyer's time. However, as we have seen in debt cases, clients often wanted their lawyers to wage holy war in pursuit of their due. Clients like Thomas B. Dibblee took litigation personally and wanted victory at all costs. In 1866, Dibblee wrote from Santa Barbara to his brother:

> Since he has chosen to disregard the letter which I wrote to him before he commenced proceedings, proposing an interview with the desire of an amicable arrangement, and has preferred a law suit, I think we may with good heart give him plenty of it. He has the name of being very litigious and is much disliked, and feared—and by his getting thor-

oughly beat in a law suit, it will give him a good lesson, and great satisfaction to us and many people. . . . I never want a fight, but if we have
to go into it, in God's name let us have a good fight anyhow. I would
not care if it cost more than the Ranch is worth. He has got the better
of many persons here, and it will please them, and please me to let him
see that he has got somebody new to fight who will not back down.[11]

Although legal fees and court costs might take their toll on a client's pocket-
book, it was sometimes with the client's enthusiastic consent.

The press generally gave lawyers' fees negative ink. The *Mariposa Free
Press* reported an 1863 incident where an attorney charged five dollars "for
waking up in the night and thinking of your business."[12] The *Contra Costa
County Gazette* told a similar tale in 1870.

A well known young lawyer obtained a divorce for a pretty and wealthy
client. He sent in a bill for $1,000. The next day the lady called on him,
and inquired if he was in earnest in proposing to her. "Propose to you,
Madam! I didn't propose to you," replied the astonished attorney.
"Well, you asked for my fortune, and I thought you would have the
grace to take me with it," was the calm reply. The lawyer wilted.[13]

In the journalist's view, fees also could corrupt. The *Placer County Republican* saw such an instance on more than one occasion. In the 1891 grand
jury inquest into the death of Ah Loy, the *Republican* questioned the motives
of the defense attorneys. "Nobody doubts that except the lawyers hired to
make it appear that Ah Loy stabbed himself in the stomach, and their doubts
are presumably purely professional as such as find hospitable lodgement in
the attny mind when accompanied by a sufficient fee for the attorney's
pocket."[14] Even more caustic was an 1885 story lifted from the *Arkansas
Travelor* by the *Republican* about a lawyer-client conversation.

Lawyer: Well sir, what can I do for you?
Client: I want to sue General Bogleton.
Lawyer: For how much?
Client: Well, say about two thousand dollars.
Lawyer: That's pretty good. State your case.
Client: I haven't got any case, particularly. He's got lots of money and
I haven't. Thought I'd better go to law about it.

Lawyer: How's your proof?

Client: First rate.

Lawyer: All right. We'll show the General what it is to beat a poor man out of his hard earnings.

Client: Don't know the General, do you?

Lawyer: No.

Client: Well, I'm the man, and the truth is, I owe Tom Kaine two thousand dollars and don't want to pay him, and he has sued me.

Lawyer: Well, by George, sir, we'll show the impudent fellow what it is to be presumptuous.[15]

The message was clearly negative: lawyers were not trustworthy. But such was not always the story.

Six weeks earlier, the *Republican* had run a story with exactly the opposite slant. Entitled "Lawyers, Origin of the Popular Prejudice Against a Useful Profession," the article found that public bias was based on the failure of only a few lawyers to uphold their moral obligations in the bar and community. The article attacked as false the literary misrepresentations about lawyers and concluded on a positive note. "The current literature of the day shows how prevalent is the desire to scoff at the lawyer; but when it becomes necessary or convenient, this indifference is replaced by an implicit trust and a slavish dependence."[16] With the exception of articles such as this one, the journalistic messages were generally negative and directed at individual attorneys as well as the legal system.

Clients and journalists were vocal about the legal system as an institution of California society. Again, the distrust of the system was of earlier origins and part of a Jacksonian and later a Populist critique of institutional arrangements.[17] The *Alta California* ran an editorial in 1852 that criticized bench and bar for being "smitten with . . . the desire to be profound . . . [rather than seeing] a question in plain sensible light."[18] This was the common sense, plain folk argument so popularly cast against the bar. The *Contra Costa County Gazette's* 1860 column entitled "Keep out of Law" was the other extreme, an antiestablishment critique.

Law is like a pocket with a hole in it and those who risk their money therein are very apt to lose it. Law is like a lancet, dangerous in the hands of the ignorant, doubtful in the hands of the adept. Law is like a box trap, easier to get into than out of. Law is like a sieve; you may see through it, but you will be considerably reduced before you can get throught it.

The law was not hopeless, but it was not instrumental in this view. The *Gazette* ran stories holding the legal system up to public ridicule throughout the period. Clients, on the other hand, often acknowledged the necessity of lawsuits under some circumstances. In 1888 Albert Dibblee, a San Francisco commission merchant, explained to Edward Greene of New York, "We always deprecate litigation unless necessary" and in this instance he agreed with William duPont, a party to the transaction in litigation, that settlement was wise. Dibblee also wrote to Charles Fernald, a Santa Barbara attorney, "For myself, although it has been my fortune to be a party to rather numerous law suits, I have never had any such differences with counsel."[19] To Dibblee, who was also the president of the Atlantic Dynamite Company and a real estate investor, litigation was part of doing business. Understanding the civil litigation system from the inside gave a far clearer perspective than the carping view from afar.

The journalistic pen slashed away at lawyers and judges with regularity. The *Gazette* attacked lawyers' courtroom habits in the 1870s.[20] In 1880 the paper noted judges cheating at cards, squabbling over judicial power, slinging political mud, needlessly delaying justice, and benefiting land-grabbers.[21] An 1885 article entitled "Lawyers' Morals" stridently blasted lawyers who defended robber barons.[22] Five years later the editors ran a caustic portrait lifted from the *New York Weekly*:

> Lawyer—who discovered America?
>
> Witness—Some say Christopher Columbus, and some say the old Norsemen.
>
> Lawyer—When the deceased was murdered, on the night of February 1, at the corner of A and Fourth streets, were you anywhere in the neighborhood?
>
> Witness (who was near by, saw the blows struck, knows who committed the crime, and is anxious that the prisoner should be brought to justice)—On that night I was standing . . .
>
> Opposing Counsel—I object y'r Honor. The question as to whether the witness was standing or sitting is irrelevant.

Judge—That part of the testimony is ruled out.

Witness—On that night I was at the corner of . . .

Opposing Counsel—I object. The words 'at the corner' are too indefinite. If the witness were trying to tell the truth he would be more explicit.

Judge—The witness need not answer the question in that way.

Lawyer—(to witness) How is the weather outside.

Witness—It is raining.

Lawyer—How is the presence of large bowlders in open fields on clay or sandy soil explained?

Witness—By the ice drift theory.

Lawyer—On the night the deceased was murdered, did you hear any disturbance?

Opposing Counsel—I object.

Lawyer—Did you see any thing which would lead any one to assume that a crime . . .

Opposing Counsel—I object.

The Court—Objections sustained. Those are leading questions.

Lawyer—Where did you get that hat?

Witness—At Sharp, Bargain & Co's.

Lawyer—Were you near the scene of the murder when it was committed?

Witness—I was.

Opposing Counsel—I move the testimony of this witness be stricken out. . . .

And so on for ten days. Verdict, Not Guilty.[23]

The *Gazette* kept the defects of the legal system in the public arena and, to a degree, represented to the public the image of legal uncertainty and technicalities thwarting justice.

Others saw the process of law costing them more than the results were worth. As we have seen in our discussion of legal fees, some clients and their lawyers did not agree upon the value of counsel or representation. Others, like G. L. Russell of Santa Ana, saw the process of law as the problem. In 1873 he wrote to John D. Bicknell, presenting the problems of his water company.

We have the right of way guaranteed by nearly all the parties on the line of our now proposed line. Our main opposition will come from Chapman & Glassell, they have said to us that they would law us to the last inch, in fact we expect no other opposition only in crossing his lands.

We wish to pursue a different course this time. Our idea is this (time) to go before the district court & ask the court to grant us the right of way by condemning the lands to the use of the ditch and paying the damage if any something similar to obtaining a right of way for a road.

Now we have had so much law and been so badly imposed upon that most of our members are shakey about trusting any lawyers.[24]

Russell's attitude and the *Gazette*'s 1860 story were not far apart, yet both recognized that law was a necessary, if at times difficult, part of social and economic transactions. Despite such a recognition, lawyers still faced an undercurrent of attitudes that were adverse to their interests and that had to be overcome. One of the ways that the bar overcame such attitudes was through civic activity.

California lawyers were joiners in the nineteenth century. They joined social clubs, fraternal organizations, civic groups, religious bodies, and charitable drives. Not only did they join, but they also led local efforts. One of the early types of groups to which lawyers gravitated was the library committees of their communities. A key interest of these committees soon became the purchase of a community law library. Daniel Cleveland was an active and founding member of the San Diego Library Association in the 1870s.[25] Samuel Denson was a superior court judge, director of the Sacramento Free Library Association, and director of the People's Savings Bank in 1879.[26] However, in the small towns of frontier California, it was difficult to stimulate interest in the creation of a library. Charles Enoch Huse complained in 1857 that "there was little need for the application of legal principles of this sort [commercial business] in this town." But he regretted that he did "not have [such] questions . . ." to stimulate his intellectual curiosity. Huse believed Santa Barbara did not have the community interest sufficient to stimulate interest in learning, but by 1869 he would join with others to form a stock company to found the College of Santa Barbara.[27] Whereas this kind of joining was typical for lawyers in nineteenth-century California, some members of the bar penetrated civic organizations. Los Angeles attorneys William Henry O'Melveny and George Smith Patton were members of the Hispanic Society of California. With Reginaldo F. del Valle they helped to found the Southwest Society in 1915, which became the Southwest Museum, with Hector Alliot as curator.[28] The social penetration of lawyers into Hispanic civic organizations was not particularly unusual because of the proclivity of the Hispanic community to welcome the participation of Anglos.[29] However, the membership per se demonstrated the diversity of social penetration of the period. This participation in community affairs was both civic-minded and good advertising, but in most instances it contributed to the civic and cultural advancement of the communities.

The first lawyers in a community frequently were the first organizers of social, fraternal, or civic organizations. The first lawyers of Los Angeles, J. Lancaster Brent and Lewis Granger were school commissioners in 1853. E.S.C. Kewen was superintendent of Los Angeles schools in 1858. Jonathan R. Scott's partner, Ezra Drown, organized the first Los Angeles lodge of Odd Fellows.[30] Leland Stanford, an attorney admitted in New York and Wisconsin, helped found the Sacramento Library Association and was elected to its first board of trustees.[31] Joseph Webb Winans, a prominent Sacramento attorney, won election to the presidency of the library association in 1858. He practiced with John G. Hyer in Sacramento until 1862, when he moved to San Francisco and founded the firm of Winans, Belknap and Godoy. Winans also served as president of the Society of California Pioneers (1864), president of the San Francisco Board of Education (1865–70), treasurer of the San Francisco Law Library, and president of the Society for the Prevention of Cruelty to Animals.[32] The activities of some attorneys in the service of the community interest were phenomenal.

The rural bar was equally involved in the social, civic, and cultural life of the community. William Branson Lardner seemingly was omnipresent in Auburn's community activities. Lardner was from Iowa and a college graduate with a law degree. In 1877 he came to Auburn, opened a practice, and settled down.[33] Lardner was an officer in the Auburn Lodge of Red Men and of the Auburn Opera House and Pavillion Association.[34] He continued his civic activities throughout his career.[35] Jeremiah Burckhalter was the main speaker at the 1863 Sons of Temperance Festival and Ball in Mariposa. His address praised the growth of Mariposa and the beneficial impact the Sons of Temperance had on the populace.[36] The same day that the *Mariposa Free Press* reported Burckhalter's speech, the editors noted that two other attorneys, J. O. Lovejoy and A. Washburn were among the managers

*4. Reginaldo F. del Valle, pioneer Los Angeles attorney and civic activist.
Reproduced by permission of The Huntington Library, San Marino, California.*

of the second annual St. Patrick's Day ball.[37] The rural bar was a civically active group, regardless of varying views on demon rum.

The early bar also had a tendency to draw attention because of their social activities. William Morris Stewart's home in Nevada City became the center of social life in the area.[38] David Colton, chief counsel for the Southern Pacific Railroad, built his home on Nob Hill in San Francisco.[39] Nob Hill became the residence of preference of the rich and powerful. When Fred Pierson Tuttle, an Auburn attorney, gave a party or played on the local baseball team, the *Placer County Republican* made public note of his activities.[40]

Lawyers like Charles Enoch Huse turned their interest in education into action on behalf of education. Huse, as mentioned above, was active in establishing the College of Santa Barbara. Solomon Heydenfeldt, a San Francisco attorney and justice of the state supreme court, was a significant moving force in the establishment of kindergartens in the Bay City.[41] Wigginton E. Creed, a Fresno native, New York University Law School graduate, and president of several corporations, was a University of California regent and president of the university.[42] Clara Shortridge Foltz was a trustee of the State Normal School of Los Angeles.[43] These are notable examples, but the efforts of lawyers on local school boards contributed equally to the advancement of education in California.

Although lawyers contributed substantially to California's history, one lawyer, Theodore H. Hittell, was one of the state's early historians. Hittell was part of what Ralph J. Roske has called "the second generation Californians" of the period 1875–1920. These people contributed to the rise of culture, the creative arts, journalism, and higher education. Hittell was a San Francisco attorney as well as the newspaper editor of the *San Francisco Bulletin*. He wrote twelve volumes on California and Nevada law as well as a history of California.[44] Hittell was part of this second generation that contributed to the cultural maturation of the state.

Public service and public notice for scholarship, public addresses, and social conversation put lawyers in a positive public light. Another print medium that advertised an attorney's trade was the legal directory. John Livingston of New York worked on one such resource in 1856, depicting it as a "catalogue of Reliable practicing attorneys." He wrote to Charles Fernald in Santa Barbara, soliciting the inclusion of Fernald's name. Fernald wrote "I cannot accept your proposal, nor can I approve of your design." He termed Livingston's "catalogue . . . valueless as evidence of reliability."[45] But times changed. Fernald's name found its way into *Hubbell's Legal Directory* and in 1877, on the basis of his inclusion in the directory, he received two promissory notes for collection from George W. Gere of Champaign, Illinois, with a 25 percent collection fee.[46] By the 1870s the lawyers directory and the credit bureau had become fixtures of the debt collection system.

The Mercantile Agency of San Francisco was a clearing-house for merchant-creditors and California's bar. Much of John Daniel Goodwin's debt collection practice was a direct result of referrals from the agency.[47] In remote Plumas County that kind of business made the difference between success and alternative career pursuits. The advertising value of such directories or agencies was most pronounced for the rural practitioner.

For all lawyers the referrals made within networks was the most important method of getting clients. An attorney named Sexton, of the firm Burt and Sexton in Oroville, wrote to John D. Goodwin in 1870 seeking a piece of the practice pie. Sexton had formed his law partnership

> for the purpose of assisting any poor devil to swindle any other poor devil, provided [that] one first aforesaid has costs—or to assist any poor devil to get swindled provided he is willing to pay for such a luxury. In fact we might indulge in something of a swindle ourselves, provided we could see spoundulics [*sic*] gleaming in silver and golden sheen in sufficient quantities to cast a respectable rainbow here over the dark cloud of the swindle—Eh?
>
> In short we are going to work and if assiduous and attentive labor will command success, by God we will have [it].[48]

With that said, Sexton wanted any referrals Goodwin could send their way. R. E. Arick of Panamint was thrilled to be "found" by the Los Angeles firm of McConnell, Bicknell and Rothchild in 1875. Unfortunately, the debtors had "left our diggins" and Arick would have to await future business to practice the art of collecting.[49] John B. Clark, Jr., who practiced before the U.S. Court of Claims, was "getting business far beyond [his] most sanguine expectations" and asked John D. Bicknell for a list of attorneys in California "to whom I can send my cards and circulars."[50] Their professional relationship could help Clark to expand his network through direct-mail advertising.

Other lawyers used the mail to solicit business on an individual basis. Collis P. Huntington found a letter of H. W. Latham, a Los Angeles attorney, persuasive enough to order Bicknell to send Latham Southern Pacific's overflow business.[51] Some attorneys found business through the newspaper. The death of a letter carrier at the wheels of a Southern Pacific train brought a deluge of letters to his mother's house.[52] Land-title litigation would create sufficient interest to keep many attorneys busy in the pursuit of justice.[53] The more practiced law firms combed the legal record for possible clients. The Graves, O'Melveny and Shankland partnership of Los Angeles was very skilled with solicitation letters based on the legal record, as an 1891 letter to the Main Street Savings Bank and Trust Company evidenced.

> We noticed by the real estate record the filing in the Recorder's Office quite a number of certificates of tax sale of property wherein you are interested. Regarding the same we would suggest that, finding it very difficult to keep run of taxes, especially on mortgages, we have, for the Farmers' and Merchants' Bank, the Los Angeles Savings Bank and the Security Savings Bank and Trust Company, encouraged the practice of having a search made once a year as to taxes only. . . . We are satisfied that we saved them many hundreds of dollars this spring by so doing, and we would advise you to do the same thing. . . .
>
> This may seem to you an unecessary expense, but [if you do not] you will be put to the necessity of an expensive litigation or settling with the tax debtors upon their own terms.[54]

The skillful soft sell to potential clients, coupled with courteous and careful service, built up a law firm's fortunes. Further, Graves was not content to rest on current clients or client types. When an opportunity arose to represent seven different New York clients in a local bankruptcy, the firm had a form letter sent to each, soliciting their business.[55] Building a law practice required the continuing attention of lawyers to ensure long-term growth and stability.

Although a public attitude of cynicism occasionally found expression in the press, California's lawyers were civically active and professionally astute in maintaining a reputable public and professional image, attorneys like Sexton notwithstanding. As the century closed, the bar could consider its public efforts to improve its image and improve the socioeconomic climate to be successful. Lawyers had become an integral part of the business and social life of the state.

CHAPTER

11

Conclusion

The West is dead my friend,/
But writers hold the seed/
And what they sow will live and grow/
Again to those who read./
—Charles M. Russell

Law in nineteenth-century California was part of the social fabric and the lives of its pioneers. The struggle to bring civilization to people was a struggle to bring the values inherent in law to the people. Much of that law was external to events. The law that was part of the culture of the people, the rule of law, was in their minds and part of the way they did business. Sometimes the tension between the law in books and the law in action, whether in a mining camp in the mother-lode country or an Antelope Valley squatter's shack, created confrontations between people. Courts and lawyers ultimately helped to decide the questions and reduce the tensions. Despite vigilante action, the due process that law afforded would prevail. Despite the lengthy processes of law, the property-law principles would prevail in the conflicts over title. On these levels, California's lawyers and clients worked within the institutional setting to settle disputes and to assert rights. Law protected and fostered a developing economic and social fabric.

The bar reached far beyond the confines of courts and law offices to have an impact on the development of California. They formed firms as well as professional contacts in their communities. They became part of the social life of their villages, towns, and cities. They entered public office for service and personal security. Lawyers became journalists, bankers, merchants, farmers, ranchers, and literary figures. While they expanded their personal and public horizons, their education and profession increasingly narrowed in scope. Specialization in legal expertise limited the reach of generalists in the bar at a time when lawyers expanded their public roles.

The roots of the profession of law in California were the liberal education of classic literature and the legal treatises of the times. The rhetoric of lawyers that touched the minds of jurors was the stuff of gold-rush practice. Slowly the technically trained attorney replaced those who read the classics and the law. We sense that the cultivated human being who emerged from a liberal university education and became a capable and sensitive lawyer lost out to the technically trained law school product. But the Henry O'Melvenys of the bar certainly stand out as exceptions, if the generalization was demonstrable. Rather, California's bar became increasingly college-educated as well as law school-educated. What was lost was the legal culture of the early national period and with it the rhetoric that could sway a jury. What emerged was an expanding law-mindedness without the client expertise of a David Jacks. Clients like Jacks purchased law books, attended court, and read newspaper articles on law, thereby maintaining an informed opinion regarding the state of the law. However, lawyers increasingly appropriated the knowledge and expertise about law for themselves, just as they separated themselves from their gold-rush colleagues.

Lawyers, and clients dealing with private law were Mad Hatter's tea party participants who won and lost within the rule of law that Alice could not see. The law was mysterious to some, but most adhered to its command in the lawful West of nineteenth-century California. Lawyers and clients met and resolved conflict as well as structured change on the table set by the legal culture of their times.

NOTES

INTRODUCTION

1. John Philip Reid, *Law for the Elephant*, 10–11.
2. Ibid, 362.
3. David M. Trubek and John Esser, "'Critical Empiricism' in American Legal Studies: Paradox, Program, or Pandora's Box?," 3, 33.
4. Hendrik Hartog, "The End(s) of Critical Empiricism," pp. 53, 54.
5. William C. Whitford, "Critical Empiricism," 61, 63.
6. Ibid, 65.
7. Patricia Nelson Limerick, *Legacy of Conquest*.
8. See Theodore S. Hamerow, *Reflections on History and Historians*, 205–43. In attempting generalizations, I acknowledge the limitations of historical methodology, yet accept the challenge to study lawyers engaged in broad-ranging legal activities in turbulent economic and social times. In contrast, Gail Williams O'Brien's study of the Guilford County, North Carolina, bar, 1848–1882, ends as industrialization begins. Gail Williams O'Brien, *The Legal Fraternity and the Making of a New South Community, 1848–1882*. Despite the differences in the periods studied, her conclusions regarding the increased specialization of the bar, lawyers as officeholders, and her focus on wealth accumulation are similar to ones found in this volume.
9. James A. Henretta, "Social History as Lived and Written," 1293–1322.
10. Ibid, 1311.
11. Hamerow, *Reflections on History and Historians*.
12. Ibid, 241–43.
13. Robert Clark, "In Critical Legal Studies, the West Is the Adversary," *Wall Street Journal*, Feb. 23, 1989. For a more detailed exploration see Nelson and Gordon, "Exchange on Critical Legal Studies," 139–86. Mark Kelman, *Guide to Critical Legal Studies*.
14. Edward P. Thompson, *Whigs and Hunters*, 266.
15. C. Robert Haywood, *Cowtown Lawyers* is the notable exception. Generally, see also Larry D. Ball, "The Lincoln County War: An Enduring Fascination," 303–12; Kermit L. Hall, "Hacks and Derelicts Revisited: The American Territorial Judiciary, 1789–1959," 273–90; Ralph J. Mooney, "Formalism and Fairness: Matthew Deady and the Federal Public Land Law in the Early West," 317–70; Stuart H. Traub, "Rewards, Bounty Hunting, and Criminal Justice in the West: 1865–1900," 287–302; and John R. Wunder, "Chinese in Trouble: Criminal Law and Race on the Trans-Mississippi West Frontier," 25–42.

16. Andrew R. L. Cayton, *The Frontier Republic: Ideology and Politics in the Ohio Country, 1800–1825*, 145.

17. Limerick, *Legacy of Conquest*, 32.

18. Ibid, 39.

19. Ibid, 291. The problem for western historians working in this field is that a great deal of the literature is found in law reviews, not an obvious source to many historians. For example, the best work done on Clara S. Foltz, the first female lawyer in California, is Barbara Allen Babcock, "Clara Shortridge Foltz: 'First Woman,'" 673–717. Much of the critical legal studies debate also is in law reviews. See Richard A. Posner, "The Jurisprudence of Skepticism," 827–91, and Jay M. Feinman, "Practical Legal Studies and Critical Legal Studies," 724–31. Even an important bibliography of the subject is found in a law review. Charles F. Wilkinson, "The Law of the American West: A Critical Bibliography of the Nonlegal Sources," 953–1011. We are accustomed to digging for nuggets like information about Charles E. DeLong in obscure veins like Carl I. Wheat "California's Bantam Cock," 193–98, but western historians also must familiarize themselves with the rich lodes in law reviews.

CHAPTER I

1. The bibliography contains more than thirty titles on the subject. Of particular interest are the works of Gary B. Nash, John Heinz and Edward O. Lauman, Gerald L. Geison, Gerard W. Gawalt, Walter J. Leonard, Maxwell Bloomfield, Jerome F. Carlin, Michael De Landon, E. Lee Shepart, W. Hamilton Bryson, Barbara J. Harris, R. Kent Newmyer, Kermit Hall, and John Phillip Reid.

2. Gerard W. Gawalt, *The Promise of Power* and Gerard W. Gawalt, ed., *The New High Priests*.

3. Lawrence M. Friedman and Robert V. Percival, *The Roots of Justice*, 56.

4. William Kramer, "Ex Post Facto," *Los Angeles Daily Journal*, Oct. 21, 1985.

5. Reprint found in *Magazine of History* 48 (1933): 104–7. The *San Francisco Herald* reported only sixty-four attorneys in town on December 25, 1855. Adams Co. Collection Scrapbook, vol. 6, p. 49, Huntington Library.

6. Charles E. DeLong practiced law in the gold-rush country prior to admission. DeLong Diaries, vols. 1856 and 1857, Charles E. DeLong Collection, California Section.

7. Friedman and Percival, *Roots of Justice*, 58.

8. Robert A. Burchell, "The Character and Function of a Pioneer Elite: Rural California, 1848–1880," 377–90, develops the concept of the bar as a significant elite in California. The biographies in my study are taken from the following: Thomas H. Thompson and Albert A. West, *History of Sacramento County*; *San Francisco: Its Builders, Past and Present*; *Past and Present of Alameda County, California*; George C. Mansfield, *History of Butte County*; *San Joaquin County, California*; *History*

of San Mateo County, California; Baily Millard, *History of the San Francisco Bay Region*; *San Diego County, California*; William L. Willis, *History of Sacramento County, California*; Eugene T. Sawyer, *History of Santa Clara County, California*; John Brown, Jr. and James Boyd, *History of San Bernardino and Riverside Counties*; William B. Lardner and M. J. Brock, *History of Placer and Nevada Counties, California*; Paul E. Vandor, *History of Fresno County, California*; *A History of Los Angeles, California, and Environs*; *A History of Monterey and Santa Cruz Counties, California*; Tom Gregory, *History of Solano and Napa Counties, California*; idem, *History of Sonoma County, California*; Kathleen E. Small and Larry J. Smith, *History of Tulare and Kings Counties, California*; *History of Long Beach and Vicinity*; John Outcalt, *History of Merced County, California*; J. P. O'Brien, ed., *History of the Bench and Bar of Nevada*; Annie L. Morrison and John H. Haydon, *History of San Luis Obispo County and Environs*; Will S. Green, *The History of Colusa County, California*; Frederick J. Hulaniski, ed., *The History of Contra Costa County, California*; Leigh H. Irvine, *History of Humboldt County, California*; Finis C. Farr, ed., *The History of Imperial County*; Wallace M. Moran, *History of Kern County, California*; Samuel Armor, *History of Orange County, California*; Willoughby Rodman, *History of the Bench and Bar of Southern California*.

9. Sepulveda to Joseph L. Brent, Feb. 6, 1878, Joseph L. Brent Collection, box 3, Huntington Library. The land-title practice was still thriving and complex in the late 1880s. In 1888 George Smith terms California titles "complicated." George H. Smith to George S. Patton, Aug. 3, 1888, George Smith Patton Collection, private letters no. 2, Huntington Library. The anxiety about titles is also evidenced in a letter Patton wrote in 1889: "Mr. Glassell, Col. Smith and I had a full discussion this morning regarding the title to the Hayes Tract. We do not think it advisable to submit the Abstract as it stands, to a possible lender, at least until we have made further effort to discover the facts regarding the original locators. We suggest that between now and our coming up, you make further inquiry from all possible sources as to this matter. Examine the records of the Recorder's office for deeds, mortgages or other instruments by any of these parties, as well as the records of the Clerk's office for any possible suits to which they may have been parties. . . . In the meantime, Col. Smith has prepared a bill to be presented to the Legislature, following the suggestions of Justice Field of the Supreme Court, to cover just such a case as ours. . . . The bill is one which is approved by all lawyers, and is really necessary under the present state of our law." George S. Patton to Arthur J. Hutchinson, Feb. 25, 1889, Patton Collection, private letters no. 2, Huntington Library.

10. Bruce Dorsey, "The Los Angeles Bar in the Nineteenth Century," California State University, Fullerton. The Los Angeles bar was particularly crowded by the 1890s. Jackson A. Graves wrote to William M. Aydellotte in 1896, "We have twice as large a bar as the business will justify. The result is that competition is very close and the outlook for a newcomer by no means encouraging." Graves to Aydellotte, Feb. 24, 1896, Jackson A. Graves Collection, 1895–97 letterbook, Huntington Library.

11. Unfortunately, the data for the 1850s and 1860s are sporadic and not useful for comparative purposes.

12. W. Turrentine Jackson, ed., *Twenty Years on the Pacific Slope*, 35, 37.

13. Haywood, *Cowtown Lawyers*, 104.

14. Eastman (Boston) to Fernald (Santa Barbara), Mar. 13, 1877, Charles Fernald Collection, box 3, Huntington Library.

15. Agreement to Dissolve Practice, May 1, 1872, John D. Bicknell Collection, box 1, Huntington Library.

16. Orner to Bicknell, Aug. 14, 1875, Ibid.

17. Threasher to Bicknell, Dec. 20, 1874, Ibid.

18. Richardson to Bicknell, Feb. 24, 1875, Ibid.

19. Ward to Bicknell, Apr. 14, 1875, Ibid.

20. Friedman and Percival, *Roots of Justice*, 56.

21. Kennedy to Bicknell, Sept. 12, 1874, Bicknell Collection, box 1, Huntington Library.

22. Friedman and Percival, *Roots of Justice*, 57.

23. John Bauer, *The Health Seekers of Southern California, 1870–1900*.

24. Oscar T. Shuck, *Bench and Bar in California*, 417–23; Leland G. Stanford, *Footprints of Justice . . . in San Diego*, 38–40.

25. Smith to Bicknell, Aug. 21, 1888, Bicknell Collection, box 5, Huntington Library.

26. Bryan to Bicknell, Jan. 29, 1890, Ibid., box 6.

27. Bicknell to Bryan, Mar. 19, 1890, Ibid., letterbook no 6.

28. Jackson A. Graves, *Seventy Years in California*, 286, 293.

29. Gerard W. Gawalt, "The Impact of Industrialization on the Legal Profession in Massachusetts, 1870–1900," in *New High Priests*, ed. Gawalt, 99. Haywood, *Cowtown Lawyers*, 224.

30. Montgomery (Santa Ana) to Patton, July 9, 1895, Patton Collection, private letters no. 8, Huntington Library.

31. William Uberti, "Oliver S. Witherby, First State District Judge of San Diego, 221–35.

32. Leland G. Stanford, "Devil's Corner and Oliver S. Witherby," 236–53. Other lawyers created positions for themselves. George Goucher was a Mariposa County lawyer who moved to Fresno County and won election to the state senate. There he introduced a bill to create Madera County. Later he became Madera County district attorney. Robert M. Wash, "Our County's Yesterdays," 5. Goucher was aided in his efforts by William Maxwell Conley. Conley was born in Dog Town, Mariposa County in 1866, educated in the Merced public school, and graduated from Stockton Business College. In 1890 he turned from teaching and public service to reading law. Admitted to the bar in 1891, he practiced in Bakersfield and waged an unsuccessful campaign for district attorney in 1892. In December 1892 he moved to Madera and lobbied for the creation of the county of Madera. In 1893 he was elected

superior court judge and held the job for twenty-eight years, trying over thirteen hundred cases. Ibid., 8: "There Came a Young Man," 1–9.

33. William Wilcox Robinson, *Lawyers of Los Angeles*, 236.

34. Letterhead of M. L. Wicks, 1900, Graves Collection, box 10, Huntington Library.

35. Higby to his father, Jan. 23, 1851, William Higby Collection, box 218, California State Library, California Section.

36. Roger W. Lotchin, *San Francisco, 1846–1856*, 3–82.

37. Terry to Cornelia R. Terry, June 29, 1852, David Smith Terry Collection, box 1, Huntington Library.

38. Terry to Cornelia R. Terry, May 12, 1870, Ibid., box 3.

39. John N. Howell, "Continuity and Persistence: A History of the Placer County, California Bar, 1850–1900," 19, California State University, Fullerton.

40. Oscar Shuck, ed., *History of the Bench and Bar of California*, 777.

41. Ibid., 529–31. Robinson, *Lawyers of Los Angeles*, 234. *Contra Costa County Gazette*, Dec. 23, 1865.

42. Andrew F. Rolle, *An American in California: The Biography of William Heath Davis*; William E. Smythe, *History of San Diego, 1542–1907*; Robert Mayer, ed., *San Diego*; Leland G. Stanford, *Tracks on the Trial Trail in San Diego*; Wallace W. Elliot, *History of San Bernardino and San Diego Counties*; Leland G. Stanford, *San Diego Lawyers You Should Have Known*; Clarence A. McGrew, *City of San Diego and San Diego County*; Leland G. Stanford, *San Diego's Legal Lore and the Bar*; Effie Enfield Johnston, "Wade Johnston Talks to His Daughter," 25.

43. Shuck, *History of Bench and Bar*, 495–99.

44. Ibid., 714.

45. Ibid., 707–8.

46. Ibid., 695–99.

47. The *Gazette* contains many stories about lawyers leaving town. J. O. Lovejoy started a lumber mill in Visalia in 1872. He left Mariposa in 1873 and started the Lovejoy Hotel in Tulare that same year. Jeremiah Burckhalter was a physician who turned to law. He won election as county judge in 1861, but lost the justice of the peace election in 1863. He then turned to the practice of law until 1873, when he moved to Visalia and returned to medicine. J. B. Cambell was Burckhalter's partner in 1865 and held the posts of districit attorney, sheriff, and district judge. In 1880 he moved to Fresno and in 1891 was counsel for the Southern Pacific Railroad. George G. Goucher moved to Fresno in 1887 after over a decade of private practice and public service in the area. W. J. Howard was an assemblyman in 1857 and district attorney in 1876. In 1881 he was declared insolvent. Subsequently, he was a justice of the peace and undersheriff prior to employment as a Folsom Prison guard in 1895. Newman Jones found employment as district attorney in the mid-1880s, but moved to Hanford in 1890. W. H. Larew was school supervisor in 1884 and 1885, but moved to Madera after a series of trials in 1885 and 1886 for misconduct in office.

J. H. Lawrence, editor of the *Gazette* from 1871–75, was admitted to the Mariposa bar in 1866 and moved to San Francisco in 1875. Samuel Merritt left Mariposa County after over a decade of practice and public service. He later became chief justice of the Utah Supreme Court. Angevine Reynolds was a forty-niner who left Mariposa in 1851 to work on a stage out of Stockton. Later he and Lovejoy erected a sawmill. Reynolds published the *Mariposa Mail* from 1868 until 1875. He bought the *Gazette* in 1874 and entered law practice three years later. In 1887 he departed for San Francisco. See *Mariposa Gazette*, November 24, 1888, Biography section. John Wilcox, a sheriff and assemblyman, left for San Francisco in 1878. John F. Cassell left in 1870 when the Oak and Reese mine he was managing played out. Thomas Long moved to Nevada in 1868 after a dozen years of practice. Jewitt Adams left for Nevada four years later. Eldridge Farnsworth was sponsored by George Goucher to bar membership in 1884 but only lasted four years. And so it went from the late 1870s on until the county was nearly devoid of legal counsel in the 1890s. Lawyers followed law business or diversified. This phenomena was very similar to that observed by Maxwell Bloomfield in Floyd County, Texas. It was difficult to establish and maintain a practice in any new frontier community. Maxwell Bloomfield, "The Texas Bar in the Nineteenth Century," 261–76. Other lawyers did not stay in any one place for any great length of time. Ezekiel Ewing Calhoun was one such attorney. A second cousin of John C. Calhoun, Ezekiel was born in Kentucky and was a graduate of the University of Louisville Law School in 1850. After one year of practice in Kentucky, he came to San Bernardino, but settled in San Diego county at farming. In 1854 Calhoun traveled to the San Joaquin Valley to seek his fortune and settled in Visalia in 1855. He won election as town clerk and as county judge for a three year term. In 1866 he was Kern County's first district attorney. Calhoun also served as county surveyor, county auditor, and county school superintendent. Later he wandered up to Santa Clara County and in 1884 to Fresno county, finally settling in Selma in 1887. Later he moved to Hildreth in Madera County and resided there until his death in 1896. "Judge E. E. Calhoun," 1–3.

48. *Who's Who in the Pacific Southwest*, 141 and Gawalt, "Industrialization," 102.

49. Shuck, *Bench and Bar in California*, 691–92.

50. Ibid., 553.

51. Ibid., 582–83. There are numerous other examples. The most amusing is of Dan M. Baker, who held a law degree from the University of Indiana and practiced in Lucas County, Iowa. Baker became the editor of the *Chariton Leader* in Iowa and moved to Santa Ana in 1883. He purchased the *Santa Ana Weekly Standard* to pursue his love of newsprint. The lure of the law enticed him to schedule a bar examination in August 1889, but he did not make an appearance. He was admitted two years later. For a popular biography, see Jim Sleeper, *Turn the Rascals Out*. See also Haywood, *Cowtown Lawyers*, 149, 156, 163, 190, 197, 211–20.

52. Green, *History of Colusa County, California*, 150.

53. Stickney to John F. Miller (Napa), Apr. 4, 1874, John F. Miller Collection, box 449, California State Library, California Section.

54. Bicknell to D. A. DeArmond (Butler, Mo.), May 23, 1891, Bicknell Collection, Letterbook no. 7, Huntington Library.

55. Thomas Garden Barnes, *Hastings College of Law: The First Century*, 48.

56. Ibid., 49–50. Karen Berger Morello, *The Invisible Bar: The Woman Lawyer in America, 1638 to the Present*, 59–64.

57. Barnes, *Hastings College*, 57–60. Gawalt, "Industrialization," 104.

58. Barnes, *Hastings College*, 56.

59. Limerick, *Legacy of Conquest*, 39.

CHAPTER 2

1. Robert Stevens, *Law Schools: Legal Education in America from the 1850's to the 1900's*; Elizabeth G. Brown, *Legal Education in Michigan, 1859–1959*; William R. Johnson, *Schooled Lawyers: A Study in the Clash of Professional Cultures*; W. Hamilton Bryson, *Legal Education in Virginia, 1779–1979*; Alfred Z. Reed, *Training for the Public Profession of the Law*; Beatrice Doerschuck, *Women in the Law*; David Wigdor, *Roscoe Pound: Philosopher of Law*.

2. Daniel H. Calhoun, *Professional Lives in America*, 59–87.

3. Robert A. Ferguson, *Law and Letters in American Culture*.

4. Charles E. DeLong diary, July 30, 1855, DeLong Collection, box 212, 1854–55 diary, California State Library.

5. Ibid., 1856 diary, Feb. 23, 1856.

6. Ibid., May 13, 1856.

7. Ibid., Sept. 8 and 9, 1856.

8. Ibid., 1857 Diary, Mar. 5, 1857.

9. Ibid., Apr. 23, 1857.

10. Ibid., May 4, 13, 14, 16, 17, 18, and 21, 1857.

11. Ibid., May 25, 1857.

12. Ibid., June 6, 1857. John R. Wunder, *Inferior Courts, Superior Justice*, 30, 118–28.

13. DeLong diary, June 18 and 28, 1857, DeLong Collection, box 212, 1857 diary, California State Library, California Section.

14. Ibid., July 8, 1857.

15. Ibid., July 11, 1857.

16. Ibid., Sept. 5, 1857.

17. Ibid., Sept. 30, 1857 and 1858 and 1859 diaries.

18. J. M. Guinn, *Historical and Biographical Record of Los Angeles and Vicinity*, 752–54.

19. M. M. Estee, "Early History and Early Day Lawyers," in *History of the Bench and Bar*, ed. Shuck, 292. Also see Ralph W. Yarborough, "A History of Law Licensing in Texas," in *Centennial History of the Texas Bar, 1882–1982*, ed. Taylor Russell, 186.

20. Graves, *Seventy Years in California*. Also see Gawalt, "Industrialization," 105.

21. Estee in Shuck, *History of the Bench and Bar*, 393.

22. Ibid., 388.

23. Ibid., 400.

24. DeLong diary, Dec. 24, 1856, Delong Collection, box 212, 1856 diary, California State Library, California Section. The 1856 and 1857 diaries have most of the social entries of note.

25. Ibid., 1859 diary, May 17, 1859.

26. Ibid., 1857 diary, May 20 and 22, 1857.

27. Ibid., June 20 and 22, 1857.

28. Ibid., Dec. 14, 15, and 16, 1857. James Alexander Watson's law practice in Shasta in 1851–52 was very similar. Rhetoric and the theatre of the courtroom were very much a part of practice. Judson Grenier, *California Legacy*, 67–70. Also see Ferguson, *Law and Letters* and Haywood, *Cowtown Lawyers*, 84–85.

29. H. K. S. O'Melveny lawyer's common place book, 1860, Henry W. O'Melveny Collection, Huntington Library.

30. O'Melveny notes on Kent, 2 vols., 1874–76 journal, 1877 diary, Ibid.

31. O'Melveny, "Solitude," a speech delivered to the Sunset Club on June 30, 1940, Ibid.

32. Murray to Bicknell, July 9, 1877, Bicknell Collection, box 2, Huntington Library.

33. McDowell to Bicknell, Oct. 27, 1872, Ibid., box 1.

34. Ibid.

35. McDowell to Bicknell, Jan. 17, 1873 and Mar. 22, 1873, Ibid.

36. Compare Gawalt, *Promise of Power*; Gawalt, *New High Priests*; Jackson Turner Main, *The Social Structure of Revolutionary America*; Gary B. Nash, *Class and Society in Early America*; Edward Pessen, *Riches, Class, and Power Before the Civil War*.

37. See Barnes, *Hastings College* and Gawalt, *New High Priests*, 105–6, 120.

38. Lawrence M. Friedman, *A History of American Law*, 326–33.

39. Currey to Catlin, July 2, 1850, Amos Parmalee Catlin Collection, box 1, Huntington Library. The problem of obtaining law books in the antebellum period was one of transportation. The West was only a tertiary market for eastern publishers who awaited railroad development to seek new markets. Ronald J. Zboray, "The Transportation Revolution and Antebellum Book Distribution Reconsidered," 53–71. On the law books of the first decade see Alfred C. Skaife, "Early California Law Books (1847–1850)," *San Francisco Bar* 1 (February 1937): 12–16; "Early California Law Books (1850–51)," *SFB* 1 (June 1937): 7–13; "Early California Law Books (1852–53)," *SFB* 1 (October 1937): 8–10; "Early California Law Books (1854)," *SFB* 1 (December 1937): 5–7; "Early California Law Books (1855–56)," *SFB* 2 (April 1938): 11–14; "Early California Law Books (1857)," *SFB* 2 (August 1938): 6–9; "Early California Law Books (1858)," *SFB* 3 (February 1939): 14–16; "Early California Law Books," *SFB* 5 (April 1941): 12–14.

40. Adams Co. Collection Scrapbook, vol. 1, p. 53, Huntington Library.

41. Gardiner to Mandeville, Jan. 15, 1852, James W. Mandeville Collection, box 1, Huntington Library.

42. Huse to Fernald, Apr. 3, 1853, Fernald Collection, box 3, Huntington Library.

43. Edith Boyd Conkey, ed., *The Huse Journal*, 99.

44. Ibid., 135.

45. Ibid., 138.

46. Ibid., 139.

47. Ibid., 110.

48. Ibid., 126.

49. Ibid., 177.

50. Ibid., 185.

51. Ibid., 204.

52. Kenneth M. Johnson, *Bar Association of San Francisco*, 10.

53. Ibid. On the origins of the *Daily Journal* see Robinson, *Lawyers of Los Angeles*, 81.

54. Scott and Montgomery to Bicknell, Feb. 24, 1879, Bicknell Collection, box 3, Huntington Library.

55. L. W. Mason to Bicknell, Apr. 2, 1874, Ibid., box 1.

56. F. J. Gallagher to Fernald, Dec. 15, 1876, Fernald Collection, box 2, Huntington Library.

57. Sanborn to Bicknell, Jan. 16, 1889, Bicknell Collection, box 6, Huntington Library.

58. Beattie to Bicknell, June 12, 1889, Ibid., box 6.

59. *Placer County Argus*, Feb. 7, 1884. We must take seriously the problem of finding the law and the ability of the practicing bar to deal with current practice problems. As we will remember, Charles Huse was frustrated by the limited legal literature in Santa Barbara in the 1850s. He was particularly frustrated by the California *Reports*. My prior research revealed that in 39.93 percent of the contract cases and in 24 percent of the landlord and tenant cases the California Supreme Court gave absolutely no legal citations. My study contained cases for 1850–90. Gordon Morris Bakken, *Development of Law in Frontier California*, 7, 38.

60. Charles Warren, *A History of the American Bar*, 557.

61. Friedman, *History of American Law*, 624.

62. Warren, *History of the American Bar*, 547–50.

63. Shuck, *Bench and Bar in California*, 417–23.

64. John Downey Works Dictation, Bancroft Library.

65. Stanford, *San Diego's Legal Lore*, 171. Stanford, *Footprints of Justice*, 38–40. Charles F. Lummis, *Out West*, 420.

66. See James C. Fifield, ed., *The American Bar*.

67. Smith Biography, Patton Collection, box 15, Huntington Library.

CHAPTER 3

1. Wayne K. Hobson, "Symbol of the New Profession: Emergence of the Large Law Firm, 1870–1915," in *New High Priests*, ed. Gawalt, 3–27.

2. *Guide to American Historical Manuscripts in the Huntington Library*, 146–47.

3. Harlan L. Hoffman, "Pistols and Coffee for Two: A History of the Santa Barbara County Bar, 1850–1900," California State University, Fullerton.

4. William Farley Mauck III and Susan Maslin, "Mariposa County, 1850–1900: A Study of Rural California Law," California State University, Fullerton.

5. Howell, "Continuity and Persistence: A History of the Placer County Bar, 1850–1900," California State University, Fullerton; Bloomfield, "The Texas Bar," 261–76; and Haywood, *Cowtown Lawyers*, 220–24.

6. Denise Mougey, "The San Diego Bar: A Study in Professionalization and Economic Developments," California State University, Fullerton.

7. Ibid. Also see Hobson, "Symbol," 5 and Bloomfield, "Texas Bar," 265.

8. Graves, *Seventy Years in California*, 286.

9. Ibid., 288–90.

10. Ibid., 293. By the late nineteenth century, O'Melveny's land-title work turned to creating and managing land companies. Judson Grenier has ably chronicled this process in Grenier, *California Legacy*, 291–409.

11. *San Francisco Chronicle*, Jan. 24, 1952.

12. Robert Glass Cleland and Frank B. Putnam, *Isaias Hellman and the Farmers and Merchants Bank*, 80–85, 88–90, 93–94, 107–10 and Gawalt, *The Promise of Power*, 177.

13. Shuck, *History of the Bench and Bar*, 907–8; *Morrison & Foerster, Reference Guide*, 5; and Morrison and Foerster, "The Morrison Firm," unpublished typescript, 1–3.

14. Burnham Enersen, "The McCutchen Law Firm—Its First Century," unpublished typescript, Aug. 10, 1983, and Enerson to Beverly B. Turley, Nov. 12, 1987, letter in author's possession.

15. E. G. Chandler, *A History of the Law Firm Now Known as Athearn, Chandler, Hoffman, and Angell*, 2–13 and Shuck, *History of the Bench and Bar*, 806, 853.

16. Eric Sutcliffe, "Acknowledgement by Eric Sutcliffe of One-Hundred-Year Award to Orrick, Herrington, and Sutcliffe from the California Historical Society" and Robert W. Gordon, "The Ideal and the Actual in the Law," in *New High Priests*, ed. Gawalt, 51–74.

17. John A. Matzko, "'The Best Men of the Bar': The Founding of the American Bar Association," in *New High Priests*, ed. Gawalt, 77–78 and Friedman, *History of American Law*, 305–10. Also see George Martin, *Causes and Conflicts: The Centennial History of the Bar Association of the City of New York, 1870–1970*; and Herman Kogan, *The First Century: The Chicago Bar Association, 1874–1974*.

18. Johnson, *Bar Association of San Francisco*, 1.

19. Ibid., 2–4.

20. Ibid., 4.

21. Ibid., 5.

22. Robinson, *Lawyers of Los Angeles*, 4–7.

23. Ibid., 81.

24. Ibid., 81–83.

25. Ibid., 98.

26. Gary B. Nash, "The Philadelphia Bench and Bar, 1800–1861," 203–220. Also see Jerold S. Auerbach, *Unequal Justice* and Gawalt, *Promise of Power*, 103–116.

27. Robert W. Gordon, "Legal Thought and Legal Practice in the Age of Enterprise, 1870–1920," in *Professions and Professional Ideologies in America*, ed. Gerald L. Geison, 70–110.

28. DeLong diary, Feb. 14, 1857, DeLong Collection, box 212, 1857 diary, California State Library, California Section.

29. Ibid., Feb. 15, 1857.

30. Wilson to Dibblee, Feb. 5, 1877, Fernald Collection, box 3, Huntington Library.

31. Clark to Bicknell, Nov. 2, 1873, Bicknell Collection, box 1, Huntington Library.

32. Hayford to Bicknell, May 11, 1889, Bicknell Collection, box 6, Huntington Library. Communications could be hampered by weather, as Bicknell indicated in an 1891 letter regarding a delinquent tax case. "Owing to recent floods my communications with your office has been somewhat delaid. I am directed by telegram from Mr. Craig (SP Law Dept.) to communicate directly with you in relation to these cases. Monday is our law day. The demurrer in all these cases will be brought up next Monday. In the ordinary course of practice, we will have ten days. Thereafter to file our answers. It will be well, however, to have the answers ready to file next week." Bicknell to Judge H. S. Brown, Mar. 2, 1891, Ibid., letterbook no. 7.

33. Steward to Bicknell, May 12, 1889, Ibid.

34. Hayford to Bicknell, Apr. 16, 1889, Ibid.

35. Stewart to Bicknell, Sept. 16, 1889, Ibid. and Hayford to Bicknell, June 5, 1889, Ibid.

36. Stewart to Bicknell, Dec. 17, 1889, Ibid.

37. Hayford to Bicknell, Jan. 14, 1890, Ibid. and Hayford to Stewart, Jan. 21, 1890, Ibid.

38. Stewart to Bicknell, Feb. 3, 1890, Ibid.

39. Forsyth to Bicknell, Feb. 8, 1890, Ibid.

40. Roger D. McGrath, *Gunfighters, Highwaymen, and Vigilantes*, 256.

41. Curtis to Bicknell, Aug. 22, 1889, Bicknell Collection, box 6, Huntington Library.

42. Towne to Bicknell, July 17, 1889, Ibid.

43. O'Brien, Morrison and Daingerfield to Bicknell, Nov. 8, 1890, Ibid., box 7.

44. Haymond to Bicknell, Sept 16, 1889, Ibid., box 6.

45. Larrabee to Bicknell, Jan. 5, 1873, Ibid., box 1.

46. Luco to Bicknell, Dec. 9, 1880, Ibid., box 3.

47. Keech to Bicknell, Oct 27, 1890, Ibid., box 7.

48. Montgomery to Bicknell, Oct. 27, 1890, Ibid., box 7.

49. Fawcett to Fernald, May 17, 1876, Fernald Collection, box 3, Huntington Library.

50. 51 Cal. 222 (1876).

51. 80 Cal. 104, 107 (1889).

52. 83 Cal. 438, 439 (1890).

53. 78 Cal. 389, 398 (1889).

54. 78 Cal. 113, 115 (1889).

55. 82 Cal. 193, 197–98 (1889).

56. For other examples see *Cummings* v. *Dudley*, 60 Cal. 383 (1882); *Patten* v. *Hicks*, 43 Cal. 509 (1872); *Joseph* v. *Holt*, 37 Cal. 250 (1869); *Thompson* v. *McKay*, 41 Cal. 221 (1871); *Happe* v. *Stout*, 2 Cal. 460 (1852); *Baughman* v. *Reed*, 75 Cal. 319 (1888); *Easton* v. *O'Reilly*, 63 Cal. 305 (1883); *Creighton* v. *Pragg*, 21 Cal. 115 (1862); *Murphy* v. *Napa County*, 20 Cal. 497 (1862).

57. 50 Cal. 585 (1875).

58. 82 Cal. 474, 480 (1890).

59. 43 Cal. 458, 462 (1872).

60. 14 Cal. 146, 147–48 (1859).

61. 31 Cal. 333 (1866) (1866).

62. A review of the literature on the development of law reveals that most scholars neglect the aspect of counsel error as an element of judicial behavior or the practice of law. See Robert W. Gordon, "Critical Legal Histories," 57–125; Gordon, "Legal Thought and Practice," in *Professions*, ed. Geison, 71–139; Morton J. Horwitz, "The Historical Contingency of the Role of History," 1057–63; Richard A. Posner, "The Present Situation in Legal Scholarship," 1113–30; Kenneth J. Vandelde, "The New Property of the Nineteenth Century: The Development of the Modern Concept of Property," 325–65; G. Edward White, "Truth and Interpretation in History," 595–615; and Wilkinson, "Law of the American West," 953–1011. Excepting Wilkinson, much recent scholarship has advocated ideology or empiricism in the debate over critical legal studies.

63. Reid, *Law for the Elephant*, 362.

CHAPTER 4

1. Peter R. Decker, *Fortunes and Failures*, 91. Lotchin, *San Francisco, 1846–1856*, 60.

2. See *Scarborough* v. *Duncan*, 10 Cal. 305 (1858).

3. *Eck* v. *Hoffman*, 55 Cal. 501 (1880).

4. Waldron to Rothchild, Aug. 2, 1875, Bicknell Collection, box 1, Huntington Library.

5. Davis to Goodwin, Nov. 28, 1882, John D. Goodwin Collection, box 729, California State Library, California Section.

6. Larrobee to Bicknell, July 21, 1873, Bicknell Collection, box 1, Huntington Library.

7. Jenkins to Jenks, Sept. 19, 1884, Goodwin Collection, box 732, California State Library, California Section.

8. Cushman to Jacks, Sept. 1, 1890, David Jacks Collection, box C(8), Huntington Library.

9. Graves and O'Melveny to Merchants Protective and Collection Agency, Dec. 1, 1885, Graves Collection, 1885–86 letterbook, Huntington Library. Also see letter of Dec. 17, 1885, Ibid.

10. Graves to Lilienthal and Co., Dec. 27, 1881, Ibid., 1881–83 letterbook.

11. Graves to Howe and Hass, July 3, 1878, Ibid., 1878–79 Letterbook.

12. See Douglas & Co. to Bicknell, Dec. 12, 1874, Bicknell Collection, box 1, Huntington Library; Boren and Curtis to Bicknell, Feb. 20, 1874 Ibid.; and M. H. Myers to J. M. Rothchild, July 19, 1875, Ibid.

13. Richards to Sheriff of Plumas Co., Aug. 16, 1865, Goodwin Collection, box 735, California State Library, California Section.

14. Reed to Bicknell, Jan. 14, 1880 and Feb. 11, 1880, Bicknell Collection, box 3, Huntington Library.

15. Ah Jake to Hai Loe, Oct. 30, 1874, Albert Dressler Collection, box 756, California State Library, California Section.

16. Tie Yuen to Kong Yuen and Co., Nov. 27, 1874, Ibid.

17. Collins and Company Collection account book, Bancroft Library.

18. L. B. Clark Ledger, Bancroft Library. The flow of business was irregular, but the problems with the formal legal system were few. Also see the Baker and Hamilton Collection, Bancroft Library and the Wellman, Peck and Company Collection, Bancroft Library. Baker and Hamilton were Sacramento importers of agricultural implements and Peck was a San Francisco mercantile house. Also see the D. W. Earl Collection, Bancroft Library. The Earl firm was in the San Francisco and Sacramento forwarding and commission merchant business. The Keller Collection, Huntington Library, contains the San Francisco Store ledger with entries for all types of merchandise showing payment in money, labor, "by lumber," "by a bay horse," and "by chickens and eggs." After 1876 the frequency of cash payments increased dramatically in Keller's store. Life in the country store was somewhat similar in transactions, but not in lifestyle. William Warner wrote to his son and wife on July 15, 1877, "I have long since found out one fact which is as true as the gospel—and that is: a half day sometimes passes away without a customer—but the moment we set down to dinner a half dozen are sure to pop in and are in a great hurry for a can of oysters, a pound of crackers and a like quantity of cheese and crackers." William Warner Collection, box 327, California State Library, California Section. On San Francisco commission merchants and their practices see the Albert Dibblee Collection, particularly Dibblee to George Woodman (Boston), July 30, 1852, Dibblee

Collection, carton 11, vol. 191, Bancroft Library; Crosby and Dibblee to Harbeck and Co., Dec. 25, 1852, Ibid., vol. 191; Crosby and Dibblee to Winsor, Jr. and Co., July 19, 1857, Ibid., vol. 192; Crosby and Dibblee to Woodman, Dec. 4, 1857, Ibid.; and Crosby and Dibblee to Henry Hastings, Jan. 20, 1858, Ibid.

19. Chapelain to Goodwin, May 10, 1864, Goodwin Collection, box 728, California State Library, California Section.

20. Carpenter to Bicknell, Apr. 27, 1878, Bicknell Collection, box 2, Huntington Library.

21. Davis and Crowell to Bicknell, Dec. 9, 1876, Ibid.

22. Graves to Soto, July 21, 1879, Graves Collection, 1879–80 letterbook, Huntington Library.

23. Graves to Dinkelspiel, Sept. 26, 1879, Ibid.

24. Ellison to Bicknell, Mar. 23, 1875, Bicknell Collection, box 1, Huntington Library.

25. Ellison to Bicknell, June 28, 1876 and Sept. 14, 1876, Ibid., box 2.

26. Biddle to Bicknell, Feb. 10, 1875, Ibid., box 1.

27. Forbes to Ledyard, Nov. 10, 1875, Ibid.

28. Cave Couts to Bandini, Feb. 6, 1865, Cave Johnson Couts Collection, box 19, Huntington Library.

29. Sitler, Price and Co. to Wells and Haight, June 19, 1854, Henry H. Haight Collection, box 3, Huntington Library.

30. Lotchin, *San Francisco, 1846–1856*, 77.

31. William Issel and Robert W. Cherny, *San Francisco, 1865–1932*, 23; Crosby and Dibblee to Belden, Oct. 31, 1852, Dibblee Collection, carton 11, vol. 191, Bancroft Library; and Dibblee to Stone and Stone, July 30, 1877, Ibid., vol. 221. The relation of East and West on financial markets was significant in the 1850s and 1860s. For example, Crosby and Dibblee wrote to Harbeck and Co. on Nov. 20, 1857, and stated, "the money troubles at the East have considerably affected our market, by creating great scarcity of money." Ibid., vol. 191.

32. Robert Glass Cleland, *The Cattle on a Thousand Hills*, 108–137.

33. Glenn S. Dumke, *The Boom of the Eighties in Southern California*.

34. *San Francisco Evening Bulletin*, Apr. 19, 1878, in First National Gold Bank Scrapbook, Santa Barbara Historical Society. Also see Decker, *Fortunes and Failures*, 87–105.

35. Cleland and Putnam, *Isaias W. Hellman*, 31–69.

36. Isaias W. Hellman to Matthew Keller, Oct. 3, 1877, Apr. 3, 1878, and Apr. 29, 1878, Matthew Keller Collection, box 1, Huntington Library.

37. See Gordon M. Bakken, "Law and Legal Tender in California and the West," 239–59.

38. Heimann and George to Bicknell, Jan. 3, 1874, Bicknell Collection, box 1, Huntington Library.

39. Warren A. Beck and David A. Williams, *California*, 299–304. Also see Rich-

ard B. Rice, William A. Bullough, and Richard Orsi, *The Elusive Eden*, 237–85.

40. William Warner to Alice and Elsie Warner, Oct. 23, 1887, Warner Collection, box 327, California State Library, California Section.

41. Graves to F. A. Hihn, Nov. 10, 1887, Graves Collection, 1885–88 letterbook, Huntington Library.

42. Studebaker to Bicknell, Aug. 24, 1888, Bicknell Collection, box 5, Huntington Library.

43. Graves to Bartlett, Dec. 6, 1889, Graves Collection, 1888–90 letterbook, Huntington Library.

44. Bacon to Samuel Barlow, Aug. 30, 1879, Samuel Barlow Collection, box 125, Huntington Library.

45. Holladay, Saunders and Cary to John Studer, Sept. 6, 1855, Holladay Family Papers, letterbook no. 5, Huntington Library.

46. Coffman to Darling, July 29, 1882, and Arrollee to Darling, Aug. 24, 1882, Ebin O. Darling Collection, box 485, California State Library, California Section.

47. *Los Angeles Star*, July 28, 1855; (Stearns v. Aguire), for Stearns, Aug. 4, 1855; July 23, 1855 (Wheeler v. Muchado); and Nov. 24, 1855, Dec. 8, 1855 (Drown v. Sexton). There also are stories of debtors winning. July 24 and 28, 1855.

48. Sweeney, et al. to Bicknell, Mar. 28, 1881, Bicknell Collection, box 3, Huntington Library.

49. W. G. Wood of J. M. Bradstreet and Son to J. M. Rothchild, June 8, 1875, Ibid., box 1.

50. W. Cornell to Bicknell, Oct. 16, 1876, Ibid., box 2.

51. John McKillop and Co. to Goodwin, Sept. 22, 1875, and John P. Manny to Goodwin, Jan. 18, 1881, Goodwin Collection, box 733, California State Library, California Section.

52. See James H. Shankland Collection, box 1, Huntington Library.

53. Beach to Bicknell, July 7, 1880, Bicknell Collection, box 3, Huntington Library. Also see Charles A. Eaton (Wentworth, Dakota Territory) to Bicknell, Sept. 25, 1886, Ibid., box 5; John P. Brockley (Lancaster, Pa.) to Bicknell, May 1, 1886, Ibid.; Granville H. Oury (Phoenix, Arizona) to George Hanson, July 30, 1875, Ibid.; Oury to Bicknell, Aug. 25, 1875, Ibid., box 1; R. Straham (Albany, Oregon) to Bicknell, Jan. 15, 1876, Ibid., box 2; and Graves and O'Melveny to Atlantic and Pacific Fiber Co., Apr. 2, 1887, Graves Collection, 1885–88 letterbook, Huntington Library.

54. Graves, et al. to Cook, May 7, 1889, Graves Collection, 1888–90 letterbook, Huntington Library.

55. Cain to Bicknell, July 19, 1887, Bicknell Collection, box 5, Huntington Library.

56. Day to Wells, Mar. 24, 1854, Haight Collection, box 2, Huntington Library.

57. Thompson and Davis to John D. Goodwin, Sept. 12, 1874, Goodwin Collection, box 735, California State Library, California Section. Goodwin also obtained

judgments against promissory notes to preserve them beyond the original statute of limitations. See note of Dec. 6, 1871, and letter to Clough and Goodwin of Oct. 16, 1871, Ibid.

58. See Samuel Way of Boston to Henry Haight, Jan. 2, 1856 and May 30, 1856, Haight Collection, box 4, Huntington Library.

59. See correspondence on the Connelly notes: Thomas H. O'Connor of New York to Bicknell, Nov. 11, 1887, Bicknell Collection, box 5, Huntington Library; O'Connor to Bicknell, June 8, 1889, Ibid, box 6; Bicknell to O'Connor, Jan. 2, 1889, Ibid., letterbook no. 4; and A. H. Loughborough to Bicknell, Feb. 5, 1890, Ibid., box 6.

60. James A. Clayton to Jacks, Nov. 2 and 26, 1889, Jacks Collection, box C(7), Huntington Library.

61. Shankland to Ulman and Remington, July 30, 1877, Shankland Collection, box 1, Huntington Library.

62. Graves to Parks, Dec. 6, 1888 and Jan. 8, 1889, Graves Collection, 1888–90 letterbook, Huntington Library.

63. Goodman to Goodwin, Dec. 21, 1883, Goodwin Collection, Box 730, California State Library, California Section.

64. Graham to Leander Bushon, Feb. 8, 1885, Bicknell Collection, box 4, Huntington Library. Also see Bushon to Bicknell, July 8, 1883, May 11, 1884, and Mar. 15, 1885, Ibid.

65. Abbott to David Jacks, Apr. 23, 1878, Jacks Collection, box C(2), Huntington Library.

66. Albon to David Jacks, July 27, 1878, Ibid.

67. Fairchild to A. L. Rhodes, Dec. 18, 1859, Goodwin Collection, box 730, California State Library, California Section.

68. Callahan to John Goodwin, May 28, 1883, Ibid., box 728.

69. Bates to Goodwin, July 14, 1883, Ibid., box 727.

70. Hall to Goodwin, May 29, 1883, Ibid., box 730.

71. Hall to Goodwin, Apr. 9, 1882, Ibid., box 731.

72. Rosecrans to Bicknell, Mar. 5, 1874, Bicknell Collection, box 1, Huntington Library.

73. Fiske to D. W. Jenks, Feb. 24, 1883, Goodwin Collection, box 730, California State Library, California Section.

74. Bicknell to Cadman, Aug. 13, 1890, Bicknell Collection, letterbook no. 6, Huntington Library.

75. Letters of demand were the first salvo that lawyers leveled at late payers and recalcitrant debtors. See, for example, the form demand letters of Jackson A. Graves to nine separate debtors dated July 3, 1878, Graves Collection, 1878–79 letterbook, Huntington Library. Also see Graves to Egan, Feb. 24, 1885, Ibid., 1883–85 letterbook.

76. Butler to Bicknell, June 5, 1876, Bicknell Collection, box 2, Huntington Library.

77. Charles C. Johnson to John D. Goodwin, Dec. 31, 1885, Goodwin Collection, box 732, California State Library, California Section. Also see Bakken, *Frontier California*, 99–101. High-volume commercial transactions had different instruments of credit and peculiar cash-flow problems. An excellent manuscript collection to follow such transactions is the Philip T. Southworth Collection, box 309, California State Library, California Section. Also see Roger W. Lotchin, *San Francisco, 1846–1856*, 53–60 and 77–78.

78. Graves, O'Melveny and Shankland to Fairview Development Co., Dec. 6, 1888, Graves Collection, 1888–90 letterbook, Huntington Library.

79. See Lotchin, *San Francisco, 1846–1856*, 54–60, 77–78, 155–56, 249, and 268–71 and Decker, *Fortunes and Failures*, 46–52, 91–95, and 148–50, 178. Mansel G. Blackford, *The Politics of Business in California, 1890–1920*, 96–99 and 117–26.

80. Hopkins to Bicknell, Oct. 3, 1879, Bicknell Collection, box 3, Huntington Library.

81. Graves to Ellis, July 9, 1888, Graves Collection, 1888–90 letterbook, Huntington Library.

82. Lotchin, *San Francisco, 1846–1856*, 249.

83. Hackett and Casserly of Janes, Doyle, Barber and Boyd to Adams, Feb. 25, 1855, Adams and Company Collection, box 22, Huntington Library. Also see Adams Company Scrapbook, vol. 2, pp. 139–40; vol. 3, p. 153; vol. 4, pp. 108–10, 112–15, and 117–20; and vols. 5 and 6, Adams and Company Collection, Huntington Library, for newspaper clippings and other documents pertaining to the legal problems.

84. Also see Albert Shumate, *The Notorious I. C. Woods of the Adams Express*.

85. Decker, *Fortunes and Failures*, 49.

86. Friedman, *History of American Law*, 549.

87. Ibid, 551.

88. McGee to Goodwin, Nov. 16, 1875, Goodwin Collection, box 733, California State Library, California Section.

89. Bransford to Goodwin, Nov. 3, 1875, Ibid., box 727.

90. Graves and O'Melveny to Shankland, Aug. 25, 1885, Graves Collection, 1883–85 letterbook, Huntington Library.

91. Roberts to Bicknell, Aug. 18, 1881, Bicknell Collection, box 3, Huntington Library.

92. Banning to Bicknell, Aug. 18, 1881, Ibid.

93. Fawcett to Fernald, Oct. 12, 1877, Fernald Collection, box 3, Huntington Library.

94. Larrobee to Bicknell, July 18, 1873, Bicknell Collection, box 1, Huntington Library. Also see letters of Aug. 20 and Aug. 21, 1873, Ibid.

95. David Jacks's debtors used bankruptcy on occasion, to his substantial detriment. For one such case see Warrant of Bankruptcy of Peter Heron, Aug. 18, 1878, Jacks Collection, box C(2), Huntington Library. Also see correspondence with T. Wood, assignee, Ibid. Jacks's legal entanglement with Heron went on into the next decade. See *Townsend Wood* v. *Chris Franks*, 67 Cal. 32 (1885) and *Woods* v. *Franks*,

56 Cal. 217 (1880). M. H. Myers, Secretary of the Commercial Association of San Francisco sent such a letter to Helling and Strauss giving notice that McCain, Flood and McClure had filed for bankruptcy and also warning, "you have been attached." Myers to Helling and Strauss, Jan. 23, 1874, Goodwin Collection, box 733, California State Library, California Section.

96. Graves, et al. to Dalleman and Co., Oct. 26, 1889, Graves Collection, 1888–90 letterbook, Huntington Library.

97. Page, Bacon and Company paid thirty-seven cents on the dollar coming out of the financial panic of 1855. Lotchin, *San Francisco, 1846–1856*, 60. H. Behrendt to Bicknell, July 30, 1875, Bicknell Collection, box 1, Huntington Library. Also see Decker, *Fortunes and Failures*, 178. J. M. Rothchild reported to Bicknell that 25 percent was the agreed-upon amount in Herzog and Roth's insolvency. Rothchild to Bicknell, June 12, 1875, Bicknell Collection, box 1, Huntington Library. Also see Chapin to Bicknell, Dec. 4, 1878, Ibid., box 2; Watt to Bicknell, Aug. 28, 1876, Ibid.; Watt to Bicknell, Feb. 27, 1877, Ibid.; Butler to Bicknell, July 22, 1877, Ibid.; Seibert to Bicknell, Oct. 16, 1882, Ibid., box 4; Bicknell to Markham, Sept. 13, 1892, Ibid., letterbook no. 8; Jackson A. Graves to Lohrance and Coglive, Dec. 9, 1878, Graves Collection, 1878–79 letterbook, Huntington Library; Graves to J. Naphtely, Apr. 5, 1880, Ibid., 1879–80 letterbook; Graves to Conway, Posey and Hawkins, Sept. 7, 1885, Ibid., 1883–85 letterbook; and Graves to E. C. Folson, June 14, 1886, Ibid., 1885–86 letterbook. Also see Peter J. Coleman, *Debtors and Creditors in America*.

98. Graves and O'Melveny to Hendricks and Youmans, Feb. 24, 1888, Graves Collection, 1885–88 letterbook, Huntington Library.

99. Hammond to Goodwin, Feb. 28, 1869, Goodwin Collection, box 731, California State Library, California Section.

100. Gray and Sexton to Goodwin, May 2, 1882, Ibid., box 730.

101. For a more extensive analysis see Bakken, *Frontier California*, 41–72.

102. Ibid. Also see John Reynolds to David Jacks, Aug. 9, 1878, Jacks Collection, box C(2), Huntington Library; William Bromwell to Jacks, Oct. 21, 1878, Ibid., box C(2); Mrs. Lizzie L. Suedaker to Jacks, Dec. 9, 1889, Ibid., box C(7); James A. Clayton to Jacks, Jan. 10, Jan. 25, Apr. 26, May 10, and July 21, 1879, Ibid., box C(3).

103. Bakken, *Frontier California*, 58–63.

104. Bakken, *Frontier California*, 68.

105. Jackson A. Graves to J. Naphtely, Feb. 24, 1880, Graves Collection, 1879–80 letterbook, Huntington Library; Graves to Alfred Hutchins, Sept. 7, 1888, Ibid., 1888–90 Letterbook; Graves to D. N. and E. Walter and Co., Mar. 16, 1888 and May 10, 1888, Ibid., 1885–88 letterbook; Graves to Mrs. Kellogg (probate problem), Jan. 5, 1880, Ibid., 1879–80 letterbook; Graves to Klauber and Live, May 26, 1885 (homestead), Ibid., 1883–85 letterbook; Graves to J. H. Elwood, Jan. 21, 1884 (homestead), Ibid., 1883–85 letterbook; E. A. Saxe to Bicknell, Aug. 25, 1873, Bicknell Collection, box 1, Huntington Library; J. D. Hancock to Bicknell, Jan. 29, 1881, Ibid., Box 3; T. H. Laine to Bicknell, Jan. 30, 1888, Ibid., box 5; Massillon Marsteller to Goodwin, May 21, 1883, Goodwin Collection, box 733, California State

Library, California Section; and Hugh McCutcheon to Goodwin, Aug. 7 and Sept. 29, 1875, Ibid. McCutcheon got a new note and security after Goodwin threatened a lawsuit. That compromise satisfied the client. George M. Davidson to Friend Hundley, Aug. 13, 1856, Ibid., box 729 and J. M. Eastman to Goodwin, May 28, 1868, Ibid.

106. Manuscript collections are filled with stories of successful debt collections along with stories of failures. See, for example, J. R. Bucklee to Goodwin, Feb. 8, 1871, Goodwin Collection, box 727, California State Library, California Section; Walter G. Holmes to McConnell, Bicknell, and Rothchild, Aug. 9, 1875, Bicknell Collection, box 1, Huntington Library; and Certificate of Execution of Nov. 4, 1854 and Affidavit of Attachment, *Tapia* v. *Ravanale*, Dressler Collection, box 3, California State Library, California Section.

107. Hickman to Bicknell, Dec. 31, 1879, Bicknell Collection, box 3, Huntington Library.

108. White to Bicknell, July 17, 1876, Ibid., Box 2.

109. Graves to Damsel, Feb. 29, 1892, Graves Collection, 1891–92 letterbook, Huntington Library.

CHAPTER 5

1. Beck and Williams, *California*, 269–70. Also see Paul Wallace Gates, *California Ranchos and Farms, 1846–1862*.

2. Halleck to G. W. Cooley, Apr. 1, 1852, Halleck, Peachy and Billings Collection, box 1, Bancroft Library.

3. Memo of Title, Chipman-Dwinelle Collection, box 3, Huntington Library. Title problems caused by transactions that did not accurately describe the property and from deeds with similar defects were not resolved by the passage of time in the nineteenth century. In 1894 Graves, O'Melveny and Shankland of Los Angeles wrote to W. F. Whittier regarding certain lands he was considering for purchase. They found several "defects in the chain of title," such as a land grant "by the Ayuntamiento of the City of Los Angeles, in 1836, the description of which is so uncertain that it [was] impossible to locate it" and an 1843 grant "the description of which [was] so imperfect that it [was] impossible to tell from the description itself what land it [was]." Despite these defects, the law firm wrote, "[We] would not hesitate to advise you to purchase it." By century's end, the legal system had moved, along with the advent of title insurance, to secure transactions in land. Graves to Whittier, Feb. 8, 1894, Graves Collection, 1893–94 letterbook, Huntington Library.

4. Dibblee to Bicknell, Sept. 29, 1880, Bicknell Collection, box 3, Huntington Library.

5. Patton to Hutchinson, Feb. 25, 1889, Patton Collection, private letters no. 2, Huntington Library.

6. Smith to Patton, Ibid. Also see Litigation materials, Los Alamitos Rancho, Abel

Stearns Collection, box 84, Huntington Library; Henry Bacon to Samuel Barlow Correspondence, Jan.–June, 1879, Barlow Collection, box 124, Huntington Library; and various letters to Jacks, Jacks Collection, boxes C(3), C(4), and C(6), Huntington Library. John Markey's Apr. 13, 1881 letter to Jacks in Box C(4) was representative of one type of problem. "I send you deeds that MAY effect the land mortgaged to you by Mr. Little. It is hard to tell what is included in your descriptions, if anything. After some tracing back of original titles I am almost certain that the lot on Alrarado St. known as the 'Zuick House' is in Wither's mortgage but not yours."

7. Peachy to Paul L. Forbes, Apr. 26, 1852, Halleck, Peachy and Billings Collection, box 1, Bancroft Library.

8. Wilson to Halleck, et al., Dec. 21, 1855, Joseph L. Folsom Collection, box 200, California State Library, California Section.

9. Lotchin, *San Francisco, 1846–1856*, 144–48. The Van Ness ordinance of 1855 relinquished all city titles to lands within the 1851 city charter limits "to such persons as had been in actual bona fide possession thereof from the first of January 1855, to June 20th of the same year, or could show by legal adjudication that they were entitled to such possessions" except those lands set aside for public purpose. This ordinance, in addition to a series of court decisions, supported the claims of those holding under Mexican claims and grants. The largest of these claims was that of Jose Y. Limantour. The Limantour claim put a cloud of title on lots in the established part of San Francisco and many of the possessors paid thousands to clear their titles. The Land Commissioners confirmed Limantour's grant in January 1856. In December 1856 the Limantour grant was declared to be a forgery. The combination of the Van Ness ordinance and the declaration voiding the Limantour grant gave a new level of certainty to land titles in San Francisco.

10. Irvine to Jacks, Nov. 13, 1869, Jacks Collection, box C(1), Huntington Library.

11. Bakken, *Frontier California*, 30–38.

12. Rosecrans to Bicknell, May 6, 1876, Bicknell Collection, box 1, Huntington Library.

13. O'Connor to Bicknell, May 6, 1876, Ibid., box 2.

14. O'Connor to Bicknell, Feb. 2, 1878, Ibid.

15. O'Connor to Bicknell, Jan. 24, 1880, Ibid., box 3.

16. O'Connor to Bicknell, June 12, 1880, Ibid.

17. O'Connor to Bicknell, Sept. 14, 1880, Ibid.

18. O'Connor to Bicknell, Jan. 16, 1881, Ibid.

19. O'Connor to Bicknell, Nov. 6, 1882, Ibid., box 4.

20. *Frasher* v. *O'Connor*, 115 U.S. 102 (1885).

21. O'Connor to Bicknell, Aug. 22, 1885, Bicknell Collection, box 4, Huntington Library.

22. Thornton to Bicknell, Aug. 13, 1888, Ibid., box 5.

23. Graves, *Seventy Years in California*, 141–44. Albert Dibblee to Thomas Dibblee, Dec. 4, 1877, Dibblee Collection, carton 14, vol. 221, Bancroft Library. Also see Albert Dibblee to Thomas Dibblee, Dec. 18, 1877, Jan. 4, 1878, Feb. 12,

1878, Mar. 29, 1878, vol. 221, and Jan. 29, 1879, vol. 222, Ibid.; Albert Dibblee to Sidney Smith, Sept. 2, 4, and 5, 1879, vol. 222, Ibid.; and Albert Dibblee to R. E. Jack, Apr. 8, 1878, vol. 222, Ibid.

24. Turner to Bicknell, Nov. 14, 1879, Bicknell Collection, box 3, Huntington Library.

25. See Rosecrans to Bicknell, Aug. 29, 1873, Sept. 30, 1873, and Feb. 20, 1874, Ibid.; O'Connor to Bicknell, May 20, 1875, Ibid., box 1.

26. Henry Gleason to Bicknell, Oct. 18, 1876, and William Hickman to Bicknell, June 30, 1878, Ibid., box 2; J. C. Davis to Bicknell, Nov. 18, 1880 and Dec. 11, 1880, Ibid., box 3; and Joseph Yoch to Bicknell, June 14, 1882, Ibid., box 4.

27. McDowell to Bicknell, May 2, 1877, Ibid., box 5.

28. Bicknell to Monroe, Feb. 7, 1891, Ibid., letterbook no. 7. Charles Huse, a Santa Barbara attorney, performed similar functions for Albert Dibblee of San Francisco and his brother, Thomas Dibblee, of Santa Barbara. See Albert Dibblee to W. W. Holister, Oct. 28, 1869, Albert Dibblee to Huse, Dec. 30, 1869, and Albert Dibblee to Ellwood Cooper, Dec. 31, 1869, Dibblee Collection, carton 12, vol. 221, Bancroft Library.

29. See generally Bakken, *Frontier California*, 29–40.

30. In addition to the extensive materials in the Bicknell Collection on point, also see the Goodwin Collection, box 731, California State Library, California Section; Jacks Collection, box C(6), Huntington Library; and the Jasper O'Farrell Collection, box 1, Huntington Library. Often the tasks were completely secondary. For example, A. Glassell Patton wrote to George Smith Patton on June 2, 1892 that he was "very busy at present on a law suit and [would] not be able to see [the] tenant at once." Patton Collection, private letters no. 5, Huntington Library.

31. Burke to Joseph J. and Sarah Jones, Oct. 21, 1868, Elbert P. Jones Collection, box 1, Huntington Library.

32. O'Connor to Bicknell, May 20, 1875, Bicknell Collection, box 1, Huntington Library.

33. Jacks to Houghton, Apr. 3, 1886, Jacks Collection, box C(5), Huntington Library.

34. The Monterey City Tract Two litigation is an example of how expensive and time consuming the process was. Jacks Collection, box B(v)(2)(11), Huntington Library. Also see box C(5) for more Houghton–Jacks correspondence on this point.

35. James Willard Hurst, *The Growth of American Law*, 319. Jackson A. Graves, *Seventy Years in California*, 286–93.

CHAPTER 6

1. Bakken, *Frontier California*, 74–77.

2. Ibid., 77.

3. Robert L. Kelley, *Gold* vs. *Grain*. Also see Mark Brumagin to Ebin Orvis

Darling, Aug. 14 and Sept. 7, 1872, Darling Collection, box 481, California State Library, California Section, for representative expressions of attitudes about property rights.

4. Southern Pacific Company Engineer's Report of Stock Killed, Bicknell Collection, box 6, Huntington Library.

5. Engineer's Report, Aug. 17, 1889, Ibid.

6. Bicknell to Muir, Sept. 6, 1889, Ibid.

7. Bicknell to Haymond, Mar. 27, 1890, Ibid.

8. Haymond to Bicknell, Apr. 2, 1890, Ibid. Also see George C. Fabens to Bicknell, May 23, 1889 and Nov. 13, 1889, Ibid. The experience of Jackson A. Graves was similar. With livestock cases, even of trespass rather than industrial accident, settlement was best. On Sept. 15, 1894, Graves wrote to J. Hugh Jones: "You had better go and settle with the Chinaman on the best terms possible, if not, give them the hogs. I don't want anything to do with this kind of a racket, and while the damages may look slight to you, anybody on earth would give the Chinamen damages for 14 pigs rooting around a vegetable garden; so my advice to you is to get out of the muss upon the most favorable terms you can make with the Chinamen, and either keep your hogs at home or turn them into bacon." Graves Collection, 1894 letterbook, Huntington Library.

9. Bicknell to George C. Fabens, Aug. 2, 1889, Bicknell Collection, box 6, Huntington Library.

10. An all too common story can be found in the *Placer County Republican* of Sept. 2, 1885. Pierre Sewain was driving his wagon home with his wife, three children, and a passenger named Baptiste. The paper reported, "Sewain had just lost a lawsuit and it is said he was so wrapped up in his disappointment that he was oblivious to the danger." Everyone in the wagon was injured in the collision and Sewain died within minutes. A coroner's jury "found that Sewain came to his death through his own carelessness."

11. See, for example, George C. Fabens to Bicknell, July 5, 1888, Bicknell Collection, box 5, Huntington Library.

12. Bicknell to Rankin, Apr. 9, 1889, Ibid., letterbook no. 4.

13. Rankin to Bicknell, Mar. 23, 1889, Ibid., box 6.

14. Rankin to Bicknell, June 16, 1889, Ibid.

15. Rankin to Bicknell, June 4, 1889, Ibid.

16. Bicknell to Rankin, June 10, 1889, Ibid., letterbook no. 4.

17. Rankin to Bicknell, July 13, 1889, Ibid., box 6.

18. Fabens to Bicknell, Dec. 31, 1889, Ibid.

19. Bicknell to E. L. Craig, June 10, 1891, Ibid., letterbook no. 7. Jackson A. Graves' experience was similar. Although he had won the case of *Carter* v. *Wells, Fargo and Company* at trial when the jury returned a plaintiff's verdict of a mere dollar in damages, the court granted a new trial. The plaintiff's attorney had approached Graves with a $2,500 settlement offer which he subsequently reduced to $1,500. Graves countered with $1,250, but was willing to go to $1,500 because he feared a

$10,000 verdict if the case went to a second jury. The plaintiff was a black man who had worked as a whitewasher, brick carrier, and furniture mover. He had been knocked from a scaffold and made an invalid with limited mobility. In the first trial, Graves had convinced the jury that the physical problems stemmed from a pre-existing condition. Now he wrote E. S. Pillsbury in San Francisco, "I am not ordinarily an alarmist, but I have given this matter very close attention," determining that settlement was a necessity. Graves to Pillsbury, Dec. 10, 1894, Graves Collection, 1894 letterbook, Huntington Library.

20. Bicknell to Creed Haymond, Mar. 18, 1889, Bicknell Collection, letterbook no. 4, Huntington Library.

21. Bicknell to George C. Fabens, July 7, 1890, Ibid., letterbook no. 6.

22. Bicknell to Creed Haymond, Aug. 9, 1890, Ibid.

23. Bicknell to E. E. Keech, Aug. 13, 1890, Ibid.

24. Bicknell to E. L. Craig, Sept. 23, 1891, Ibid., letterbook no. 7.

25. Bicknell to Haymond, Nov. 4, 1891, Ibid. Also see Bicknell to E. L. Craig, Mar. 7, 1891 and Apr. 8, 1891, Ibid. Creed Haymond wrote to Bicknell on Aug. 27, 1890: "I concur with you in the suggestion which you make as to fastening turntables in towns like Santa Ana." Ibid., box 7.

26. Bicknell to M. G. Watson, July 29, 1890, Ibid., letterbook no. 6.

27. Bicknell to George C. Fabens, Nov. 15, 1890, Ibid., letterbook no. 6, and Jan. 6, 1891, Ibid., letterbook no. 7.

28. Bicknell to Fabens, Nov. 4, 1892, Ibid., letterbook no. 8, and Bicknell to W. S. Millspaugh, Oct. 7, 1893, Ibid., letterbook no. 9.

29. George J. Denis to Bicknell, July 23, 1889, and George C. Fabens to Bicknell, Aug. 5, 1889, Ibid., box 6.

30. Bakken, *Frontier California*, 76.

31. Ibid., 83.

CHAPTER 7

1. William W. Clary, *History of the Law Firm of O'Melveny and Myers, 1895–1965*, 82.

2. Ibid., 92–94.

3. Ibid., 110–12.

4. James Norris Gillette Collection, boxes 1076–1108, California State Library, California Section.

5. Alfred D. Chandler, Jr., *The Visible Hand: The Managerial Revolution in American Business*, 293.

6. Ibid., 323.

7. Hurst, *Growth of American Law*, 347.

8. The development of irrigation also had a dramatic impact on agriculture. See Donald J. Pisani, *From the Family Farm to Agribusiness*.

9. See Hurst, *Growth of American Law*, 334–41.

10. Bicknell to Mayberry, Feb. 24, 1896, Bicknell Collection, letterbook no. 13, Huntington Library.

11. O'Melveny Journal, Feb. 4, 1899, O'Melveny Collection, 1899 journal, Huntington Library.

12. O'Melveny Journal, Apr. 13, 1903, Ibid., 1903 journal.

13. Bicknell to W. F. Herrin, Mar. 26, 1894, Bicknell Collection, letterbook no. 9, Huntington Library. Also see Bicknell to Herrin, May 17, 1894, Ibid., letterbook no. 10.

14. Bicknell to Herrin, July 27, 1894, Ibid., letterbook no. 10.

15. Bicknell to Crawley, Jan. 17, 1894, Ibid., letterbook no. 9.

16. Bicknell to J. A. Muir, Nov. 30, 1896, Ibid., letterbook no. 14.

17. Graves, et al. to Farmers and Merchants Bank of Los Angeles, July 31, 1890, Graves Collection, 1890–91 letterbook, Huntington Library.

18. Bicknell to Morris, Oct. 24, 1896, Bicknell Collection, letterbook no. 14, Huntington Library.

19. Bicknell to Banning, Feb. 6, 1897, Ibid., letterbook no. 15.

20. Smith to Patton, June 21, 1889, Patton Collection, private letters no. 2, Huntington Library.

21. Crittenden to Wilson, Feb. 19, 1869, Benjamin D. Wilson Collection, box 13, Huntington Library. Also see Curtis Lucien to Wilson, Mar. 12, 1869, Ibid., and James de Barth Shorb to Wilson, April 30, 1869, Ibid.

22. Bicknell to Huntington, Apr. 13, 1893, Bicknell Collection, letterbook no. 8, Huntington Library; Bicknell to J. E. Foulds, May 18, 1893, Ibid.; Bicknell to J. A. Muir, July 20, 1893, Ibid.; and Bicknell to Huntington, July 25, 1893, and Oct. 14, 1893, Ibid., letterbook no. 9.

23. Bicknell to A. H. Payson, Apr. 30, and Oct. 19, 1897, Ibid., letterbook no. 15. Also see Bicknell to J. T. Burke, Oct. 8, 1895, Ibid., letterbook no. 12. This is a five-page letter about corporate strategy. Also see letterbook no. 11 on L.A. Consol. R.R. Co. and a five-page opinion letter from Bicknell and Trask to a Montreal firm regarding stockholder and director liability. As usual they assessed the law as well as the practicalities of the situation. See Bicknell and Trask to Chapleau, Bisaillon, Brosseau and Lajoie, Dec. 7, 1893, Ibid., letterbook no. 9.

24. Bicknell to F. W. Wood, Apr. 22, 1895, Ibid., letterbook no. 11.

25. Bicknell to Henry C. Campbell, May 16, 1895, Ibid.

26. Bicknell to Campbell, July 2, 1895, Ibid.

27. Bicknell to J. T. Burke, Aug. 21, 1895, Ibid., letterbook no. 12. Also see Bicknell to J. M. Allen, Aug. 31, and Sept. 4, 1895, and Bicknell to Morris Trumbull, Sept. 15, 1895, Ibid.

28. Bicknell to Hellman, Oct. 6, 1891, Ibid., letterbook no. 7.

29. Bicknell to W. H. Perry, Jan. 4, 1892, Ibid.

30. Bicknell to T. W. Bullit, Aug. 17, 1891, and to E. L. Craig, Aug. 17, 1891, Ibid.

31. W. L. Witherbee's letter to Bicknell in 1888 was typical of the questions that started to flow into the office. Witherbee was chairman of the Santa Ana Valley Irrigation Co. and wanted to know what authority his corporation had to borrow money, issue bonds, and conduct certain business. If the articles of incorporation were deficient, he asked, "what steps can the Company take to put itself on a sound legal and financial basis to dispose of its bonds?" Witherbee to Bicknell, Oct. 9, 1888, Ibid., box 5. Corporate interpretation and litigation came from all quarters in the next decade.

32. Bicknell to Curtis, Oct. 11, 1893, Ibid., letterbook no. 9.

33. Bicknell to J. N. Crawley, Feb. 17, 1891, Ibid., letterbook no. 7.

34. See Bicknell to Thomas Brown, Sept. 18, 1895, Ibid., letterbook no. 12; Bicknell to Morris Trumbull, Oct. 8, Nov. 2, and Nov. 5, 1895, Ibid.; Bicknell to Edwin B. Smith, Nov. 30, 1895, Ibid.; Bicknell to William F. Herrin, July 20, 1894 (about cooperation with Santa Fe Co. to end a strike), Ibid., letterbook no. 10; and Bicknell to Thomas Brown, Jan. 10, 1896, Ibid., letterbook no. 12.

35. See Walter Nugent, *Structures of American Social History*.

36. A similar finding for an Illinois railroad attorney may be found in Maurice G. Porter, "Portrait of a Prairie Lawyer: Cliften H. Moore, 1850–61 and 1870–80, A Comparative Study," Ph.D. dissertation, University of Illinois, 1960.

37. See Chandler, *Visible Hand*, 167, 204–5, 292–302, 323, and 323–33. Although limited in data, the work of Hall McAllister of San Francisco and Charles Huse of Santa Barbara for Albert and Thomas Dibblee was very similar. McAllister handled the admiralty, commercial, and contract law problems of Albert Dibblee's commission mercantile business in San Francisco. Charles Huse superintended the real estate enterprises of the brothers Dibblee in Santa Barbara County. The admiralty business ranged from simple problems of charter parties to the complex issues of general average. See Crosby and Dibblee to Harbeck and Co., Apr. 22, 1853, Dibblee Collection, carton 11, vol. 191, Bancroft Library, and Albert Dibblee to Dibblee and Hyde, Sept. 2, 1864, Jan. 25, Feb. 1, Feb. 12, and Feb. 21, 1865, Ibid., carton 16, vol. 243. The volatile commodities market of the 1850s and 1860s exhibited legal problems of price, merchantability, and fitness for purpose that casebooks are made of today. The price of potatoes and flour fluctuated with each cargo or storm at sea. See Crosby and Dibblee to Harbeck and Co., Aug. 11, 1852, Ibid., carton 11, vol. 191; Crosby and Dibblee to A. W. McPherson, Nov. 25, 1852, Ibid.; and Crosby and Dibblee to Harbeck and Co., Dec. 25, 1852, Ibid.

CHAPTER 8

1. H. Jon Rosenbaum and Peter C. Sederberg, "Vigilantism: An Analysis of Establishment Violence," in *Vigilante Politics*, ed. H. Jon Rosenbaum and Peter C. Sederberg, 4.

2. Ibid., 10.

3. Ibid., 12.

4. Ibid., 17.

5. Richard Maxwell Brown, "The History of Vigilantism in America," in *Vigilante Politics*, ed. Rosenbaum and Sederberg, 81.

6. Ibid., 81. Also see Reid, *Law for the Elephant*. Reid's thoroughly documented work clearly and convincingly established that the overland trail pioneers held legal values relating to private property that elevated its status beyond the current judicial views of the sanctity of property.

7. Brown, "History of Vigilantism," 81.

8. Ibid., 85. Also see Richard Maxwell Brown, *Strain of Violence*; David A. Johnson, "Vigilance and the Law: The Moral Authority of Popular Justice in the Far West," 558–86; Nathaniel Pitt Langford, *Vigilante Days and Ways*; Alan Valentine, *Vigilante Justice*; Hoffman Birney, *Vigilantes*; Joan Bishop, "Vigorous Attempts to Prosecute: Pinkerton Men on Montana's Range, 1914," 2–15; Larry V. Bishop and Robert A. Harvie, "Law, Order, and Reform in the Gallatin," 16–25; and Jacob Mathews Powers, "Montana Episodes: Tracking Con Murphy," 52–56.

9. Richard Maxwell Brown, "Legal and Behavioral Perspectives on American Vigilantism," in *Perspectives in American History*, vol. 5, ed. Donald Fleming and Bernard Bailyn, 96–97.

10. Brown, "History of Vigilantism," 86.

11. Rodman, Paul, *California Gold: The Beginning of Mining in the Far West*, 203–5.

12. Register of Suits, Yuba County records, pages 112–17 reproduced in part in Peter J. Delay, *History of Yuba and Sutter Counties, California*, 122.

13. Lardner and Brock, *History of Placer and Nevada Counties*, 386.

14. Ferguson, *Law and Letters*, 66–72.

15. Ibid., 73.

16. Maurice Glen Baxter, *One and Inseparable: Daniel Webster and the Union*, 160–61.

17. Ibid., 161.

18. Ferguson, *Law and Letters*, 69.

19. The mother-lode attorney had to be very good with words because trials were very short. In researching criminal trials in Butte County, Kristin Kindig has observed, "Justice was usually swift; trials were often held the same day the defendant first appeared in court. Sometimes a trial was set for the next day, and witnesses were called in to testify. Records reflect cases being called at 3:00 p.m. and then continued to 8:00 p.m. for sentence. Court was often held in the evening." Kristin Kindig, "Court Is Now in Session," 20–22.

20. Friedman and Percival, *Roots of Justice*, 171. Haywood, *Cowtown Lawyers*, 242.

21. Kermit L. Hall, *The Magic Mirror*, 179.

22. Friedman and Percival, *Roots of Justice*.

23. Reid, *Law for the Elephant*, 4–25 and 345–47.

24. Friedman and Percival, *Roots of Justice*, 142–43. Reid, *Law for the Elephant*, 345–47.

25. William Henry Ellison, *A Self-Governing Dominion, California, 1849–1860*, 192–231.

26. Henry Haight to Samuel Haight, Aug. 29, 1851, Haight Collection, box 1, Huntington Library. Also see Robert M. Senewicz, *Vigilantes in Gold Rush San Francisco, 1846–1856*, and Roger W. Lotchin, *San Francisco, 1846–1856*, 193–201. Also see on vigilantes, Hubert Howe Bancroft, *Popular Tribunals*, and Zoeth Skinner Eldredge, *History of California*, vol. 3, pp. 405–15 and vol. 4, pp. 55–125. Manuscript sources may be found at several libraries. See San Francisco Committee of Vigilance (1851) Collection, 8 boxes, Bancroft Library; San Francisco Committee of Vigilance (1856) Collection, 1 box, Bancroft Library; Vigilance Committee Collection (1856), box 324, California State Library, California Section; and San Francisco Committee of Vigilance (1856) Collection, 3,750 pieces, Huntington Library.

27. Grass Valley's last vigilance committee, for example, formed in 1855. Ralph Mann, *After the Gold Rush*, 75. California had forty-three vigilante movements, twenty-seven of which occurred in the 1850s. Brown, *Strain of Violence*, 101 and 306–7. Although not all vigilante actions resulted in a hanging, as noted below, the death penalty was fitting for crimes, including grand larceny in 1851. On the death penalty generally see Louis P. Masur, *Rites of Execution*, and Thomas L. Dumm, *Democracy and Punishment*. For comparisons with the South see Richard Maxwell Brown, "Southern Violence—Regional Problem or National Nemesis?: Legal Attitudes Toward Southern Homicide in Historical Perspective," 225–250; Edward L. Ayers, *Vengeance and Justice*; Peter C. Hoffer, "Disorder and Deference: The Paradoxes of Criminal Justice in the Colonial Tidewater," in *Ambivalent Legacy: A Legal History of the South*, ed. David Bodenhamer and James W. Ely, Jr., 187–201; Bertram Wyatt-Brown, *Honor and Violence in the Old South*; Michael Stephen Hindus, *Prison and Plantation*; and William Lynwood Montell, *Killings*.

28. Ellison, *Self-Governing Dominion, California*, 67–68.

29. Friedman and Percival, *Roots of Justice*, 39–40.

30. McGrath, *Gunfighters, Highwaymen, and Vigilantes*, 120–23, 136–37, 189–90, 193–94, and 256–57.

31. "The Dill Murder Case," 13–15.

32. Charles Higby, "Biographical Sketch of William Higby," Higby Collection, box 218, California State Library, California Section.

33. Shuck, *History of the Bench and Bar*, 271.

34. Ibid., 275.

35. Ellison, *Self-Governing Dominion, California*, 196–201. Also see Brown, *Strain of Violence*, 21–22 and 306–7.

36. "Murder at San Andreas," 3.

37. Judge Ord's Statement procured by E. F. Murray, 1878, in Miscellaneous Documents for California History, Bancroft Library.

38. Joseph Lamson, "Nine Years' Adventure in California from Sept., 1852 to Sept., 1866," Bancroft Library.

39. Ibid.

40. Higby to his father, Feb. 25, 1851, Higby Collection, box 218, California State Library, California Section.

41. Higby to his father, June 21, 1851, Ibid. The punishment of death for robbery was authorized by the legislature on April 22, 1851. See Gordon Morris Bakken, "The Influence of the West on the Development of Law," 68–69.

42. Higby to his father, June 28, 1851, Higby Collection, box 218, California State Library, California Section.

43. Higby to his father, July 31, 1851, Ibid. Also see Ibid., Aug. 29, 1851.

44. Higby to his father, June 9, 1852, Ibid.

45. Ibid.

46. McGrath, *Gunfighters, Highwaymen, and Vigilantes*, 79–80.

47. Southworth to Alden R. Southworth, Oct. 27, 1850, Southworth Collection, box 309, California State Library, California Section.

48. Higby to his father, June 28, 1852, Higby Collection, box 218, California State Library, California Section.

49. Brown, *Strain of Violence*, 306.

50. Higby to his father, Feb. 20, 1853, Higby Collection, box 218, California State Library, California Section.

51. Ibid., July 26, 1853.

52. Ibid., Dec. 10, 1853.

53. Ibid., Aug. 9, 1854.

54. Ibid., Aug. 27, 1854.

55. Ibid., Oct. 10, 1854.

56. Ibid., Mar. 26, 1854.

57. Ibid., Jan. 28, 1855.

58. Ibid., Mar. 11, 1855.

59. Ibid., May 18, 1856.

60. Ibid., Apr. 16, 1857.

61. John Hume to Jane Hume Williams, Apr. 18, 1852, James B. Hume Collection, box 1, Bancroft Library.

62. The best evidence of these trials is the original trial court materials commonly found in disarray in county archives. One of the most accessible documents is the Criminal Trials at Los Angeles, Blotter Notes of Honorable Benjamin Hayes (1877), Bancroft Library. Another is the 1862–82 Justice Court Records, El Dorado County Archives Collection, Huntington Library.

63. DeLong diary, Aug. 8 and 9, 1856, DeLong Collection, box 212, 1856 diary, California State Library, California Section. Also see Ibid., Aug. 13 and 16, 1856.

64. Ibid., Sept. 6, 1856.

65. Ibid., Dec. 14–16, 1857, 1857 Diary.

66. See Ferguson, *Law and Letters*.

67. Carey to Goodwin, May 29, 1884, Goodwin Collection, box 728, California State Library, California Section.

68. Carey to Goodwin, March 15, 1885, Ibid.

69. Robert H. Tillman, "The Prosecution of Homocide in Sacramento County, California, 1853–1900," 167–82.

70. Haywood, *Cowtown Lawyers*, 242–43.

71. Dumm, *Democracy and Punishment*, 126–27 and 145–46, and Masur, *Rites of Execution*, 110–48.

72. *People v. Tanner*, 2 Cal. 257 (1852).

73. Reid, *Law for the Elephant*.

CHAPTER 9

1. Calhoun, *Professional Lives in America*, 59–87. For other insights on the eighteenth century, see Anton-Hermann Chroust, *The Rise of the Legal Profession in America*, vol. 1, pp. 159–60; vol. 2, pp. 254–55 on fees and pp. 92–128 on frontier lawyers.

2. Charles R. Johnson wrote to Abel Stearns in 1862 that he could not cash a draft until the steamer arrived. Johnson to Stearns, Aug. 14, 1862, Stearns Collection, box 37, Huntington Library.

3. Martin to Wilson, Jan. 23, 1850, Wilson Collection, box 1, Huntington Library.

4. Hereford to Ester S. Hereford, Feb. 20, 1851, Ibid., box 2.

5. Eberhart to Benjamin D. Wilson, July 16, 1863, Ibid., box 9.

6. Eberhart to Wilson, May 12, 1866, Ibid.

7. Perry and Woodworth to Wilson, Dec. 21, 1869, Ibid., box 14.

8. San Francisco Store Ledger, Keller Collection, Huntington Library.

9. Joseph Lancaster Brent, *Memoirs of the War Between the States*, 7. Also see Bakken, "Law and Legal Tender," 239–59 and Idem., *Frontier California*, 7–27.

10. J. F. Dye to Halleck, Peachy and Billings, Oct. 16, 1854, Halleck, Peachy and Billings Collection, box 1, Bancroft Library.

11. Contract of Castro, Apr. 19, 1862, Chipman-Dwinelle Collection, box 2, Huntington Library.

12. Several historians have concluded from the rapid decline of the native Californio population that legal fees paid in land and high-interest loans paid to unscrupulous Anglos caused the Californios' decline from wealth, power, and social status. See Albert Camarillo, *Chicanos in a Changing Society*, 36; James M. Guinn, "The Passing of the Cattle Barons of California," 59; and Leonard Pitt, *The Decline of the Californios*. These authors do not compare the costs of litigation with the economic fortunes of Anglos who had to defend their titles in law. Further, they do not consider the periodically high interest rates in an immature, specie-poor community. Paul Gates has established with documentary evidence that the process of adjudicating private land claims only accelerated a process of disintegration already well underway. Paul Wallace Gates, "Adjudication of Spanish-Mexican Land Claims in California," 213–36 and Idem., "California's Embattled Settlers," 99–130.

13. Hickman to Bicknell, July 29, 1879, Bicknell Collection, box 3, Huntington Library.

14. Clark to Bicknell, June 19, 1877, Ibid., box 2.

15. Ritchie to Halleck, Peachy and Billings, June 1, 1853, Halleck, Peachy and Billings Collection, box 1, Bancroft Library.

16. O'Connor to Bicknell, Sept. 23, 1876, Bicknell Collection, box 2, Huntington Library.

17. O'Connor to Bicknell, Feb. 5, 1877, Ibid.

18. O'Connor to Bicknell, Dec. 26, 1877, Ibid.

19. Graves to Amos S. Kimball, July 28, 1893, Graves Collection, 1893–94 letterbook, Huntington Library.

20. Larrobee to Bicknell, Feb. 28, 1874, Bicknell Collection, box 1, Huntington Library.

21. Wadham to Bicknell, Feb. 18 and 20, 1890, Ibid., box 6.

22. Graves, et al. to Hooper, Nov. 12, 1897, Graves Collection, 1897–98 letterbook, Huntington Library.

23. Bicknell to White, Feb. 15, 1889, Bicknell Collection, letterbook no. 4, Huntington Library.

24. Bicknell to Pope, Aug. 31, 1894, Ibid., letterbook no. 10.

25. Stanford and King to Bicknell, Oct. 16, 1875, Ibid., box 1.

26. Clark to Bicknell, Oct. 17, 1875, Ibid. Also see Clark to Bicknell, Apr. 20, 1874, Ibid. The Washington, D.C., attorneys did not always satisfy land claimants. Charles Larrobee wrote to Bicknell in 1874, "these people have been sadly fooled, and will ascertain at the trial that they threw away their money in paying Thompson, Brittan, and Gray. But they must pay me for my services—which were promptly and efficiently performed." Larrobee to Bicknell, Feb. 17, 1874, Ibid.

27. Graves to Hellman, Mar. 28, 1893, Graves Collection, 1893–94 letterbook, Huntington Library. Juan M. Luco offered John D. Bicknell a structured fee in an estate case. "You will only be required to aid Col. Irving in the trials that may take place in the County of Los Angeles, and keep the general run of the case and help prepare the case for the Supreme Court. You will be required to attend to the case in the Supreme Court. For your services the sum of five hundred dollars in case of final success in gaining the case [setting aside the will of Mateo Luna Franco]. If the case should be compromised you will be allowed two hundred and fifty dollars. There will be no retainer paid." Juan M. Luco (San Francisco) to Bicknell, Aug. 6, 1874, Bicknell Collection, box 1, Huntington Library. Bicknell found some levity in estate cases. For example, he wrote to Benson Wood in Effingham, Illinois: "If there is any subject in the world that an average California lawyer is competent to solve, it is in finding out the true wife of a dead man. Our court spent four solid weeks recently in determing whether a squaw was the lawful wife of a man who died worth about a half a million of money, and the jury in its wisdom pronounced them to be married and gave her a community interest in the property, which is likely to enlarge the brush shanty into a fine residence and will probably materially assist her attor-

neys. There is no individual that is considered a better client than some poor woman who is not certain whether she was married or not to some rich man who has recently died." Bicknell to Wood, June 22, 1891, Bicknell Collection, letterbook no. 7, Huntington Library.

28. *California Session Laws* (1873–74), ch. 474, p. 707.

29. Graves, et al. to Michigan Trust, Dec. 23, 1896, Graves Collection, 1895–97 letterbook, Huntington Library.

30. Bicknell to Simona A. Bradbury, June 30, 1894, Bicknell Collection, letterbook no. 10, Huntington Library.

31. Johnson to Hatfield, Aug. 29, 1893, Cyrus T. Wheeler Collection, box 1073, California State Library, California Section.

32. Bicknell to Champlin, July 15, 1889, Bicknell Collection, letterbook no. 5, Huntington Library.

33. Geis to Darling, May 12, 1883, Darling Collection, box 486, California State Library, California Section.

34. For example, D. English and Son wrote to Halleck, Peachy and Billings in San Francisco in 1857, requesting the collection of two hundred dollar notes made in 1849, simply wanting to pay Halleck, Peachy and Billings their fee and for the law firm to remit the balance. English to Halleck, et al., Apr. 15, 1857, Halleck, Peachy and Billings Collection, box 1, Bancroft Library. N. H. Dodson made an alternative arrangement with John D. Bicknell in 1872. He allowed Bicknell "one half the amount clear of attorneys fees." This incentive plan was the alternative to Dodson's usual "Settle with yourself and send the balance to me." Dodson to Bicknell, Aug. 31, Sept. 6, and Sept. 20, 1872, Bicknell Collection, box 1, Huntington Library. Crosby and Dibblee, San Francisco Commission merchants, held back commercial account funds "to cover law expenses" and handled referrals to local firms for out-of-state clients. Crosby and Dibblee to Mumford and Bros., New York, June 4, 1857, Dibblee Collection, carton 11, vol. 192, Bancroft Library.

35. Hoffman to Hundley, July 25, 1862, Goodwin Collection, box 731, California State Library, California Section.

36. Gere to Fernald, Nov. 3, 1877, Charles Fernald Collection, box 3, Huntington Library.

37. Waldron to Bicknell, July 8, 1875, Bicknell Collection, box 1, Huntington Library.

38. Waldron to Bicknell, July 10, 1875, Ibid. Also see letter of July 30, 1875, Ibid.

39. Fargo to John D. Bicknell, Sept. 1, 1873, May 26, 1874, and July 24, 1874, Bicknell Collection, box 1, Huntington Library. Similarly, Holladay, Saunders and Cary of San Francisco deducted their fee when a note was collected. Holladay, et al. to John Stuber, Sept. 6, 1855, Holladay Family Papers, Holladay, Saunders and Cary letterbook, vol. 5, Huntington Library.

40. Ellison letterhead, Bicknell Collection, box 3, Huntington Library.

41. William J. O'Connor to Bicknell, May 20, 1875, Ibid., box 1.

42. Thomas H. O'Connor to Bicknell, Mar. 14, 1885, Ibid., box 4.

43. William S. Rosecrans to Bicknell, Sept. 30, 1873, Ibid., box 1.

44. O'Connor to Bicknell, Feb. 26, 1887, Ibid., box 5.

45. Stephen C. Foster to Halleck, Peachy and Billings, Sept. 24, 1853, Halleck, Peachy and Billings Collection, box 1, Bancroft Library.

46. Jackson A. Graves to George K. Porter, Mar. 11, 1892, Graves Collection, 1891–92 letterbook, Huntington Library.

47. 1851–55 McGay, Holladay and Saunders Book of Accounts, Holladay Family Papers, vol. 4, Huntington Library.

48. See John Wipple Dwinelle to Samuel Cassidy, June 27, 1872, Chipman-Dwinelle Collection, box 2, Huntington Library; *Robert Watt* v. *S. A. Miller*, Plumas Co. Superior Court, Mar. 29, 1880, Goodwin Collection, box 746, California State Library, California Section; and John S. Runnells to John D. Bicknell, Aug. 9, 1889, Bicknell Collection, box 6, Huntington Library.

49. Houghton and Reynold to David Jacks, Dec. 10, 1872, Jacks Collection, box C(1), Huntington Library and Graves, O'Melveny and Shankland to Courtney Clark, Oct. 7, 1891, Graves Collection, 1891–92 letterbook, Huntington Library.

50. John D. Bicknell to WCTU of Southern California, Apr. 11, 1889, Bicknell Collection, letterbook no. 4, Huntington Library.

51. Graves, O'Melveny and Shankland to George Smith Patton, Nov. 5, 1894, Patton Collection, receipt book no. 4, Huntington Library.

52. Rosecrans to Bicknell, Sept. 30, 1873, Bicknell Collection, box 1, Huntington Library. Also see Bicknell to M. J. O'Connor, May 10, 1875, Ibid., letterbook no. 1 and Rosecrans to Bicknell, Nov. 22, 1882, Ibid., box 4. O'Connor's fee structure was as follows: "I accept the terms on which you are hereafter to attend to my business in your county, viz: Fifty dollars per month for attending to the general business, including the renting of the land and collecting the rents. I [agree] to pay for the extra help necesssary in the harvest and thrashing season. Also five percent to be allowed you on sales of Land; and ordinary charges for suits pending or hereafter brought; it being understood that all charges heretofore incurred in my business have been settled by our late verbal agreement—the balance due you to be paid out of the grain now on hand, when sold." See O'Connor to Bicknell, July 5, 1881, Ibid., box 3.

53. Bicknell to Creed Haymond, Jan. 21, 1889 and Apr. 8, 1890. Ibid., letterbook no. 4.

54. Graves to C. A. Hooper, July 16, 1897, Graves Collection, 1897–98 letterbook, Huntington Library.

55. Bicknell to Owen, Apr. 12, 1892, Bicknell Collection, letterbook no. 8, Huntington Library.

56. 1851 Billings, 1851–55 Book of Accounts, Holladay Family Papers, vol. 4, Huntington Library.

57. Carillo to Halleck, Sept. 27, 1853, Halleck, Peachy and Billings Collection, box 1, Bancroft Library.

58. Blume to Halleck, Oct. 1, 1853, Ibid.

59. Huse diary, May 7 and 8, 1855, Edith B. Conkey, ed., *Huse Journal*, 85.

60. *Los Angeles Star*, Aug. 2, 1856.

61. Bellah to Bicknell, May 31, 1874, Bicknell Collection, box 1, Huntington Library.

62. Bicknell to Armstrong, Oct. 2, 1893, Ibid., letterbook no. 8. Bicknell wrote to J. A. Gibson of San Diego on April 3, 1895 about a similar problem. "The general rule . . . [is that] it is very difficult to collect proper fees unless the full amount is collected before the judgment is obtained. Mr. Morrison had assurances that certain persons and corporations would contribute to our fees who now fail to respond, and he finds himself very much embarrassed from that fact." Ibid., letterbook no. 11.

63. Bicknell to Canfield, Aug. 16, 1890, Ibid., letterbook no. 6.

64. Graves to Curtis, Jan. 6, 1893, Graves Collection, 1892–93 letterbook, Huntington Library.

65. Graves to Dorsey, Oct. 6, 1897, Ibid., 1897–98 letterbook.

66. For another such instance see Howe to Bicknell, June 30, 1886, Bicknell Collection, box 5, Huntington Library.

CHAPTER 10

1. Hurst, *Growth of American Law*, 249–52.

2. Hinton Helper, *Dreadful California*, 46–50.

3. *Mariposa Gazette*, June 17, 1862.

4. *Contra Costa County Gazette*, Aug. 26, 1865.

5. Ibid., July 27, 1895.

6. Estee, "Early Day Lawyers," 393.

7. Ibid., 400. Albert Dibblee to Thomas Dibblee, Apr. 18, 1879, Dibblee Collection, carton 14, vol. 222, Bancroft Library and Cooper to Dibblee, Dec. 13, 1880, Ibid., carton 24, folder 300B.

8. *Contra Costa County Gazette*, Apr. 8, 1865.

9. *Los Angeles Star*, Feb. 14, 1852.

10. *Contra Costa County Gazette*, Feb. 2, 1861.

11. Ibid., Aug. 26, 1865. Thomas Dibblee to Albert Dibblee, July 26, 1866, Dibblee Collection, carton 23, folder 296B, Bancroft Library.

12. *Mariposa Free Press*, May 2, 1863.

13. *Contra Costa County Gazette*, Feb. 26, 1870.

14. *Placer County Republican*, Mar. 4, 1891.

15. Ibid., July 5, 1885.

16. Ibid., May 27, 1885.

17. Hurst, *Growth of American Law*, 251. Ferguson, *Law and Letters*, 230 and 279–90. Also see Laurence Veysey, ed., *Law and Resistance*, 1–36.

18. *Alta California*, Dec. 1, 1852.

19. *Contra Costa County Gazette*, Oct. 27, 1860. Also see *Los Angeles Star*, "Beauties of the Law," May 17, 1851; Dibblee to Greene, Apr. 28, 1888, Dibblee Collec-

tion, carton 16, vol. 246, Bancroft Library; Dibblee to duPont, Apr. 28, 1888, Ibid.; and Dibblee to Fernald, May 15, 1878, Ibid., carton 14, vol. 221.

20. *Contra Costa County Gazette*, June 25 and Aug. 14, 1870.

21. Ibid., Feb. 28, May 1, July 3, Oct. 16, and Nov. 27, 1880.

22. Ibid., Jan. 10, 1885.

23. Ibid., Mar. 1, 1890. Also see "Image of Court Procedure," Ibid., June 18, 1890; "An Excitement in the Court Docks," Ibid., May 10, 1890; and "Tax Cases," Ibid., Mar. 15, 1890.

24. Russell to Bicknell, Dec. 9, 1873, Bicknell Collection, box 1, Huntington Library.

25. McGrew, *City of San Diego*, vol. 1, p. 295. *San Diego Union*, Feb. 17 and 24, and Apr. 7, 1870. Denise Mougey, "San Diego Bar," California State University, Fullerton.

26. J. C. Bates, *History of the Bench and Bar*, 145.

27. Conkey, *Huse Journal*, 99 and 177. Walker A. Tompkins, *Santa Barbara History Makers*, 117. Huse also wrote: "I send you the Statutes of last year in Spanish. There are here no copies of the Practice Act in Spanish, but you will find this published in the Los Angeles Star, which is on file in the office of the County Clerk." Charles Huse (Benicia) to Charles Fernald (Santa Barbara), Apr. 3, 1853, Fernald Collection, box 3, Huntington Library.

28. See, generally, Patton Collection, box 5, Huntington Library.

29. Richard Griswold del Castillo, *The Los Angeles Barrio, 1850–1890*, 151.

30. Robinson, *Lawyers of Los Angeles*, 31–34, 43, 45–46, and 225–27. Maurice and Marco Newmark, eds., *Harris Newmark: Sixty Years in Southern California*, 45–46.

31. See George T. Clark, *Leland Stanford*. Stanford was a local merchant at the time and would later become significant in railroad development and politics.

32. See Lotchin, *San Francisco, 1846–1856*; Issel and Cherny, *San Francisco, 1865–1932*; Johnson, *Bar Association of San Francisco*, 3 and 9; Shuck, *History of the Bench and Bar*, 410–11; and Noel C. Stevenson, "The Glorious Uncertainty of the Law, 1846–1851," 374 and 380.

33. Lardner and Brock, *History of Placer and Nevada Counties*, 141–42 and 320–21.

34. *Placer County Republican*, Sept. 30, 1885.

35. Howell, "Continuity and Persistence," California State University, Fullerton.

36. *Mariposa Free Press*, Feb. 21, 1863. In the movement for temperance in Mariposa, Angevine Reynolds, Newman Jones, J. J. Farnsworth, R. Daly, E. O. Lovejoy, and G. G. Goucher were all officers for the cause in the Sons of Temperance Encampment. Mauck and Maslin, "Mariposa County," California State University, Fullerton.

37. *Mariposa Free Press*, Feb. 21, 1863. Burckhalter was a frequent speaker at civic and fraternal events. He also made the rounds of Democratic Party events. *Mariposa*

Free Press, June 13, 1863. Lovejoy and William Guard, a county attorney, were officers in the Mariposa Forester's Lodge No. 39. *Mariposa Gazette*, June 7, 1859.

38. Ruth Hermann, *Gold and Silver Colossus*, 79–99. Also see Ralph Mann, "The Decade after the Gold Rush: Social Structure in Grass Valley and Nevada City, California, 1850–1860," 484–504.

39. Issel and Cherny, *San Francisco, 1865–1932*, 69.

40. *Placer County Republican*, Sept. 30, 1885.

41. Issel and Cherny, *San Francisco, 1865–1932*, 105.

42. Ibid., 36.

43. Robinson, *Lawyers of Los Angeles*, 228.

44. Ralph J. Roske, *Everyman's Eden: A History of California*, 425.

45. Fernald to Livingston, Nov. 20, 1856, Fernald Collection, box 1, Huntington Library.

46. Gere to Fernald, Nov. 3, 1877, Ibid., box 3. Similarly, in 1877 Bromwell and Sleeth of Denver found the services of John D. Bicknell in the Commerical Law and Bank Directory. Bromwell and Steeth to Bicknell, July 31, 1877, Bicknell Collection, box 2, Huntington Library. The Merchants' Law and Collection Association of New York solicited the inclusion of the Plumas County firm of Clough and Goodwin in 1871. For an annual fee of five dollars, the firm would be widely known, or so the three-page pamphlet represented. Merchants Law and Collection Association of Clough and Goodwin, Sept. 15, 1871, Goodwin Collection, box 727, California State Library, California Section.

47. See the Mercantile Agency (R. G. Dunn and Co.) to Goodwin Correspondence, 1871–75, Goodwin Collection, box 729, California State Library, California Section and Joseph Bremer and Co. to Goodwin, Sept. 8, 1883, Ibid., box 727.

48. Sexton to Goodwin, Jan. 4, 1870, Ibid., box 735.

49. Arick to McConnell, et al., July 14, 1875, Bicknell Collection, box 1, Huntington Library.

50. Clark to Bicknell, Jan. 16, 1876, Ibid., box 2.

51. Huntington to Bicknell, Dec. 12, 1889, Ibid., box 6.

52. Bicknell to George C. Fabens, July 22, 1891, Ibid., letterbook no. 7.

53. T. H. Laine to Bicknell, Nov. 25, 1889, Ibid., box 6.

54. Graves to Main Street Bank, Aug. 28, 1891, Graves Collection, 1891–92 letterbook, Huntington Library.

55. Graves to Maurice Jacob and Company, and others, Mar. 18, 1892, Ibid., 1891–92 letterbook.

BIBLIOGRAPHY

MANUSCRIPTS

The Bancroft Library, University of California, Berkeley, California
  Baker and Hamilton Collection
  L. B. Clark Ledger
  Collins and Company Collection
  Albert Dibblee Collection
  D. W. Earl Collection
  Halleck, Peachy and Billings Collection
  Honorable Benjamin Hayes, Blotter Notes (1877)
  James B. Hume Collection
  Joseph Lamson, "Nine Years' Adventure in California"
  Miscellaneous Documents for California History, Judge Ord's Statement
  San Francisco Committee of Vigilance (1851) Collection
  San Francisco Committee of Vigilance (1856) Collection
  Wellman, Peck and Company Collection
  John Downey Works Dictation
California State Library, California Section, Sacramento, California
  Ebin O. Darling Collection
  Charles E. DeLong Collection
  Albert Dressler Collection
  Joseph L. Folsom Collection
  James Norris Gillette Collection
  John D. Goodwin Collection
  William Higby Collection
  John F. Miller Collection
  Philip T. Southworth Collection
  Vigilance Committee (1856) Collection
  William Warner Collection
  Cyrus T. Wheeler Collection
California State University, Chico, Special Collections
  John J. Bogard Scrapbook
Henry E. Huntington Library, San Marino, California
  Adams Company Collection
  Samuel Barlow Collection
  John D. Bicknell Collection
  Joseph L. Brent Collection

Amos Parmalee Catlin Collection
Cave Johnson Couts Collection
Chipman-Dwinelle Collection
El Dorado County Archives Collection
Charles Fernald Collection
Jackson A. Graves Collection
Henry Haight Collection
Holladay Family Papers
David Jacks Collection
Elbert P. Jones Collection
Matthew Keller Collection
James W. Mandeville Collection
Jasper O'Farrell Collection
Henry W. O'Melveny Collection
George Smith Patton Collection
San Francisco Committee of Vigilance (1856) Collection
James H. Shankland Collection
Abel Stearns Collection
David Smith Terry Collection
Benjamin D. Wilson Collection
Santa Barbara Historical Society
First National Gold Bank Scrapbook

NEWSPAPERS

Alta Calfornia, 1852
Contra Costa County Gazette, 1860–90
Los Angeles Daily Journal, 1985
Los Angeles Star, 1851–56
Mariposa Free Press, 1863
Mariposa Gazette, 1859–62
Placer County Argus, 1884
Placer County Republican, 1885–91
San Diego Union, 1870
San Francisco Chronicle, 1952
Wall Street Journal, 1989

OTHER PRIMARY SOURCES

History of Long Beach and Vicinity. 2 vols. Chicago: S. J. Clarke Publishing Co., 1927.
A History of Los Angeles, California, and Environs. Los Angeles: Historic Record Co., 1915.

A History of Monterey and Santa Cruz Counties, California. Chicago: S. J. Clarke Publishing Co., 1925.
History of San Mateo County, California. 2 vols. Chicago: S. J. Clarke Publishing Co., 1928.
Past and Present of Alameda County, California. 2 vols. Chicago: S. J. Clarke Publishing Co., 1914.
San Diego County, California. 2 vols. Chicago: S. J. Clarke Publishing Co., 1913.
San Francisco: Its Builders, Past and Present. 2 vols. Chicago: S. J. Clarke Publishing Co., 1913.
San Joaquin County, California. Chicago: Lewis Publishing Co., 1890.

BOOKS

Armor, Samuel. *History of Orange County, California.* Los Angeles: Historic Record Co., 1911.
Auerbach, Jerold S. *Unequal Justice.* New York: Oxford University Press, 1974.
Ayers, Edward L. *Vengeance and Justice.* New York: Oxford University Press, 1984.
Bakken, Gordon Morris. *The Development of Law in Frontier California 1850–1890.* Westport, Conn.: Greenwood Press, 1985.
Bancroft, Hubert Howe. *Popular Tribunals.* 2 vols. San Francisco: The History Co., 1887.
Barnes, Thomas Garden. *Hastings College of Law: The First Century.* San Francisco: Hastings College of Law Press, 1978.
Bates, J. C. *History of the Bench and Bar.* San Francisco: Bench and Bar Publishing Co., 1912.
Bauer, John. *The Health Seekers of Southern California, 1870–1900.* San Marino, Calif.: Huntington Library Publications, 1959.
Baxter, Maurice Glen. *One and Inseparable: Daniel Webster and the Union.* Cambridge: Harvard University Press, 1984.
Beck, Warren, and David Williams. *California.* Garden City, N.Y.: Doubleday, 1972.
Birney, Hoffman. *Vigilantes.* Philadelphia: Penn Publishing Co., 1929.
Blackford, Mansel G. *The Politics of Business in California, 1890–1920.* Columbus: Ohio State University Press, 1977.
Blaustein, Albert P., and Roy M. Mersky. *The First Hundred Justices: Statistical Studies of the Supreme Court of the United States.* Hamden, Conn.: Archon Books, 1978.
Bledstein, Burton J. *The Culture of Professionalism.* New York: Norton, 1976.
Bloomfield, Maxwell. *American Lawyers in a Changing Society.* Cambridge: Harvard University Press, 1976.
Bodenhamer, David, and James W. Ely, Jr., *Ambivalent Legacy: A Legal History of the South.* Jackson: University of Mississippi Press, 1984.
Brent, Joseph Lancaster. *Memoirs of the War Between the States.* New Orleans: Fontana Printing Co., 1940.

Brown, Elizabeth G. *Legal Education in Michigan, 1859–1959.* Ann Arbor: University of Michigan Press, 1959.

Brown, John, Jr., and James Boyd. *History of San Bernardino and Riverside Counties.* Chicago: Lewis Publishing Co., 1923.

Brown, Richard Maxwell. *Strain of Violence.* New York: Oxford University Press, 1975.

Bryson, W. Hamilton. *Legal Education in Virginia, 1779–1979, A Biographical Approach.* Charlottesville: University of Virginia Press, 1982.

———. *The Virginia Law Reporters before 1880.* Charlottesville: University of Virginia Press, 1977.

Calhoun, Daniel H. *Professional Lives in America.* Cambridge: Harvard University Press, 1965.

Camarillo, Albert. *Chicanos in a Changing Society.* Cambridge: Harvard University Press, 1979.

Carlin, Jerome F. *Lawyers on Their Own: A Study of Individual Practitioners in Chicago.* New Brunswick, N.J.: Rutgers University Press, 1962.

Cayton, Andrew R. L. *The Frontier Republic: Ideology and Politics in the Ohio Country, 1800–1825.* Kent, Ohio: Kent State University Press, 1986.

Chandler, Alfred D., Jr., *The Visible Hand: The Managerial Revolution in American Business.* Cambridge: Harvard University Press, 1977.

Chandler, E. G. *A History of the Law Firm Now Known as Athearn, Chandler, Hoffman, and Angell.* San Francisco: Privately printed, 1950.

Chroust, Anton-Hermann. *The Rise of the Legal Profession in America.* 2 vols. Norman: University of Oklahoma Press, 1965.

Clark, George T. *Leland Stanford.* New York: Oxford University Press, 1974.

Clary, William W. *History of the Law Firm of O'Melveny and Myers, 1895–1965.* Los Angeles: Privately printed, 1966.

Cleland, Robert Glass. *The Cattle on a Thousand Hills.* San Marino, Calif.: Huntington Library Publications, 1975.

Cleland, Robert Glass, and Frank B. Putnam. *Isaias W. Hellman and the Farmers and Merchants Bank.* San Marino, Calif.: Huntington Library Publications, 1965.

Coleman, Peter J. *Debtors and Creditors in America.* Madison: University of Wisconsin Press, 1974.

Conkey, Edith Boyd, ed. *The Huse Journal.* Santa Barbara: Santa Barbara Historical Society, 1977.

Decker, Peter R. *Fortunes and Failures.* Cambridge: Harvard University Press, 1978.

De Landon, Michael. *The Honor and Dignity of the Profession.* Jackson: University of Mississippi Press, 1979.

Delay, Peter J. *History of Yuba and Sutter Counties, California.* Los Angeles: Historic Record Co., 1924.

Del Castillo, Richard Griswold. *The Los Angeles Barrio, 1850–1890.* Berkeley: University of California Press, 1979.

Doerschuck, Beatrice. *Women in the Law: An Analysis of Training, Practice, and Salaried Positions.* New York: Bureau of Vocational Information, 1920.

Dumke, Glenn S. *The Boom of the Eighties in Southern California.* San Marino, Calif.: Huntington Library Publications, 1944.

Dumm, Thomas L. *Democracy and Punishment.* Madison: University of Wisconsin Press, 1987.

Eldredge, Zoeth Skinner. *History of California.* 5 vols. New York: The Century History Co., 1915.

Elliott, Wallace W. *History of San Bernardino and San Diego County.* Riverside, Calif.: Riverside Museum Press, 1965.

Ellison, William Henry. *A Self-Governing Dominion, California, 1849–1860.* Berkeley: University of California Press, 1950.

Farr, Finis C., ed. *The History of Imperial County.* Berkeley: Elms & Franks Publishers, 1918.

Ferguson, Robert A. *Law and Letters in American Culture.* Cambridge: Harvard University Press, 1984.

Fifield, James C., ed. *The American Bar.* Minneapolis: J. C. Fifield Co., 1919.

Fleming, Donald, and Bernard Bailyn, eds. *Perspectives in American History.* Vol. 5. Cambridge: Harvard University Press, 1971.

Friedman, Lawrence M. *A History of American Law.* 2d ed. New York: Simon and Schuster, 1985.

Friedman, Lawrence M., and Robert V. Percival. *The Roots of Justice: Crime and Punishment in Alameda County, California, 1870–1910.* Chapel Hill: University of North Carolina Press, 1981.

Friedman, Leon, and Fred L. Israel, eds. *The Justice of the Supreme Court, 1789–1978.* 5 vols. New York: Chelsea House, 1969–78.

Gates, Paul Wallace. *California Ranchos and Farms, 1846–1862.* Madison: University of Wisconsin Press, 1967.

Gawalt, Gerald W., ed. *The New High Priests.* Westport, Conn.: Greenwood Press, 1984.

———. *The Promise of Power.* Westport, Conn.: Greenwood Press, 1979.

Geison, Gerald L. ed. *Professions and Professional Ideologies in America.* Chapel Hill: University of North Carolina Press, 1983.

Graves, Jackson A. *My Seventy Years in California, 1857–1927.* Los Angeles: Times-Mirror Press, 1927.

Green, Will S. *The History of Colusa County, California.* Sacramento: Sacramento Lithograph Co., 1950.

Gregory, Tom. *History of Solano and Napa Counties, California.* Los Angeles: Historic Record Co., 1912.

———. *History of Sonoma County, Califoria.* Los Angeles: Historic Record Co., 1911.

Grenier, Judson. *California Legacy.* Los Angeles: Watson Land Co., 1987.

Guide to American Historical Manuscripts in the Huntington Library. San Marino: Huntington Library Press, 1979.

Guinn, J. M. *Historical and Biographical Record of Los Angeles and Vicinity.* Chicago: Chapman Publishing Co., 1901.

Hall, Kermit. *The Magic Mirror.* New York: Oxford University Press, 1989.

———. *Politics of Justice.* Lincoln: University of Nebraska Press, 1979.

Hall, Kermit. *The Magic Mirror.* New York: Oxford University Press, 1989.

Hamerow, Theodore S. *Reflections on History and Historians.* Madison: University of Wisconsin Press, 1987.

Harris, Barbara J. *Beyond Her Sphere: Women and the Professions in American History.* Westport, Conn.: Greenwood Press, 1977.

Haywood, C. Robert. *Cowtown Lawyers.* Norman: University of Oklahoma Press, 1988.

Heinz, John, and Edward O. Lauman. *Chicago Lawyers.* New York: Russell Sage Foundation and the American Bar Foundation, 1982.

Helper, Hinton. *Dreadful California.* New York, 1855. Reprint, Indianapolis: Bobbs-Merrill, 1948.

Hermann, Ruth. *Gold and Silver Colossus: William Morris Stewart and His Southern Bride.* Sparks, Nev.: Dave's Printing and Publishing Co., 1975.

Hindus, Michael Stephen. *Prison and Plantation: Crime, Justice, and Authority in Massachusetts and South Carolina, 1767–1878.* Chapel Hill: University of North Carolina Press, 1980.

Hulaniski, Frederick J., ed. *The History of Contra Costa County, California.* Berkeley: Elms Publishing Co., 1917.

Hurst, James Willard. *The Growth of American Law.* Boston: Little, Brown, 1950.

Irvine, Leigh H. *History of Humboldt County, California.* Los Angeles: Historic Record Co., 1915.

Issel, William, and Robert W. Cherny. *San Francisco, 1865–1932.* Berkeley: University of California Press, 1986.

Jackson, W. Turrentine, ed. *Twenty Years on the Pacific Slope.* New Haven: Yale University Press, 1965.

Johnson, Kenneth M. *The Bar Association of San Francisco: The First Hundred Years, 1872–1972.* San Francisco: Bar Association of San Francisco, 1972.

Johnson, William R. *Schooled Lawyers: A Study in the Clash of Professional Cultures.* New York: New York University Press, 1978.

Kelley, Robert. *Gold vs. Grain.* Glendale, Calif.: Arthur Clark Co., 1959.

Kelman, Mark. *A Guide to Critical Legal Studies.* Cambridge: Harvard University Press, 1987.

Kogan, Herman. *The First Century: The Chicago Bar Association, 1874–1974.* Chicago: Rand McNally, 1974.

Lardner, Nathaniel Pitt. *Vigilante Days and Ways: The Pioneers of the Rockies, the Makers and Making of Montana, Idaho, Oregon, Washington, and Wyoming.* 2 vols. Boston: J. G. Cupples Co., 1890.

Lardner, William B., and M. J. Brock. *History of Placer and Nevada Counties, California.* Los Angeles: Historic Record Co., 1924.

Leonard, Walter J. *Black Lawyers: Training and Results, Now and Then*. Boston: Senna and Shih, 1977.

Limerick, Patricia Nelson. *The Legacy of Conquest: The Unbroken Past of the American West*. New York: Oxford University Press, 1987.

Lotchin, Roger W. *San Francisco, 1846–1856: From Hamlet to City*. New York: Oxford University Press, 1974.

Lummis, Charles. *Out West*. Los Angeles: Outwest Magazine Co., 1909.

McGrath, Roger D. *Gunfighters, Highwaymen, and Vigilantes*. Berkeley: University of California Press, 1984.

McGrew, Clarence A. *City of San Diego and San Diego County*. 2 vols. Chicago: American Historical Society, 1922.

Main, Jackson Turner. *The Social Structure of Revolutionary America*. Princeton: Princeton University Press, 1965.

Mann, Ralph. *After the Gold Rush*. Stanford: Stanford University Press, 1982.

Mansfield, George C. *History of Butte County*. Los Angeles: Historic Record Co., 1918.

Martin, George. *Causes and Conflicts: The Centennial History of the Bar Association of the City of New York, 1870–1970*. Boston: Houghton Mifflin, 1970.

Mason, Alpheus T. *William Howard Taft, Chief Justice*. New York: Simon and Schuster, 1965.

Masur, Louis P. *Rites of Execution*. New York: Oxford University Press, 1989.

Mayer, Robert., ed. *San Diego*. Dobbs Ferry, N.Y.: Oceana, 1978.

Millard, Bailey. *History of the San Francisco Bay Region*. San Francisco: American Historical Society, 1924.

Montell, William Lynwood. *Killings: Folk Justice in the Upper South*. Lexington: University Press of Kentucky, 1986.

Moran, Wallace M. *History of Kern County, California*. Los Angeles: Historic Record Co., 1921.

Morello, Karen Berger. *The Invisible Bar: The Woman Lawyer in America, 1638 to the Present*. New York: Random House, 1986.

Morrison, Annie L., and John H. Haydon. *History of San Luis Obispo County and Environs*. Los Angeles: Historic Record Co., 1917.

Morrison and Foerster Reference Guide. San Francisco: Privately printed, 1987.

Nash, Gary B. *Class and Society in Early America*. Englewood, N.J.: Prentice-Hall, 1970.

Newmark, Maurice, and Marco Newmark, eds. *Harris Newmark: Sixty Years in Southern California*. 4th ed. Los Angeles: Zeitlin & Ver Brugge, 1970.

Newmyer, R. Kent. *Supreme Court Justice Joseph Story*. Chapel Hill: University of North Carolina Press, 1985.

Nugent, Walter. *Structures of American Social History*. Bloomington: Indiana University Press, 1981.

O'Brien, Gail Williams. *The Legal Fraternity and the Making of a New South Community, 1848–1882*. Athens, Ga.: University of Georgia Press, 1986.

O'Brien, J. P., ed. *History of Bench and Bar of Nevada: Included in this Volume is the Bench and Bar of California.* San Francisco: Bench and Bar Publishing Co., 1913.

Outcalt, John. *History of Merced County, California.* Los Angeles: Historic Record Co., 1925.

Paul, Rodman. *California Gold: The Beginnings of Mining in the Far West.* Cambridge: Harvard University Press, 1947.

Pessen, Edward. *Riches, Class, and Power before the Civil War.* Lexington, Mass.: D. C. Heath, 1973.

"Pile"; or, A Glance of the Monied Men of San Francisco and Sacramento County. Also an Accurate List of Lawyers. 1851. Reprinted in *Magazine of History* 48 (1933): 104–7.

Pisani, Donald J. *From the Family Farm to Agribusiness.* Berkeley: University of California Press, 1984.

Pitt, Leonard. *The Decline of the Californios.* Berkeley: University of California Press, 1970.

Reed, Alfred Z. *Training for the Public Profession of the Law.* New York: Carnegie Foundation, 1921.

Reid, John Phillip. *Law for the Elephant.* San Marino, Calif.: Huntington Library Publications, 1980.

Rice, Richard B., William A. Bullough and Richard Orsi. *The Elusive Eden.* New York: Alfred A. Knopf, 1988.

Robinson, William Wilcox. *Lawyers of Los Angeles: A History of the Los Angeles Bar Association and of the Bar of Los Angeles County.* Los Angeles: Los Angeles Bar Association, 1959.

Rodman, Willoughby. *History of the Bench and Bar of Southern California.* Los Angeles: W. J. Porter, 1909.

Rolle, Andrew F. *An American in California: The Biography of William Heath Davis.* San Marino, Calif.: Huntington Library Publications, 1956.

Rosenbaum, H. Jon and Peter C. Sederberg, eds. *Vigilante Politics.* Philadelphia: University of Pennsylvania Press, 1976.

Roske, Ralph J. *Everyman's Eden: A History of California.* New York: Macmillan, 1968.

Russell, Taylor., ed. *Centennial History of the Texas Bar, 1882–1982.* Burnet, Tex.: Eakin Press, 1981.

Sawyer, Eugene T. *History of Santa Clara County, California.* Los Angeles: Historic Record Co., 1922.

Senewicz, Robert M. *Vigilantes in Gold Rush San Francisco, 1846–1856.* Stanford: Stanford University Press, 1985.

Shuck, Oscar T. *Bench and Bar in California.* San Francisco: Occident Printing House, 1889.

———, ed. *History of the Bench and Bar of California.* Los Angeles: Commercial Printing House, 1901.

Shumate, Albert. *The Notorious I. C. Woods of the Adams Express.* Glendale: Arthur H. Clark Co., 1986.

Sleeper, Jim. *Turn the Rascals Out*. Trabuco Canyon, Calif.: California Classics, 1973.

Small, Kathleen E., and J. Larry Smith. *History of Tulare and Kings Counties, California*. Chicago: S. J. Clarke Publishing Co., 1926.

Smythe, William E. *History of San Diego, 1542–1907*. San Diego: The History Co., 1907.

Stanford, Leland G. *Footprints of Justice . . . in San Diego and Profiles of the Senior Members of the Bench and Bar*. San Diego: San Diego County Law Library, 1960.

———. *San Diego Lawyers You Should Have Known*. San Diego: San Diego Law Library Justice Foundation, 1971.

———. *San Diego's Legal Lore and the Bar. A History of Law and Justice in San Diego County*. San Diego: San Diego Law Library Justice Foundation, 1968.

———. *Tracks on the Trial Trail in San Diego*. San Diego: San Diego Law Library Justice Foundation, 1963.

Stevens, Robert. *Law Schools: Legal Education in America from the 1850s to the 1900s*. Chapel Hill: University of North Carolina Press, 1983.

Thompson, Edward P. *Whigs and Hunters*. London: Allen Lane, 1975.

Thompson, Thomas H., and Albert A. West. *History of Sacramento County*. 1880. Reprint, Berkeley: Howell-North, 1960.

Tompkins, Walker A. *Santa Barbara History Makers*. Santa Barbara: McNally & Loftin, 1983.

Unger, Roberto. *The Critical Legal Studies Movement*. Cambridge: Harvard University Press, 1986.

Urofsky, Melvin I. *Louis D. Brandeis and the Progressive Tradition*. Boston: Little, Brown, 1981.

Valentine, Alan. *Vigilante Justice*. 1929. Reprint, New York: Reynal, 1956.

Vandor, Paul E. *History of Fresno County, California*. Los Angeles: Historic Record Co., 1919.

Veysey, Laurence, ed. *Law and Resistance*. New York: Harper and Row, 1970.

Warren, Charles. *A History of the American Bar*. Cambridge: Harvard University Press, 1912.

Who's Who in the Pacific Southwest. Los Angeles: Times-Mirror Printing House, 1923.

Wigdor, David. *Roscoe Pound: Philosopher of Law*. Westport, Conn.: Greenwood Press, 1974.

Willis, William L. *History of Sacramento County, California*. Los Angeles: Historic Record Company, 1913.

Wunder, John R. *Inferior Courts, Superior Justice*. Westport, Conn.: Greenwood Press, 1979.

Wyatt-Brown, Bertram. *Honor and Violence in the Old South*. New York: Oxford University Press, 1986.

ARTICLES

Babcock, Barbara Allen. "Clara Shortridge Foltz: 'First Woman.'" *Arizona Law Review* 30 (1988): 673–717.

Bakken, Gordon Morris. "The Influence of the West on the Development of Law." *Journal of the West* 24 (January 1985): 66–72.

———. "Law and Legal Tender in California and the West." *Southern California Quarterly* 62 (Fall 1980): 239–59.

Ball, Larry D. "The Lincoln County War: An Enduring Fascination." *New Mexico Historical Review* 62 (1987): 302–12.

Bishop, Joan. "Vigorous Attempts to Prosecute: Pinkerton Men on Montana's Range, 1914." *Montana* 30 (April 1980): 2–15.

Bishop, Larry V., and Robert A. Harvie. "Law, Order, and Reform in the Gallatin." *Montana* 30 (April 1980): 16–25.

Bloomfield, Maxwell. "The Texas Bar in the Nineteenth Century." *Vanderbilt Law Review* 32 (1979): 261–76.

Brown, Richard Maxwell. "Southern Violence—Regional Problem or National Nemesis?: Legal Attitutdes toward Southern Homicide in Historical Perspective." *Vanderbilt Law Review* 32 (1979): 225–50.

Burchell, Robert A. "The Character and Function of a Pioneer Elite: Rural California, 1848–1880." *American Studies* (1981): 377–90.

"The Dill Murder Case." *Las Calaveras* 18: 13–15 (January 1958).

Feinman, Jay M. "Practical Legal Studies and Critical Legal Studies." *Michigan Law Review* 87 (December 1988): 724–31.

Gates Paul Wallace. "Adjudication of Spanish-Mexican Land Claims in California." *Hastings Law Quarterly* 21 (1958): 213–36.

———"California's Embattled Settlers." *California Historical Society Quarterly* 61 (1962): 99–130.

Gordon, Robert W. "Critical Legal Histories." *Stanford Law Review* 36 (1984) 57–125.

Guinn, James M. "The Passing of the Cattle Barons of California." *Historical Society of Southern California* 8 (1909–11) 59–70.

Hall, Kermit. "The Children of the Cabins: The Lower Federal Judiciary, Modernization, and the Political Culture." *Northwestern University Law Review* 75 (1980): 432–65.

———"Hacks and Derelicts Revisited: The American Territorial Judiciary, 1789–1959." *Western Historical Quarterly* 12 (1981): 273–90.

Hartog, Hendrik. "The End(s) of Critical Empiricism." *Law and Social Inquiry* 14 (Winter, 1989) 53–59.

Henretta, James A. "Social History as Lived and Written." *American Historical Review* 84 (1979): 1293–1322.

Horwitz, Morton J. "The Historical Contingency of the Role of History." *Yale Law Journal* 90 (1981): 1057–63.

Johnson, David A. "Vigilance and the Law: The Moral Authority of Popular Justice in the Far West." *American Quarterly* 33 (Winter 1981): 558–86.

Johnston, Effie Enfield. "Wade Johnston Talks to His Daughter." *Las Calaveras* 19 (1971): 25.

"Judge E. E. Calhoun." *The Madera County Historian* 10 (January 1970): 1–3.

Kindig, Kristin. "Court Is Now in Session." *Tales of the Paradise Ridge* 29 (June 1988): 20–22.

Mann, Ralph. "The Decade after the Gold Rush: Social Structure in Grass Valley and Nevada City California, 1850–1860." *Pacific Historical Review* 41 (November 1972): 484–504.

Mooney, Ralph J. "Formalism and Fairness: Matthew Deady and the Federal Public Land Law in the Early West." *Univeristy of Washington Law Review* 63 (1988): 317–70.

"Murder at San Andreas." *Las Calaveras* 6 (January 1958): 3.

Nash, Gary B. "The Philadelphia Bench and Bar, 1800–1861." *Comparative Studies in Society and History* 7 (1965): 203–220.

Nelson, William and Robert W. Gordon. "An Exchange on Critical Legal Studies." *Law and Society Review* 6 (1988): 139–86.

Posner, Richard A. "The Jurisprudence of Skepticism." *Michigan Law Review* 86 (April 1988): 827–91.

———. "The Present Situation in Legal Scholarship." *Yale Law Journal* 90 (1981) 1113–30.

Powers, Jacob Mathews. "Montana Episodes: Tracking Con Murphy." *Montana* 30 (October 1980): 52–56.

Russell, Peter E. "The Development of Judicial Expertise and Eighteenth Century Social Change." *Journal of Social History* 16 (1983): 143–55.

Shepart, E. Lee. "Breaking into the Profession: Establishing a Law Practice in Antebellum Virginia." *Journal of Southern History* 48 (1982): 393–410.

Skaife, Alfred C. "Early California Law Books." *San Francisco Bar* 1 (February 1937): 12–16; 1 (June 1937): 7–13; 1 (October 1937): 8–10; 1 (December 1937): 5–7; 2 (April 1938): 11–14; 2 (August 1938): 6–9; 3 (February 1939): 14–16; 5 (April 1941): 12–14.

Stanford, Leland G. "Devil's Corner and Oliver S. Witherby." *Journal of San Diego History* 24 (Spring 1978): 236–53).

Stevenson, Noel C. "The Glorious Uncertainty of the Law, 1846–1851." *Journal of the State Bar of California* 28 (1953): 374–80.

"There Came a Young Man." *The Madera County Historian* 14 (April 1974) 1–9.

Tillman, Robert H. "The Prosecution of Homocide in Sacramento County, California, 1853–1900." *Southern California Quarterly* 68 (Summer 1986): 167–82.

Traub, Stuart H. "Rewards, Bounty Hunting, and Criminal Justice in the West: 1865–1900." *Western Historical Quarterly* 19 (1988): 287–302.

Trubek, David M., and John Esser. "'Critical Empiricism' in American Legal

Studies: Paradox, Program, or Pandora's Box?" *Law and Social Inquiry* 14 (Winter 1989): 3–52.

Uberti, William. "Oliver S. Witherby, First State District Judge of San Diego." *Journal of San Diego History* 24 (Spring 1978): 221–35.

Vandelde, Kenneth J. "The New Property of the Nineteenth Century: The Development of the Modern Concept of Property." *Buffalo Law Review* 29 (1980): 325–65.

Wash, Robert M. "Our County's Yesterdays." *The Madera County Historian* 8 (October 1968): 1–5.

Wheat, Carl I. "California's Bantam Cock." *Quarterly of the California Historical Society* 8 (September 1929): 193–98.

White, G. Edward. "Truth and Interpretation in History." *Michigan Law Review* 79 (March 1981): 595–615.

Whitford, William C. "Critical Empiricism." *Law and Social Inquiry* 14 (Winter 1989): 61–67.

Wilkinson, Charles F. "The Law of the American West: A Critical Bibliography of the Nonlegal Sources." *Michigan Law Review* 85 (April–May 1987): 953–1011.

Wunder, John R. "Chinese in Trouble: Criminal Law and Race on the Trans-Mississippi West Frontier." *Western Historical Quarterly* 17 (1986): 25–42.

Zboray, Ronald J. "The Transportation Revolution and Antebellum Book Distribution Reconsidered." *American Quarterly* 38 (Spring 1986): 53–71.

UNPUBLISHED PAPERS

Dorsey, Bruce. "The Los Angeles Bar in the Nineteenth Century." California State University, Fullerton.

Enersen, Burnham. "The McCutchen Law Firm—Its First Century." McCutchen, Doyle, Brown, and Enersen, San Francisco, Calif., Aug. 10, 1983.

Hoffman, Harlan L. "Pistols and Coffee for Two: A History of the Santa Barbara County Bar, 1850–1900." California State University, Fullerton.

Howell, John N. "Continuity and Persistence: A History of the Placer County, California Bar, 1850–1900." California State University, Fullerton.

Mauck, William Farley III, and Susan Maslin. "Mariposa County, 1850–1900: A Study of Rural California Law." California State University, Fullerton.

Mougey, Denise. "The San Diego Bar: A Study in Professionalization and Economic Developments." California State University, Fullerton.

Morrison and Foerster, San Francisco, Calif. "The Morrison Firm."

Porter, Maurice G. "Portrait of a Prairie Lawyer: Cliften H. Moore, 1850–61 and 1870–80, A Comparative Study." Ph.D. diss., University of Illinois, 1960.

Sutcliffe, Eric. "Acknowledgement by Eric Sutcliffe of One-Hundred-Year Award to Orrick, Herrington and Sutcliffe from the California Historical Society," Speech given November 19, 1984 in San Francisco. Orrick, Herrington, and Sutcliffe, San Francisco, Calif.